A publication of the

INSTITUTE OF HIGHER EDUCATION

Teachers College, Columbia University

Dynamics
of
Academic
Reform

FOREWORD BY

Earl J. McGrath

JB Lon Hefferlin

Dynamics
of
Academic
Reform

Jossey-Bass Inc., Publishers
615 Montgomery Street • San Francisco • 1969

DYNAMICS OF ACADEMIC REFORM
by JB Lon Hefferlin
Foreword by Earl J. McGrath

Copyright © 1969 by Jossey-Bass, Inc., Publishers

Copyright under Pan American and
Universal Copyright Conventions

Jossey-Bass, Inc., Publishers
615 Montgomery Street
San Francisco, California 94111

Library of Congress Catalog Card Number 76-92895

Standard Book Number SBN 87589-048-2

Manufactured in the United States of America
Composed and printed by York Composition Company, Inc.
Bound by Chas. H. Bohn & Co., Inc.

JACKET DESIGN BY WILLI BAUM

FIRST EDITION

6916

THE JOSSEY-BASS SERIES IN HIGHER EDUCATION

General Editors

JOSEPH AXELROD *and* MERVIN B. FREEDMAN
San Francisco State College

Foreword

The study reported in *The Dynamics of Academic Reform* has been concerned with the vitality of American institutions of higher education. The use of the term *vitality* is not without its disadvantages, for it has come to have two accepted meanings that if used interchangeably, especially in the context of this inquiry, can cause operational confusion. In one connotation vitality means the mere capacity to endure or survive with no implication of growth or change. In this sense the word is often used in referring to an old person who continues to live with unusual physical vigor. There is no suggestion that he seeks new experiences or alters any of his lifelong habits to adjust to the changing conditions of the world around him.

Vitality may mean something quite different. It may connote the capacity to grow and to adapt to new social demands. The history of American higher education shows that most colleges and universities have been extremely vital institutions in the first sense. Although a number of those established in the nineteenth century failed to survive, hundreds of others clung to life with an amazing vitality and now appear to be immortal. Among these older establishments are many which today enjoy a celebrated name in the academic world. Yet these venerable centers of learning may exhibit little vitality in the sense of making persistent efforts to change their purposes and practices in terms of the changing character of American society and its emerging educational needs.

In the use of the word *vitality* in this study the emphasis has not been put on the capacity to exist at a high level of efficiency simply by carrying on the ordinary day-by-day activities of a college or a university. The study reported here has been more concerned with the capacity of an academic enterprise continuously to reorganize its program and to redistribute its resources in such ways as to encourage the most promising innovations in the theory and practice of higher education. An even more important objective has been to discover the factors in the life of an educational community which are conducive to the maintenance of productive vitality over a period of years. In simple terms the purpose has been to uncover the forces within institutions which tend to preserve and nourish a readiness to change as they face new social conditions, new types of students, and new developments in teaching methods and materials.

At no point in the history of American higher education could such a book have been more timely. In the first place the swift and ever-accelerating changes in the conditions of life at home and abroad will require related innovations in the programs of the institutions whose responsibility it is to prepare each new generation to live and to work amid the rapid ebb and flow of human events. Some few colleges and universities may be able and satisfied to continue their traditional ways until the worth of new practices has been indisputably established, or until external developments force internal alterations of structures and functions. Some institutions took such self-satisfied positions for years after the appearance, in the second half of the nineteenth century, of entirely new disciplines in the liberal arts and professional fields of learning. They adhered to the ancient classical tradition. But today imperative social demands and institutional self-interest will require most colleges and universities to keep their own programs abreast—if not ahead—of the rapidly emerging needs of society. Moreover, if this book proves anything it is that the necessary readjustments will occur neither automatically nor by force of local circumstances. If imaginative adaptations of services are to be accomplished in an orderly and sound manner, the ideas and energies of the entire academic establishment must become involved.

Second, the two major academic bodies in colleges and universities, the faculty and the students, are now more than ever before demanding a larger role in the determination of academic policies and practices. Student activists, especially, believe that institutions of higher education as a whole are not sufficiently in touch with the conditions of life in the circumambient society. They are firmly convinced that the entire range of purposes of American higher education, of its instructional programs, of its teaching staff and facilities, of its relationships to the community—all these features of the higher education enterprise—are urgently in need of reexamination, reevaluation, and modification. Many faculty members are raising similar questions and proposing changes in their role in academic government. They feel, for example, that representatives of the faculty should play a larger part in the activities of the boards of trustees. Regardless of the validity of any of these claims, an unprecedented amount of energy must be mustered in institutions which expect to come to grips with the attendant issues and problems. Business-as-usual procedures will not be adequate to the reorganizational tasks ahead.

Third, there is growing evidence that the immense resources now being made available from public and private sources to institutions of higher education can hardly be expected to increase at the same rate as their expansion in size and service. Legislative bodies and private donors will doubtless continue to increase their support. There is, however, a growing tendency for such groups to become more concerned about the way in which funds which they appropriate are being spent. It seems certain that in the future institutions seeking additional support will have to show that they are already making every effort to devise and use the most advanced methods of operation not only in the narrower field of business management but also in the activities of teaching and research. In this connection it is significant that the initial interest of the officers of the Kettering Foundation in this study of vitality stemmed from their observation that some institutions were typically quick to experiment with or adopt new educational practices while others seemed unconcerned about innovations that had proved fruitful elsewhere. It is a truism that all foundations are constantly on the alert for new ideas and promising experiments. As the competition for funds grows more intense the vital institution seeking by adaptation and by experimentation to improve the effectiveness of its operations will be more likely than the self-satisfied to attract support.

Vitality has always been an institutional asset. The vital institution has not only distinguished and benefited itself; it has also set the patterns of policy and practice which other colleges and universities have emulated. Institutions like Harvard, Chicago, and Johns Hopkins in the past led the way to lasting educational reforms through innovative leadership. In the changing circumstances of contemporary academic life and of society generally the vital institution will be able to make an even larger contribution than it has hitherto been able to make.

The officers and trustees of the Kettering Foundation, especially Charles Kettering and Edwin Vause, deserve the gratitude of the academic community for having foreseen several years ago the desirability of investigating the character and conditions of educational vitality. The characteristics of institutions which make up or indicate vitality, as those who have made this study know, are complex and fugitive. They deserve continuing analysis. This study has made an initial effort to discover the factors which seem to be related to a lively concern about the validity of established educational practices and a desire to revise existing practices in any ways that seem calculated to improve educational efficiency. No one, educator or layman, can expect to find in this report a set of how-to-do-it techniques by the use of which he can overnight transform a stagnant, self-satisfied, smug educational enterprise into an exciting, forward-moving, experimental academic community. But he will find here valuable suggestions concerning the factors which seem to predispose toward such an institution and the dynamics by which forward movement can be inaugurated.

I wish to thank the officers of the Kettering Foundation for their interest in and support of this investigation of vitality which constitutes only one of three separate but related studies. Another approaches the same matter historically by analyzing the forces which from the beginning of a single college over forty years ago have been instrumental in keeping alive a spirit of innovation and experimentation. Still a third activity under the Kettering grant involved the collaboration of the Institute of Higher Education at Teachers College, Columbia University, with the Educational Testing Service of Princeton, New Jersey. This joint enterprise resulted in the development of the Institutional Functioning Inventory, an instrument with 132 items, on the basis of which institutions can get some measure of their various characteristics and capacity for change.

So many persons cooperated in this study that it would be impossible to identify all of them. The administrative officers and faculty members in the colleges and universities who supplied information deserve special thanks, as well as others who advised on procedures and criticized the early drafts of the report. JB Lon Hefferlin directed the daily activities of the staff and prepared the final report. Only his diligence and imagination could have brought the study to its present successful conclusion.

Lastly, I wish to express my personal gratitude to President John H. Fischer of Teachers College, whose administrative policies enabled the Director of the Study of Institutional Vitality and the dozens of others who worked on research projects in the Institute of Higher Education to carry on their activities with the maximum amount of freedom and self-direction. In a very real way he has provided one of the elements in institutional life which this study shows to be conducive to sustained vitality and productiveness.

Philadelphia
September, 1969

EARL J. MCGRATH, *Director*
Higher Education Center
Temple University

Preface

The whole business about a university and about education can be summed up in a question: Has the institution vitality? Is anything going on? Is there anything exciting about it? This is the only test of a good university.[1]

Robert M. Hutchins

[1] "Trees Grew in Brooklyn: Robert M. Hutchins Interviewed by Frank K. Kelly," *The Center Magazine,* Volume 1, Number 7 (November, 1968), page 21. Santa Barbara: Center for the Study of Democratic Institutions.

I f you happened to have been waiting for a train on the downtown platform of the IRT Seventh Avenue subway station at Seventy-second Street in New York City shortly after five o'clock on June 20, 1968, you would have witnessed one small incident in the four-year series of episodes that culminated in this report. A young man in a business suit was lying at the edge of the platform, surrounded by a crowd of observers and kibitzers. He was holding a broken mop handle that he had found in a nearby trash barrel, and on the end of the handle were the well-chewed remains of a nickel's worth of gum from a vending machine in the station. As each subway train left the platform, the young man used the gummed mop handle to try to catch one sheet of paper after another from the tracks before another train approached.

Arthur Shriberg, a research assistant in the Institute of Higher Education at Teachers College, Columbia University, had just spent two hours in the steaming hot animal experiment quarters on the top floor of the American Museum of Natural History, perched on a stool with a seven-foot alligator asleep in a tank at his feet. He had been interviewing a psychologist who both works at the museum and teaches at a metropolitan university, and he had the interview schedule under his arm while he waited for the subway afterwards. In the rush-hour melee, the folder was knocked into the tracks. Determined not to lose the record of that conversation, Shriberg had found the mop and gum. After a half-hour, he rescued the notes, and the sticky results were incorporated into the data reported in this book.

This report thus results both from the perseverance of Shriberg and his similarly dogged colleagues on the staff of the Institute of Higher Education at Teachers College, and from the observations of professors and administrators in some hundred colleges and universities across America, who were willing to be interviewed to give us the evidence on which it is based.

The four-year study leading to this report stemmed originally from the foresight of three men: Earl J. McGrath, the director of the Institute of Higher Education, and Charles Kettering II and E. H. Vause of the Charles F. Kettering Foundation. On October 8, 1964, they met in New York to discuss the problem of the slow adoption of innovations in higher education. It seemed to them that many colleges and universities were not employing the most efficient educational procedures possible and were unnecessarily ineffective as a result. Some of the problem appeared to lie in a lack of information among professors and administrators about effective educational practices. Part of it stemmed from a lack of funds to undertake these practices. But it seemed that many institutions, even with sufficient information and money, were unable to implement sound changes—sometimes because of a lack of leadership, sometimes a too-rigid tradition, or any of a number of infirmities.

Out of this discussion grew the project that we called the Study of Institutional Vitality. To McGrath, the problem of vitality in educational institutions was one of understanding the forces that cause educational effectiveness and the steps that could be taken to "revive the moribund and sustain the vigorous." He proposed that the central questions of the study should be these:

> What are the factors in institutional life which stimulate and sustain enterprising developments and promote educational excellence? And why do some institutions seem to maintain a spirit of experimentation and change their policies and practices in accordance with new knowledge and the emerging conditions of life, while others, no less well supported, seem to stay in an educational rut?

With the support of the Kettering Foundation, the staff of the institute under Dr. McGrath's direction has sought the answers to these questions. We have tried to learn the means that can be used to stimulate greater academic reform in American higher education and that can assure that the process of academic change becomes more continuous in more and more colleges and universities. Our basic premise has been that academic change is essential to academic vitality.

The first criterion of a vital educational institution, we imagine most everyone will agree, is that it is *effective*. In other words, it is "alive" to the degree that it influences its students and its environment for the better, it does good for people other than merely its own employees, and it affects their lives. In Robert M. Hutchins' words, it is exciting because something important is going on. But we suggest that institutional vitality is also based on *adaptability,* since a college or university cannot be effective for long without remaining adaptive to new conditions.

A vital educational institution, in other words, must be dynamic: It must be responsive to the changing intellectual needs of its students, its community, and its times. It must be able to adapt its policies and practices to keep its means consistent with its ends. In order to progress, it must change. We agree with Samuel P. Capen's observation as chancellor of the University of Buffalo that the surest index of vitality for such a university is "its readiness to alter its methods, its requirements, or the content of its curricula with a view both to offering the students richer opportunities for self-improvement and to equipping them better to perform the duties of present day citizenship and professional practice."[2]

In short, it seems to us that institutional vitality for a college or university is achieved by an institution's being as effective as possible educationally and then keeping effective through continuous adaptation to new conditions. And from our perspective, it is the second of these problems—the maintenance of adaptability—that recently has needed the most attention and research.

Other scholars, such as Kenneth Feldman, Theodore Newcomb, Joseph Katz, and Nevitt Sanford, have already been studying the educational effectiveness of colleges and universities. From their work, much can be learned about the factors that either aid or hinder an institution's educational impact and the changes that may be needed to increase its impact.[3] We at the Institute of

[2] Samuel P. Capen, "The Process of Educational Reform." Report of the Chancellor to the Council of the University of Buffalo for the Academic Year of 1947–1948. Reprinted in Capan's *The Management of Universities.* Buffalo: Foster and Stewart, 1953, p. 98.

[3] See, for example, Nevitt Sanford, *Where Colleges Fail,* 1967; Joseph Katz and Associates, *No Time For Youth,* 1968; and Kenneth A. Feldman and Theodore M. Newcomb, *The Impact of College on Students* (two volumes), 1969. San Francisco: Jossey-Bass.

Preface

Higher Education, however, are particularly concerned with *how* these needed changes come about. How is reform accomplished? And what are its causes? These seemed the most pressing unanswered questions to us and to the Kettering Foundation, and it has been to these questions that we addressed ourselves in the Study of Institutional Vitality.

For our purposes, *academic reform* means the modification and improvement of the program of an educational institution. It refers to such alterations as shifts in institutional services, revision of policies, reorganization of curricula, development of new methods of teaching, and increases in learning. It does not include other structural changes—important as they are—such as the expansion of enrollments, increases in financial resources, changes in the sources of support, turnover in the faculty, or the introduction of new budgeting procedures. These other variables are related to academic reform, but they are not themselves academic changes. They could well be the focus of attention for other studies of higher education; but in this study our prime concern is with changes in program.

To study academic reform at large in American higher education on the basis of this definition would require an examination of the whole range of programs of colleges and universities, including their extensive research enterprises, their community service projects, their ancillary operations of experimental farms, airports, wind-tunnels, and bus lines, and their extracurricular programs of student organizations, intermural activities, intercollegiate competition, volunteer work, concerts and other scheduled events, teach-ins and unscheduled education. Of all these activities, we chose to focus on the formal educational program. Our reason was simple: the curriculum remains the central means to an educational institution's ends; and if the curriculum is irrelevant, it must be changed. Rather than despairing of it as unmanageable and trying to compensate for its pickled abracadabra by making the out-of-class extracurriculum and other programs more vital, it seems to us that the curriculum itself must be revitalized.

Many students view the formal program of study as a necessary evil—griping at the "busy work" of remembering remote facts for credits and points. Many parents eye it with suspicion ("Whatever you do, just don't believe everything they tell you in class.") Faculty and administrators alike approach it with frustration ("Another decade gone and we've got to rethink it again.") But the curriculum is the battlefield at the heart of the institution. Complaints of institutional irrelevance, obscurantism, and ossification all aim here. And of all an educational institution's programs, it must be foremost in leading to the goals of education. To leave the curriculum to its own devices and try to improve its periphery of education and life beyond the classroom—as most student personnel administrators are obliged to do—is, in the vernacular of the religious fundamentalists, to whitewash the sepulcher. Whether the goals of four years of college are to "make a man or woman wiser, more sensitive, more compassionate, more responsible, more useful, and happier,"[4] or to develop "such general attributes as freedom from prejudice, depth of interest, a humanized conscience, and eagerness for continued learning,"[5] or, in William James' words, to "help you know a good man when you see him,"[6] they cannot be left to chance in the informal program but rather must be the reason for being of the required program.

For these reasons, we are particularly concerned with the options that are open to students and with the work that is expected of them in the curriculum. In the Study of Institutional Vitality, we sought to determine the changes that have been made in these options and expectations, and then we tried to account for these changes. We are not unconcerned about the other functions of colleges and universities: their dynamics are merely easier to understand. For example, research services change with the interests of

---

[4] Thomas C. Mendenhall, "The Care and Feeding of the Liberal Arts Curriculum," *The Challenge of Curricular Change.* (Report of the Colloquium on the Challenge of Curricular Change, April, 1965, Skytop, Pennsylvania). New York: College Entrance Examination Board, 1966, p. 62.

[5] Nevitt Sanford, "Discussion" in "Social Changes and the College Student: A Symposium," *Educational Record, 41,* 4, October 1960, 336.

[6] William James, "The Social Value of the College-Bred," *Memories and Studies,* New York: Longmans, Green, 1912, p. 309.

professors and financial patrons; and most universities would not be averse to accepting a cyclotron or a linear accelerator if one were offered them. Similarly the volunteer activities of the extra-curriculum have their own dynamic. They originate and operate on student energy and exist under fewer constraints than the curriculum. Change in the extracurriculum is largely a function of student desire and trends in late-adolescent culture: as interest wanes in harvest balls, freshman beanies, and foreign language clubs, it may rise in political theory, mysticism, and movie making. Thus any fraternity with an exchange student from England and a soccer ball can inaugurate a new tradition in the extracurricular codex. But change in the formal curriculum is more complex and restricted. It always slowly follows the lead that research and the extracurriculum take—since the curriculum is basically the institutionalized remains of earlier interests of professors, patrons, and students. But the curriculum usually follows their lead with some difficulty—and it is essential to understand the nature of these restrictions and difficulties.

In sum, we have not studied all of the factors that could be considered as measuring the vitality of an educational institution. We have not studied the educational effectiveness or the quality of colleges and universities. Instead we have sought to understand the forces that effect educational change within higher education in the hope of stimulating more continuous academic reform.

Work on the study took three distinct directions. One, led by Richard E. Peterson and his associates at Educational Testing Service in collaboration with Earl J. McGrath, was the development of a questionnaire called the Institutional Functioning Inventory. This instrument, which can be completed by faculty members, administrators, and other members of an institution, provides measures of several scales related to educational adaptability and excitement. It has already provided many self-study data for the institutions that have used it, and eventually these data will be related to empirical measures of institutional effectiveness and adaptability to indicate its utility as a predictive instrument.

Second, Hans Flexner and I at Teachers College undertook

a survey of existing information on organizational change in general and on academic change in particular, and then we made a series of sixteen case studies of the evolution of particular educational practices at a variety of institutions. We examined the adoption by Kalamazoo College of the Kalamazoo Plan; the creation of Justin Morrill College at Michigan State University, the Residential College at the University of Michigan, Fairhaven College at Western Washington State College, and the National Technical Institute for the Deaf at Rochester Institute of Technology; and the difficulties that several other colleges and universities experienced in reorganizing their curricula, calendar, and operations. Flexner on his own analyzed the origins and subsequent history of Bennington College as a study of changes within a particularly distinctive institution.[7] These case studies provided the staff with a number of ideas about the dynamics of academic change that are summarized in Chapters One and Two of this book. But we recognized that we could not use these examples—illuminating as they were—to test our hypotheses about change, since we had deliberately selected them for study because of their significance.

The third phase of the project thus involved the testing of our ideas about academic reform on a randomly-selected stratified sample of 110 American colleges and universities. The details of this part of the study will be found in Chapters Three, Four, and Five; and our conclusions to date from the entire project can be seen in Chapter Six.

Because these chapters could not have been written without the assistance of many people who have been involved in the study since 1964, before turning to Chapter One I wish to acknowledge their valued effort, endurance, and enthusiasm. First among them is Earl J. McGrath himself, the director of the study, the director, until 1968, of the Institute of Higher Education, and now, since his retirement from Teachers College, director of the new Higher Education Center at Temple University. His idealism, humanitarianism, and devotion to the improvement of higher education have

[7] Hans Flexner, "The Dynamics of Institutional Change at Bennington College." Ph.D. Dissertation, Columbia University, 1969.

encouraged the staff of the project just as they have his other colleagues throughout his significant career.

The other members of the institute staff served the project faithfully and energetically. Ann Ash proved the mainstay in the conduct of the study, keeping correspondence, schedules, interviews, tabulations, data, manuscripts, and morale in excellent shape— cheerfully and without apparent effort. Charles F. Fisher, Hans Flexner, Jack T. Johnson, Herman P. Kauz, Sidney S. Letter, Tetsuko Nakamura, and William R. O'Connell, Jr., proved refreshing companions during the years of the project.

Throughout 1968, Robert H. Friis and Arthur Shriberg were invaluable to the study by taking major responsibility for planning and coordinating the telephone interviews, gathering additional institutional data, and providing thoughtful criticism and suggestions, aided by a vigorous crew that included Blanche Bigelow, Helen Birnbaum, Carroll Cline, Colleen Doherty, Richard Dubow, Myrna Garvey, Joan Godshall, Bonnie Impara, Joyce McNiell, Gary Milby, Winsome Munro, Bruce Noble, Linda Ronald, Tom Rounds, Ronald Schenk, Margie Shriberg, Joyce Shue, Jane Stanicki, Marion Turpeau, Joseph Wells, and Jon Wicklund. Further facts and advice were obtained from George Nash and David Kamins of the Bureau of Applied Social Research of Columbia University and from Chiogu Ebede of the Teachers College Computer Center. The report was typed, assembled, and checked by Paula Adsit, Alan Karp, Julia Reed, Barbara Symmes, and Amelia and Hilary Hefferlin.

The several hundred professors and administrators who graciously agreed to be interviewed for the study deserve acknowledgment for their help; but since we promised them anonymity, we must here offer them only collective thanks. We can, however, personally acknowledge the aid of colleagues throughout the country whose ideas have stimulated ours. Among them are Laurence Barrett, Howard Becker, Theodore Caplow, Burton R. Clark, Terry Clark, Junius Davis, Frank G. Dickey, Robert Dreeben, Paul L. Dressel, Edwin D. Duryea, Marie Frazee, Blanche Geer, Patricia Grinager, Arden Grotelueschen, Edwin F. Hallenbeck, Fred F.

Preface

Harcleroad, Frank M. Hefferlin, Warren G. Hill, Everett C. Hughes, Morris Keeton, Charles Kletzsch, Edward O. Laumann, Martin Lichterman, Warren Bryan Martin, Elliot Maxwell, Murray Milner, Samuel Eliot Morison, C. Robert Pace, George Wilson Pierson, Lawrence A. Pervin, Gerald M. Platt, Donald L. Reidhaar, Stephen J. Stearns, Rebecca S. Vreeland, Miriam Wagenschein, Seymour Warkov, Margie Ann White, Theresa Birch Wilkins, Donald T. Williams, Jr., Logan Wilson, and J. L. Zwingle. Among the men and women who hosted us during our case study visits were J. Arnold Bricker, William Churchill, Winifred Dumphy, Carl Gatlin, Thomas H. Langevin, Howard R. Neville, Adolph J. Stern, Kay Stratton, John H. Taylor, Peter Veltman, and James W. Wilson.

Students in my classes on academic administration at Teachers College offered excellent suggestions about the report, as did the faculty members in the Seminar on Organizational Analysis and in the Department of Higher and Adult Education—chief among the latter being Walter I. Garms, Alan B. Knox, Gordon C. Lee, and W. Max Wise. Finally, five long-time friends, companions, and intellectual mentors have contributed incalculably more to the study than they realize: Franc Mason, Clayton Shaw, W. H. Cowley, William K. Selden, and Earline Dawdy Hefferlin.

Moreover, the Charles F. Kettering Foundation deserves acknowledgment for its support of this project and of other research and demonstration projects in educational innovation on many campuses. We are indebted to the officers and trustees of the foundation for their interest and financial backing—which generously included the nickel for the gum that Arthur Shriberg purchased at the Seventy-second Street subway station last June. Because of its utility to the project, we decided that it would not be inappropriate to charge the gum to "data retrieval."

JB LON HEFFERLIN

New York City
August, 1969

xxiv

Contents

Foreword by Earl J. McGrath   *ix*

Preface   *xv*

1   *Problems of Reform*   *I*

2   *Processes of Reform*   *17*

3   *Changes in Curriculum*   *50*

Contents

4 *Agents of Change* 73

5 *Correlates of Dynamism* 105

6 *Sources of Reform* 136

Appendices

A *Literature on Change* 191

B *Sampling and Analysis* 200

C *Telephone Interviews* 209

D *Variables Employed in Analysis* 222

Index 233

Dynamics
of
Academic
Reform

CHAPTER I

Problems of Reform

... Men must be discriminating appraisers of their society, knowing coolly and precisely what it is about the society that thwarts or limits them and therefore needs modification. And so must they be discriminating protectors of their institutions, preserving those features that nourish and strengthen them and make them more free. To fit themselves for such tasks, they must be sufficiently serious to study their institutions, sufficiently dedicated to become expert in the art of modifying them.[1]

John W. Gardner

[1] "Uncritical Lovers, Unloving Critics," Commencement Address, Cornell University, June 1, 1968.

1

Charles Muscatine, the chairman of the select committee that was appointed by Berkeley's Academic Senate to suggest improvements in instruction at the University of California following the student revolt of 1964, stated the central problem of academic reform in one sentence. "For the permanent health of our academic community," he wrote in the report of the committee, "we would prefer to see it change gradually and continuously rather than having to suffer the shocks of drastic adjustment following periods of quiescence."[2]

Throughout history, educational institutions have continually become inadequate for the intellectual demands of their times and as a result have suffered from the shocks of drastic adjustment. In Europe, the Renaissance developed outside the medieval universities, and it passed them and their scholasticism by. Slowly the universities adjusted to the fruits of the Renaissance, but then in the seventeenth and eighteenth centuries many of them turned their backs on the growth of science. Having once accepted Aristotle's *organum,* they had difficulty adapting to Francis Bacon's *novum organum.*

During the nineteenth and into the twentieth century, the liberal arts colleges of America finally acquiesced to the fact of science but neglected the industrialism and utilitarianism that surged around them. Having come to accept Francis Bacon, they were now unprepared for Francis Wayland.

"In the history of education," Alfred North Whitehead noted, "the most striking phenomenon is that schools of learning, which at one epoch are alive with a ferment of genius, in a succeeding generation exhibit merely pedantry and routine."[3] In every epoch, new structures have had to be created—the scientific academy, the technical institute, the normal school, the land-grant college, the research institute, the comprehensive university—to supplement the existing institutions. And the competition of these new

[2] *Education at Berkeley: Report of the Select Committee on Education.* Berkeley: University of California Press, 1966, p. 4.
[3] Alfred North Whitehead, *The Aims of Education and Other Essays.* New York: Macmillan, 1929, p. 2.

2

organizations has forced the existing institutions to adapt their functions in order to survive—a fact which has led Sir Nevill Mott, the Cavendish Professor of Experimental Physics at Cambridge, to remark that "the infallible recipe for stirring up a university is to set up a rival."[4]

The present appears to be another period in the cycle of institutional turmoil. On one campus after another, inaction has precipitated crisis. Student rebellion, faculty protests, or external intervention has been required for redress of grievances. At some colleges, declining effectiveness has been halted only by major surgery, and the prospect of collapse has forced radical retrenchment and reorganization. In the years ahead, many more colleges and universities will probably experience the same shocks of drastic adjustment unless they are able to adapt more responsively to change than they ever have until now.[5]

This all-too-common process of sporadic reform by major crisis is, of course, by no means unique to educational institutions. Many groups and organizations are unable to anticipate and adjust easily to new conditions. But it seems to us on the staff of the Institute of Higher Education that this tradition of periodic reaction to crisis is an inadequate method of change for any effective organization in as dynamic a society as ours; and we believe this is particularly true for an effective educational institution. The education of students is now too important, both to them and to all of us, for them to be exploited at institutions where discontent must accumulate for years before it reaches the bursting point of reform and where obsolete procedures lead to the production of obsolescent alumni. Not only the permanent health of the academic commu-

[4] *The New York Times,* December 12, 1965, Section E, p. 11.

[5] Burton R. Clark has noted this tendency in these words: "Many schools and colleges are unable to make a major change until confronted by crisis—near bankruptcy or an exodus of staff or an explosive split among key personnel. Crisis is the common condition under which old enterprises are reborn, allowed once more to begin anew with a sense of starting down an uncharted road." (*Educating the Expert Society.* San Francisco: Chandler, 1962, p. 194.)

nity but the continued health of the larger society now depend on the continuity of systematic academic change.

Our thesis, therefore, is *continuous adaptability*. We hope for continual academic change beyond sporadic and occasional reforms, beyond reacting to crises of "near bankruptcy or an exodus of staff or an explosive split among key personnel,"[6] beyond the fits and starts and spurts of housecleaning followed by years of inertia.

Like the Muscatine committee, we are ameliorists, not revolutionaries. When strain develops in the life of a social institution, just as in a geological formation, we prefer the occasional tremor of adjustment to the infrequent cataclysmic quake. In 1968, France needed a student rebellion to force change in its university system. Now in the United States—where Jefferson once asserted the necessity of occasional rebellions—many students are also claiming that violence is necessary for institutional reform. We would like to think that they are wrong. Just as in health, where preventive medicine is better than therapeutic and restorative medicine; just as in the upkeep of a building, where continuous maintenance can be less costly than deferred maintenance; so with institutions: we believe that their incremental change is not only possible but is less costly than their upheaval, disruption, collapse, and the creation of new substitutes.

The innovator typically builds a new institution or a new model to replace the old. The reformer revamps an existing institution to make it better. The traditionalist suspects them both of perfidy.

Americans have historically been reformers. After observing the results of the innovators, most of them have not been averse to remodeling existing institutions to serve new goals. Traditionalists, of course, have viewed such changes in higher education as debasements—leading, over the years, to humanism, science, professionalism, utility, or—worse yet—popularization. Could the B.A. or Ph.D. degrees remain pure, unsullied, and "rigorous" if the requirements for these degrees were altered? Should job retraining be of-

6 *Ibid.*

fered in the groves of academe, or be left to industry, the Job Corps, and paramilitary services? Should students from "nonstandard" backgrounds be allowed to enroll? Dare the universities undertake action projects on urban problems? Should the colleges risk corruption by trying to educate the masses?

Some observers believe not. They contend that American colleges and universities are already too accommodating to American society—too adaptive, too innovative, or at least too much so in the wrong direction. "Since 1945 the universities have been doing nothing but innovate," Jacques Barzun has been quoted as saying.[7] They have taken on projects that "they had no ability or means of performing, and that's why they are in their present mess —financially and spiritually." Other critics charge the universities with selling tradition for popularity, with mimicking the American drugstore in supplying public wants, with failing to resist the detrimental influences in American life. Instead of supposed rigidity and conservatism, such critics point to rampant academic faddism, bandwagon fashion, uncritical innovation, and helterskelter efforts at modernity in following the peddlers of untested nostrums.[8]

Certainly over the past century and a half our colleges have been more faddish than most of us realize. They have come to accept not only science but chalk and blackboards, the performing arts, research laboratories, fraternity houses, seminars, circulating and open-stack libraries, graduate study, contract research, lectures, overseas campuses, football, vocational education, academic majors and minors, and teach-ins: no small assortment of novelty. Even within the curriculum, it may seem that higher education is in a constant turmoil of self-analysis and renewal. The presidents of a number of midwestern colleges a few years ago, for example, claimed that in recent years general education at their institutions had been:

---

[7] *The New York Times,* October 25, 1968, p. 50.

[8] For example, see the critiques by Lee J. Cronbach, "The Role of the University in the Improvement of Education," *Expanding Horizons of Knowledge About Man: A Symposium.* New York: Yeshiva University, 1966, p. 8; and Paul L. Dressel and Frances H. DeLisle, *Undergraduate Curriculum Trends.* Washington, D.C.: American Council on Education, 1969, p. 2.

5

developed, introduced, reassessed, enriched, clarified, firmed-up, redistributed, initiated, required, instituted, adopted, modified, abandoned, changed, reduced, revised, studied, switched, spread over four years, reduced from four to two years, expanded, broadened, and formalized.[9]

And during the past decade, the enthusiasm about general education that blossomed after World War II has been replaced by high-pressure specialization in the colleges. While general education of the 1950s has been percolating down into the high schools, the colleges have begun preparing young undergraduate sociologists, physicists, and literary historians whose counterparts twenty years ago would have been graduate students.

From all these examples, it might be possible to conclude that the problem of academic change is only an academic issue: that the House of Intellect, even if not completely perfect, is being kept in adequate repair with occasional tinkering and home craftsmanship. We ourselves, however, are not that sanguine. Even if we disregard the youthful critics who have concluded that our existing educational institutions are too corrupt to be capable of reform and who advocate their destruction and replacement, we cannot overlook the widespread concern of otherwise moderate men, many of them from within higher education itself. Among them, Irving Kristol, co-editor of *The Public Interest,* states that "the university has been—with the possible exception of the post office—the least inventive (or even adaptive) of our social institutions since the end of World War II."[10] Goodwin Watson has observed pessimistically that the effective educational life of most new colleges seems to be about seven years, and he has suggested that unless new institutions can become more adaptive than this, they might as well be disbanded at that age and new ones created.[11] Among the historians

[9] Ida Long Rogers, *The Process of Institutional Change, with Particular Reference to Major Curricular Change in Selected Colleges.* Ph.D. Dissertation, University of Michigan, 1964, p. 14.

[10] Irving Kristol, "A Different Way to Restructure the University," *The New York Times Magazine,* December 8, 1968, p. 50.

[11] Goodwin Watson, "Experimental Colleges in America," *Confer-*

of higher education, Frederick Rudolph concludes that the policy of American colleges and universities, except on rare occasions, has been "drift, reluctant accommodation, belated recognition that while no one was looking change had in fact taken place."

> Resistance to fundamental reform was ingrained in the American collegiate and university tradition, as over three hundred years of history demonstrated. . . . Experimentation, which was the life of the university, and innovation, which was its gift to society, were seldom tried upon the colleges and universities themselves. There timidity prevailed.[12]

Bernhard J. Stern, in his historical analysis of academic change, termed the process one of "defensive concessions and progressive adjustments" to the demand for change.[13] Homer D. Babbidge, the president of the University of Connecticut, has written:

> Even the radical land-grant institutions show signs of shuddering conservatism when it comes to the educational needs of the late twentieth century. . . . Though we have concrete and disturbing instances in which the public has "shot down" educators and institutions for their failure to conform to social or political or educational convention, we have examples of many more instances in which institutions and educators have grounded themselves by playing it too safe.[14]

Alvin Eurich, at the end of his work with the Fund for the Advancement of Education, stated:

> . . . college teaching stands out as one of the few fields in which innovation and improvement are neglected. . . .

---

ence 1: *Dimensions of Changes in Higher Education.* Yellow Springs, Ohio: Union for Research and Experimentation in Higher Education, 1967, p. 31.

[12] Frederick Rudolph, *The American College and University.* New York: Knopf, 1962, pp. 491, 492.

[13] Bernard J. Stern, "Historical Materials on Innovations in Higher Education" (unpublished manuscript), May, 1953, p. 25.

[14] Homer D. Babbidge, "The Outsiders. External Forces Affecting American Higher Education," R. J. Ingham (ed.), *Institutional Backgrounds of Adult Education: Dynamics of Change in the Modern University.* Boston: Center for the Study of Liberal Education for Adults, 1966, pp. 85–86.

Clearly, a very large majority of our institutions of higher learning and faculty members have no commitment to change or to improve college and university teaching.[15]

Edmund Volkart, former dean of the faculty at Oregon State and now executive officer of the American Sociological Association, observes:

> Drastic overhaul of curricula seems necessary if succeeding generations are to cope with problems of social change, increased leisure time, a highly specialized occupational structure, and the constant shrinking of the world. It is my general impression that this is not being done. Outmoded ideas of the educated man persist, and too many professional schools seek only technical competence in their products.[16]

Sidney Sulkin makes this observation about current students in summarizing a conference sponsored by the College Entrance Examination Board and the National Association of Secondary-School Principals:

> Better prepared academically than his predecessors were, with a broader range of goals to choose from, and thus more in need of educational flexibility, today's student comes out of a radically changing secondary school system only to be confronted by the uncompromising rigidities of colleges that have not changed drastically from what they were a generation or two ago.[17]

And John Gardner, prophetically looking backward on the twentieth century from a twenty-first century perspective, has concluded that:

[15] Alvin C. Eurich, "The Commitment to Experiment and Innovate in College Teaching," *Educational Record, 45,* 1, Winter 1964, 49, 50.

[16] Edmund Volkart, "Role of the Administrator and Faculty Member in the Process of Change," R. J. Ingham (ed.), *Institutional Backgrounds of Adult Education: Dynamics of Change in the Modern University.* Boston: Center for the Study of Liberal Education for Adults, 1966, p. 54.

[17] Sidney Sulkin, "Introduction," *The Challenge of Curricular Change.* Report of the Colloquium on the Challenge of Curricular Change, April, 1965, Skytop, Pennsylvania. New York: College Entrance Examination Board, 1966, p. xviii.

Problems of Reform

Most institutions were designed to obstruct change rather than facilitate it. And that is not really surprising. The institutions were, after all, designed by human beings, and most men most of the time do not want the institutions in which they themselves have a vested interest to change. Professors were often cited as an interesting example of this tendency, because they clearly favored innovation in other parts of the society but steadfastly refused to make universities into flexible, adaptive, self-renewing institutions.[18]

We agree with these critics of inertia as well as with the critics of faddism. We believe with John Gardner that the process of self-renewal can be institutionalized in colleges and universities so that academic reform is more continuous and effective. We want organizations to build in flexibility and responsiveness, experimentation and evaluation, to ease their fluctuation between radical reconstruction and then rigid reaction. We hope to assist the development of planned change—the "conscious, deliberate, and collaborative effort to improve the operation of a system," as Warren Bennis defines it, "through the utilization of scientific knowledge."[19]

To do so, it seems to us that exhortation is inadequate. Pleas for change are insufficient. The rhetoric of complaint is vivid—"institutional stagnation," "ossification," "internal decay," "dry rot," "dead wood," "petrification," "decline and moribundity"—but such rhetoric is emotive rather than analytic. For effective reform, the process of academic change in American colleges and universities must first of all be better understood: not for the sake of change itself, but for the sake of academic progress.

To begin to learn about academic change, we examined all the information that we could gather about the process of organizational change at large—whether it was the expansion of services of libraries or hospitals, the community services of local government, the redirection of a social movement, the programming of symphony orchestras, or the tasks of research institutes. In Appen-

[18] John W. Gardner, *op. cit.*
[19] Warren G. Bennis, Kenneth D. Benne, and Robert Chin, *The Planning of Change: Readings in the Applied Behavioral Sciences.* New York: Holt, 1964, p. 3.

9

dix A we have listed some of the literature on this problem, and here we identify the major conclusions to be drawn from it. First we point to the difficulty of organizational change; then, in the next chapter, we look at the sources for change.

Organizations are inherently passive.   In contrast to congeries of individuals who do not interact or to crowds that interact only transiently, organizations consist of patterns of repetitive and continuing interaction, patterns of coordinated and ordered behavior. A liberal arts college, a family, an afternoon bridge club, and the federal government all continue in existence through the repetitive interaction of their members. They exist for the routinization of behavior. They are efficient devices for the continuing performance of some task. They organize people's interaction through such mechanisms as classroom schedules, hourly periods, semester course assignments, yearly calendars, and handbooks of regulations. And hence they are structurally passive: their procedures and goals are not altered capriciously.[20]

Moreover, organizations are hierarchical, in that some members—the faculty, an administrative council, the president, the comptroller—have more power than other members to enforce these procedures, including the procedures to screen and reject prospective applicants, and to dismiss any unsuitable members.

Voluntary organizations attract members who agree with their activities.   Organizations are self-selective. Their members recruit others who appear to be compatible with them, and new recruits join the organization because they approve of its goals. Thus, few medical students enter the medical profession in order to introduce Christian Science; and few professors enter academe to destroy it. In other words, most opponents of organizations battle them from without—not as subversives from within.

[20] For this reason, while organizations seem to have an inherent tendency to grow in size and to add to their original functions—for one reason because of safety in size and in diversification (whereby bets are hedged by spreading the possible loss)—they tend to retain their original activities until pressure forces their modification or elimination. For examples of this characteristic tendency, observe the criticisms of permanent or standing committees in organizations in contrast to the comments about ad hoc committees.

The most typical example in education of this tendency toward self-selection is for schools and colleges, whenever they have the chance, to select as students those applicants who need them the least. They establish a goal to be achieved, and then tend to admit those students who already, before entering the institution, come closest to meeting that goal.[21]

Organizations tend toward institutionalization and ritualism. Organizational activities and procedures tend over time to assume a sacred quality by a process that sociologists call the "institutionalization of means" and the "formalization of routine."[22] By this process, the methods for achieving a goal slowly come to be considered the goal itself. Administration may begin to expand for administration's sake; library policies may be enforced for enforcement's sake; and a professor who starts his career by using lectures as a means to help students learn may eventually come to the point of lecturing regardless of whether or not his students learn. In this way, the professor's original procedure—lecturing—has now supplanted his original object—learning. As Robert M. Hutchins suc-

---

[21] Ralph Tyler first alerted us to this example. We observed an illustration of it at a midwestern college that was trying to maintain its traditions by admitting only those students who appeared to share its norms. The administration was reluctant to recruit particularly bright students because of their fear that high scholastic ability was associated with the dangers of other types of deviance—such as beards, drugs, sex, and activism—and so they encouraged for admission only the blandly mediocre.

[22] Here, for example, is how Burton Clark describes the process: "Organizations become institutionalized in part through the formalizing of procedure. Out of trial and error come practices that are explicitly promoted and codified—in short, are made part of the formal arrangement of work. The practices become routines and the personnel become accustomed to their pace. The routines conserve time and energy, as habits do generally, but they tend to promote rigidity. If the personnel invest themselves emotionally in their routines, and in this way transform means into ends, then the means become fixed, resistant to change when a change in purpose or a change in the environment demands the scrapping of the old and the instituting of something new. Professors may come to love their old lectures, and teachers to feel that certain classroom techniques are a very extension of themselves. Formalization, always necessary to some degree, thus may develop to the point where it impairs the viability of the organization. . . ." (*Educating the Expert Society,* pp. 193–194.)

11

cinctly put the problem of institutionalization, "the enterprise goes on because it started and runs for the sake of running."[23]

Moreover, these practices—whether they be lecturing or rain dancing—may come to be ritualistically continued without an evaluation of their effectiveness. As Benjamin Bloom and his associates have indicated, educational institutions tend to retain educational objectives that are most easily evaluated, such as the most elemental cognitive and verbal learning, while letting their more significant objectives, such as affective value orientations, disappear over time.[24]

In addition, organizations that are livelihoods for people tend to come to exist only as livelihoods for these people. A volunteer organization disappears as soon as the volunteer effort collapses, but an organization with paid employees becomes a particularly vested interest; and any threat to procedures and rituals that provide a livelihood is likely to be resisted. R. M. Beverly noted this at Cambridge a hundred and thirty years ago in his complaint that "the system is established: it is in the interest of a swarm of useless men to keep it so, who would be ruined if it were altered."[25]

Finally, the maintenance of institutional effectiveness or achievement (such as students' learning) is only one problem that organizations must face in order to survive. Other problems may take precedence over it. Problems of recruiting members, of coordination and integration, of authority and stability—all must be attended to when they occur. For example, college and university administrators and faculty members must find applicants and resources, maintain morale, and avoid disaffection and rebellion; and thus their attention to academic reform in carrying out the institu-

---

[23] Robert M. Hutchins, "The Administrator: Leader or Officeholder?" *Freedom, Education, and the Fund: Essays and Addresses, 1946–1956.* New York: Meridian, 1956, p. 177.

[24] See David R. Krathwohl, Benjamin S. Bloom, and Bertram B. Masia, *Taxonomy of Educational Objectives: The Classification of Educational Goals. Handbook II: Affective Domain.* New York: McKay, 1964, p. 16.

[25] *A Letter to His Royal Highness, The Duke of Gloucester, Chancellor, on the Present Corrupt State of the University of Cambridge,* 1833.

tion's goals and in expanding and diffusing knowledge may of necessity be sporadic and transient.[26] The squeaking institutional imperative, in short, gets the oil.

Organizations clearly have successive stages of change and consolidation, of ferment and fixity, and it is probably unrealistic to expect any institution to be continually in experiment. Kurt Lewin and his associates concluded that after major changes, a period of "refreezing" and then unfreezing must normally occur before further changes can be made.[27] Continuous change may thus be as disruptive to students and faculty members as occasional crises. If this is always so, one major problem of change is to keep the periods of change and consolidation in balance and the periods of consolidation as temporary as possible.

For all these reasons, most organizations experience some difficulty in adapting to new conditions. Academic institutions, however, appear to have particular problems in addition because of their own distinctive characteristics:

Their purposes and support are basically conservative. Schools and colleges are essentially devices for the perpetuation of culture. Their support and governance stem from the most successful and wealthy groups in society that are naturally devoted to assuring the continuity of the present system. Most teachers and professors, in addition, are concerned with the preservation as well as the expansion of knowledge. They are members of a professional elite and of the establishment, and their academic disciplines represent a long tradition of custom and precedent.

The educational system is vertically fragmented. Under-

---

[26] For a statement of the theory of organizational equilibrium, see Talcott Parsons, "Some Considerations on the Theory of Social Change," *Rural Sociology, 26,* 3, September 1961, 219–239. Peter M. Blau and W. Richard Scott discuss the problem that "new problems are internally generated in organizations in the process of solving old ones" under the caption of "Dialectical Processes of Change" in *Formal Organizations: A Comparative Approach.* San Francisco: Chandler, 1962, pp. 250–253.

[27] See, in particular, Kurt Lewin, "Frontiers in Group Dynamics: Concept, Method, and Reality in Social Science," *Human Relations, 1,* 1, 1947, 5–42, especially pp. 33–39.

graduate colleges are trapped between the lower schools and the graduate schools: they are caught between the competencies of their applicants and the expectations of employers and graduate school admissions officers. Junior colleges, moreover, are even more seriously constrained by the narrow transfer requirements of the senior colleges. Thus many institutions of higher education operate in the tradition of a cottage industry—independently doing piece-work as part of a larger system, but with few options open to them. They must receive students, care for them, educate them, and send them along in good condition to the next stage of the process. To modify their program beyond accepted bounds would be as risky as for a typewriter manufacturer to market typewriters with an ar-rangement of keys different from that of the standard keyboard.

Within higher education, institutional reputation is not based on innovation. The accepted roads to academic prestige and advancement are not those of unconventionality. Amitai Etzioni explains the reasons well in these words:

> Businesses which do not innovate are likely to go out of busi-ness. Universities, first of all, very rarely disintegrate or are forced to disappear through mergers. Even the most tradition-alistic university continues to operate. Hence here innovation is optional and not mandatory. . . . in general, to be a late-comer to institutional innovation and even cultural innova-tion is not undermining to the operation of a university. More-over, since reputation and not profit is the main indicator of success, to "take a risk" by accepting an untested innovation is considered especially unwise. The norm is to wait and see.[28]

This fact helps explain why F. M. Cornford, the most incisive ob-server of academic politics, stated his famous axiom of academic life that "nothing should ever be done for the first time."[29]

Faculty members have observed their vocation for years as students before joining it. Thus they differ from the practitioners

[28] Amitai Etzioni, "Innovations in Universities," unpublished memo-randum.

[29] *Microcosmographia Academica: Being A Guide for the Young Academic Politician.* Cambridge, England: Bowes and Bowes, 1908. Fifth Edition, 1953, p. 15.

14

of law or medicine or most other professions, who have had little direct acquaintance with their field before entering it. As a result, the process of self-selection in college and university faculties is particularly narrow. Professors have thought highly enough of college to become academicians. Rebellious and dissatisfied students seldom have any interest in becoming professors, and thus educational institutions tend to prepare as future academicians only those students who believe in them.

The ideology of the academic profession treats professors as independent professionals. We professors tend to think of ourselves as biologists or historians who deign to associate ourselves with an institution in order to practice our profession. The tradition of classroom sanctity, once we close the door and begin our lecture, tends to insure that change will occur only voluntarily or through the slow natural process of faculty retirement and replacement. "You can make all the rules and regulations you want," one professor said to us during an interview for this study, "but if a professor of microbiology is always going to teach the way he's always taught, you're stuck." In general, a professor who receives tenure also receives tenure for his program and his techniques. His powers of passive resistance are therefore great.[30]

Academics are skeptical about the idea of efficiency in academic life. Many professors harbor a mystique about teaching and

---

[30] Commenting on the almost "Gothic-letter sanctity of the classroom of the college teacher" in comparison with the school classroom, Thomas C. Mendenhall has written, "Anyone who has attempted in-service training for college teachers knows its perils. Just try to help a younger teacher with his teaching: the possibility can create a tremor in even a strong breast." ("The Care and Feeding of the Liberal Arts Curriculum," *The Challenge of Curricular Change*, p. 65.) In addition, not only does the faculty deem itself to have "primary responsibility for determining educational policies of the institution," in the words of the AAUP Committee on Faculty Participation in College and University Government. ("Faculty Participation in College and University Government," *AAUP Bulletin, 49, 3,* Autumn 1963, 255). But most academics assume that no change in academic direction should be made until, as Kingman Brewster says, "they have become quite genuinely the will of the faculty itself." (*Yale University: 1967–68. The Report of the President.* New Haven: Yale University Press, 1968, p. 8).

education that denies the validity of measurement. In this view, education is intangible; its goals cannot be operationally defined, and hence it cannot be observed or evaluated. It is an "art," not subject to systematic analysis or investigation by the behavioral scientist. Therefore many professors grant little status to the study of education itself and do not favor the use of institutional resources for institutional research and evaluation.

Finally, academic institutions are deliberately structured to resist precipitant change. Besides their policies of academic freedom and tenure to protect against external vigilantes or internal dissension, most colleges and universities operate through a series of review and approval mechanisms: departmental faculty meetings, general faculty committees, administrative boards, senate, assemblies, and governing boards. This structure contributes to the deliberately slow adoption of change. They also are intentionally fragmented into separate specialties—programs, departments, divisions, and schools—that assure the diffusion of power. This dual pattern of extensive coordination combined with extensive decentralization to units and individuals serves to prohibit rapid alteration, subversion, or overthrow, but it prevents concerted action when action is needed. Hence even when professors desire institution-wide reform, the structure of the institution impedes it.

In short, not only do colleges and universities share the usual tendencies of any organization toward stability, but they have more than the usual number of constraints and several distinctive characteristics to safeguard their own specific function of education. Under these conditions and with these restraints, it may seem surprising that much academic change occurs at all. As a result of them, it certainly is less surprising that the process of academic change is the source of so much complaint, frustration, and ridicule.

But how, in fact, does academic change come about? That question is the topic for the following chapters.

CHAPTER II

Processes of Reform

If I read history aright, human institutions have rarely been killed while they retain vitality. They commit suicide or die from lack of vigor, and then the adversary comes and buries them. So long as an institution conduces to human welfare, so long as a university gives to youth strong, active methods of life, so long as its scholarship does not degenerate into pedantry, nothing can prevent its going on to greater prosperity.[1]

A. Lawrence Lowell

[1] Statement at the Harvard tercentenary celebration, September 18, 1936, adjourning the meeting until September, 2036.

$\mathcal{C}$hanging the curriculum, it has been said, is like moving a graveyard. In both cases, for better or worse, the content is generally lifeless. Moreover, the physical problems pall before the issues of sanctity and sacrilege. A multitude of deep-seated and traditional values are threatened. The emotions of everyone even remotely related with the enterprise need to be respected. And the onerous task is most typically referred to a committee—one that is respected, honorable, and judicious.

In either circumstance, the change is likely to be delicate, tortuous, and slow. How, then, does academic change occur? This chapter reviews the historical evidence that we have been able to gather about the process. To begin with, since academic reform is only a part of the larger process of organizational and intellectual change in society, we will first sketch out several general ideas about this total process.

Most observers of organizations and social systems tend to view the process of organizational change as a response to pressure. Institutions, they suggest, respond "homeostatically" to the influence and inspiration of their members who desire change and to the power of external forces. For example, many sociologists see organizational change, in Alvin W. Gouldner's words, as "the results of cumulative, unplanned, adaptive responses to threats to the equilibrium of the system as a whole."[2] Note the significance of the word *responses;* modifications are not random self-generated actions, initiated and emanating without cause. They occur because of discontent and effort.

In illustration, consider the evidence that social clubs and communities reluctantly drop their discriminatory practices when they judge that integration is more tolerable than the consequences of continued segregation. The threat of government regulation proves a spur for self-regulation, not only in industries ranging from motion pictures and automobiles to drugs and cigarettes, but also for voluntary accreditation in education. Ford's famous shift from

[2] Alvin W. Gouldner, "Organizational Analysis," in Robert K. Merton, Leonard Broom, and Leonard S. Cottrell, Jr. (eds.), *Sociology Today: Problems and Prospects.* New York: Basic Books, 1959, p. 405.

the Model T to the Model A stemmed from the competition of other manufacturers. Statistical quality control techniques were developed by Walter Shewhart and others in the late 1920s, but were not widely adopted in industry until pushed during World War II by the military services and the Office of Production Research and Development. Congress passed the National Defense Education Act when the threat of Russian scientific superiority seemed greatest. And colleges adapt their programs in response to public demand and institutional competition, as the history of higher education from antiquity shows and as the development of Afro-American studies and computer technology courses demonstrate today. James McCosh, the conservative president of Princeton, illustrated this fact a century ago, when his reason for having "new chairs founded to meet the wants of the times" lay in his fear that "unless this is secured without much longer delay, we shall be outstripped by other Colleges."[3]

In general, then, change occurs when the expected reward of change outweighs the reward of stability. Both in the individual and the organization, change is accepted when it seems the least of all possible evils and more desirable than any other alternative. Without the motivation of perceived benefit—prestige, economic return, enhanced self-image—it will not occur.

Observe, however, the importance of the perception of threat in stimulating change. It is the awareness of crisis, rather than crisis itself, that stimulates social action. Before it is perceived as such and counteraction taken, disaster can overwhelm an organization as well as an individual. Thus a typical reaction to a possible threat or changed condition is to disbelieve it ("Those students can't mean it."). But even if it must be believed, it is deemed irrelevant ("Why don't they attack the real cause?").[4] And even if it is deemed relevant, it seems at least transitory ("It will probably all

[3] James McCosh, "President's Report," Princeton: College of New Jersey, 1868, p. 1, quoted in Laurence R. Veysey, *The Emergence of the American University*. Chicago: University of Chicago Press, 1965, p. 11.
[4] A recent example of the problems this kind of reaction can precipitate is the "People's Park" fracas in Berkeley, May, 1969.

blow over.")'. Only belatedly does the evidence of change finally hit home. Hence the sensitivity of an organization to potential danger can determine its responsiveness to change.

Notice, too, that whether the disequilibrium stems originally from external force or internal dissatisfaction, it eventually is embodied in individual members of the organization who come to advocate change. They may be unsatisfied with the operations of the organization; they may sense a discrepancy between its reality and its potential; they may call for new responsibilities and priorities. Thus Walter Metzger has observed that "the breeding ground of institutional change is the sense of institutional failure."[5] This psychological disequilibrium or dissatisfaction with the status quo lies at the core of creativity, innovation, and leadership. Just as the greatest teachers throughout history have been considered visionary because they championed new ideals, great executives are termed leaders because they initiate action rather than waiting for circumstances to demand it.

Thus in organizations, advocacy is essential for change. An advocate wins others to his point of view, championing a vision of reality as yet unrealized, serving as the spearhead of social change —the infectious "microbe" of reform.[6] In religious movements such an advocate is proclaimed as a prophet or damned as a heretic; in politics he is labeled revolutionary, radical, or at least progressive; in science and technology he is considered a madcap or genius; in corporation life he has been termed the "product champion,"[7] the "change agent," the "innovator." And the history of American higher education is incomprehensible without these advocates— among them Benjamin Franklin and Thomas Jefferson, George Ticknor and Jonathan Baldwin Turner, Daniel Coit Gilman and William Rainey Harper, Herbert Hawkes and Alexander Meikle-

[5] Richard Hofstadter and Walter Metzger, *The Development of Academic Freedom in the United States*. New York: Columbia University Press, 1955, p. 316.

[6] See J. J. Jusserand, *English Wayfaring Life in the Middle Ages*, translated by Lucy Toulmin Smith. New York: Putnam's, 1925, p. 442.

[7] See Donald A. Schon, *Technology and Change: The New Heraclitus*. New York: Delacorte Press, 1967, pp. 115ff.

john, Robert M. Hutchins and Paul Goodman, Tom Hayden and Mike Vozick.

Francis Wayland was championing a new role for American colleges in 1842 when he proclaimed that their purpose was not to "give away a modicum of Greek and Latin and geometry to everyone who chooses to ask for it, but to foster and cultivate the highest talent of the nation, and raise the intellectual character of the whole, by throwing the brightest light of science in the path of those whom nature has qualified to lead."[8] John Erskine was advocating a broader function than most educators have when he called on us to teach science and literature "not merely as techniques, but as developers of the heart and spirit, as strengtheners of imagination and sympathy . . . to render the human heart more kindly."[9] More recently, Nevitt Sanford has been challenging the traditional limits of academic concern in his call for individual human development as the responsibility of the college. ". . . a central purpose of higher education is the fullest possible development of the whole personality," he states—not the mere exercise of cognitive skills. "Every aspect of the college environment, then, should be made to serve this purpose."[10] All of us are to some extent advocates like these. Each of us tries to change the condition of his life and his environment, although few of us are full-time revolutionaries prepared to abandon everything for a cause, regardless of the chance of success.

Looking at the targets of advocacy, it is clear that societies and institutions differ widely in their response to advocates of change. Equalitarian organizations, for example, appear in general to be most evocative of ideas from their members and lack the power to resist advocacy. They cannot prevent experimentation and change from arising continuously throughout their membership. On the

[8] Francis Wayland, *Thoughts on the Present Collegiate System . . . in the United States.* Boston: Gould, Kendall, and Lincoln, 1842, p. 48.

[9] John Erskine, "The Humanities in the New College Program," *The Journal of Higher Education, 18,* May 1947, 230.

[10] Nevitt Sanford, "General Education and the Theory of Personality Development," *Proceedings of the Symposium on Undergraduate Environment, October 18–19, 1962.* Brunswick, Me.: Bowdoin College, 1963, p. 8.

other hand, highly centralized organizations, where initiative is traditionally restricted to a small elite, appear to inhibit advocacy among their members, while advocacy from the central elite can be easily facilitated and implemented. Court martial, excommunication, and expulsion serve as devices to maintain order in hierarchical organizations, as can be illustrated by cases that range from the Edict of Worms regarding Martin Luther in 1521 to the court martial of Billy Mitchell in 1925. Yet reform can be dramatic if a visionary becomes the head of a centralized organization, as witness Pope John XXIII, Admiral John Fisher, the first Sea Lord of the Admiralty in the Royal Navy from 1904 to 1910 and 1914 to 1915, or Father Leo McLaughlin at Fordham University. "If the university were not autocratic," Elizabeth Sewell of Fordham's new experimental college says, "we would not exist."

Thus if an advocate senses little possibility of success in reforming an existing organization, he may turn instead to create a new one to accomplish his ends. Thomas Jefferson did so at Virginia, as did Jonathan Baldwin Turner at the Illinois Industrial University, and Daniel Coit Gilman at Johns Hopkins. George P. Baker left Harvard to establish his drama workshop at Yale, and William Rogers left Virginia to establish his Institute of Technology in a more receptive climate—that of Massachusetts. To create a radically new model is precarious—as the Cord automobile, the National Recovery Administration, and the University of Chicago's sophomore-year bachelor's degree of 1942 illustrate and as the difficulties of today's few upper division colleges attest.[11] But a new model may ultimately appear to be the only option for the reformer who feels thwarted in efforts to change the existing system. Just as trying a different marriage may seem easier than improving the old one, innovation may finally look more promising than reform.

Academic changes appear to take three general patterns: the creation of new institutions, the radical transformation of existing institutions, or the piecemeal alteration of institutional programs.

[11] Regarding the upper division colleges, see Robert A. Altman, *A Study of the Establishment of Upper Division Colleges in the United States.* Ph.D. dissertation, Columbia University. (Jossey-Bass, in press.)

Processes of Reform

One way to bring about reform is indeed to create a new model of an academic institution that introduces new concepts into the educational system. In Europe, the Ecole Polytechnique, the Kaiser Wilhelm University, and the University of London broke old molds; in America, so did Samuel Reed's normal school at Concord, Vermont, in 1823; Jefferson's University of Virginia and Stephen Van Rensselaer's School at Troy, New York, in 1824; the Agricultural College of the State of Michigan in 1855; Gilman's Johns Hopkins University in 1876; and what came to be the Joliet Junior College after 1902. The birth of new institutions such as these, however, is not the major means of change in higher education. They are necessary for emulation, but they are a minor part of the process. Most new colleges are created on the same educational lines as existing institutions, with the objective of simply offering the same education to a new clientele (as Smith College did in 1875, when it opened for women but with the same requirements as Yale, Harvard, and Amherst, and as most community colleges are now doing). Radically new institutions, such as Bennington, Sarah Lawrence, or newly-opening Hampshire College, influence the system primarily as their methods are adopted by other institutions.

A somewhat more frequent means of change occurs when old institutions are radically transformed, as were Brown in 1850, Antioch in 1921, St. John's in 1937, and Parsons in 1955, with the old program rejected and a new model substituted. At Brown, Francis Wayland threatened to resign as president unless the corporation approved his plans for "a radical change of the system of collegiate instruction" by adapting Brown to industrial and democratic America.[12] In 1919, Antioch had almost expired. It had been graduating fewer than a dozen students a year, and when the trustees tried to give it away to the YMCA, the YMCA returned it—whereupon Arthur Morgan, one of the trustees, agreed to become president and introduce his pet idea of cooperative educa-

[12] Francis Wayland, *Report to the Corporation of Brown University, on Changes in the System of Collegiate Education.* Providence: George H. Whitney, 1850, p. 50.

23

tion.[13] St. John's was on the verge of bankruptcy in 1937, with an endowment less than its debts of $300,000. It had lost its accreditation the year before because of an athletic scandal and its financial difficulties, and would have closed its doors in June except for the arrival of Stringfellow Barr from Chicago, who brought with him Scott Buchanan as dean and 120 classics as the new curriculum.[14] And at Parsons in 1955, Millard Roberts took over as president to introduce new funding and instructional theories to a struggling college—theories that for better or worse got embroiled in wheeler-dealing and academic nonrespectability.

The reason for such dramatic reforms as these has been suggested by Millar Upton, the president of Beloit College, in these words:

> When a college is on the verge of oblivion there is no problem in its achieving instant curricular revision, so to speak. All interested parties recognize that it is this or nothing. Dynamic, creative, dictatorial leadership is therefore welcomed by all. Time is of the essence in the abbreviated sense rather than the prolonged sense. The history of American higher education contains many evidences of the pressures of imminent failure providing the condition for immediate radical curricular change. Panic always produces action that is unobtainable during normal times.[15]

During normal times, however, the major process of academic change is that of *accretion and attrition:* the slow addition and subtraction of functions to existing structures. Accretion and

[13] See Burton R. Clark, *The Distinctive College.* Chicago: Aldine (in press).

[14] A brief reminiscence of the origins of the St. John's curriculum appears in Stringfellow Barr, "Scott Buchanan, Teacher," *The Center Magazine, 1,* 7, November 1968, 81–88. Santa Barbara: Center for the Study of Democratic Institutions.

[15] Millar Upton, "How to Achieve Acceptance of Major Curricular Change," abstract of speech at Twenty-Second National Conference on Higher Education, Chicago, March 7, 1967 (duplicated), reproduced in part in "Acceptance of Major Curricular Changes," G. Kerry Smith (ed.), *Current Issues in Higher Education, 1967.* Washington, D.C.: American Association for Higher Education, 1967, p. 101.

attrition are the most common means of academic change primarily because they are the most simple. Unlike radical reform, they are small-scale, undramatic, and often unpublicized. By accretion an institution merely encompasses a new program along with the old— a new occupational course, a research project, a new undergraduate tradition. And through attrition, other programs and functions are abandoned, either because they become outdated—like compulsory chapel—or because they come to be performed by other institutions.

The process may involve only one person: a declining major like Greek finally disappears when the classics professor retires. Or a new professor brings from graduate school an interest in solar spectroscopy. He attracts research support and assistants; he eventually may teach one or two courses in the subject; he may win the appointment of a similarly-minded colleague to the faculty; and if he moves on or retires, the central administration may find that a successor is expected to be appointed to continue the program: the field has become institutionalized. J. Harris Purks, the former provost of the University of North Carolina, satirized this process of unplanned accretion in his modern classic of "Academic Planning in Alligator Farm Management." Among the steps he noted are these: a professor gets approval to offer one course in Alligator Farm Management at an institution. A professional association of alligator farm managers is organized, and it pushes for more courses, such as "The Alligator in the Modern World" and "The Exceptional Alligator." Fellowship funds from the field lead to the appointment of a full-time professor with assistants. The staff win begrudging permission for a program leading to a Bachelor of Science in Alligator Farm Administration. The institution's president discovers the existence of the field, but by this time things are out of hand: competing programs at rival institutions arise; the National Accrediting Association for Schools and Departments of Alligator Farm Administration is organized; and ultimately—in order to prepare professors for the new programs—the institution establishes a graduate department of alligator farm administration education.[16]

[16] "Academic Planning in Alligator Farm Management," an address

Consider some actual examples of recent accretion: at Johns Hopkins University, Seymour Perlin has organized a new professional program in "suicidology" to prepare specialists in the scientific and humane study of suicide and suicide prevention.

During the past decade a new area of "sociolinguistics" has been emerging within the total field of semiotics and linguistics. It involves the study of relationships between linguistic repertoires and social roles, and one of its founders, Joshua Fishman, reports that at present between a dozen and two dozen scholars form the nucleus of the area and that nine universities have begun to offer courses in it.

Stimulated by the assassination of President Kennedy, a group of businessmen proposed to President Abram Sachar of Brandeis that the university take leadership in attacking the problem of wanton aggression. Out of initial conferences and faculty committee recommendations has come its Lemberg Center for the Study of Violence.

Northwestern University has become a center of interest in the simulated conduct of international relations since Richard C. Snyder and his colleagues in political science brought Harold Guetzkow there in 1957. Guetzkow and his associates that year developed their technique of "inter-nation simulation," which has since been adopted in the teaching of international relations elsewhere, both as other investigators in the field of simulation and reality gaming have learned of it and as Guetzkow's protégés have dispersed to other institutions.

In 1956, Edwin Land, president of the Polaroid Corporation, proposed at MIT that universities provide small groups of freshmen with a senior faculty member as an "usher" into academic life. Two years later, Harvard introduced its experimental freshman seminars as a technique of accomplishing the idea; two years after that, MIT organized a similar program; and now other institutions are adopting the plan.

At San Francisco State College in the fall of 1965, students

at the Third State of the University Conference of the University of North Carolina, March 10, 1955.

Jim Nixon and Mike Vozick organized three seminars on subjects not offered in the curriculum. By the spring, they had developed twenty more, involving 350 students, with students serving as "course organizers," thirty faculty members as resource people, and Paul Goodman as a visiting professor. The movement was named the "Experimental College," and by vote of the Academic Senate, students could receive academic credit for participating in a seminar if they could satisfy a faculty member of their accomplishment.

The most spectacular form of accretion in higher education has indeed been the continuing transformation of the college curriculum by new knowledge. If you had been John Bowden or another of the dozen or so freshmen attending little King's College in New York City—the predecessor of Columbia—two hundred years ago, you would have been required to start the day with Chapel and then spend from nine o'clock to noon translating and reciting from Caesar's *Commentaries*, Ovid's *Metamorphoses,* the *History* of Sallust, Vergil's pastoral poems, the *Ecologues,* Cornelius Nepos' *Vitae Excellentium Imperatorum,* Aesop's *Fables,* Grotius' *The Truth of the Christian Religion,* and—in Greek—the *Dialogues* of Lucian and the New Testament. You would have taken dinner at noon with the two professors, Samuel Clossy and Myles Cooper (who was also president). You would have studied during the afternoon until six, when called to required prayers. After supper (consisting, according to the college rules, of bread, butter, and cheese "or the remainder of the Dinner") you would have been on your own, as long as you were inside the college fence by nine o'clock.[17]

A hundred years later, if you had been Robert Arnold or another of forty freshmen in Columbia's "academic department," during the morning you would have also attended morning prayers, studied geometry and algebra, translated from Herodotus, Homer, and the odes of Horace, recited from textbooks on the history and customs of ancient Greece and Rome, memorized the intricacies of

---

[17] See, among other sources, *A History of Columbia University,* Appendix B. New York: Columbia University Press, 1904, and catalogs of later years.

27

their grammar, and done exercises in punctuation, simile, para-phrasing, abridging, and criticism from Quackenbow's *Course of Composition and Rhetoric.* You might have access to the college library between one and three in the afternoon, if President Barnard had so authorized you. You would not, however, have had to go to evening chapel, which had been dropped by 1817, or to Saturday morning prayers, which had been discontinued in 1844.

In 1968, if you were one of the seven hundred members of Columbia's Class of 1972, you would more than likely still have been reading Homer and Herodotus, Vergil and the Bible—but all in English, and only as four selections among some twenty-six classics ranging from the *Iliad* to Dostoyevsky in humanities and from an equal number ranging from Machiavelli to Keynes and Schupeter in contemporary civilization. In college composition you would have received "intensive training in the composition of expository and argumentative essays." You would have taken either astronomy, biological sciences, chemistry, geography-geology, mathematics, or physics, and one of eleven foreign languages. If exempted from these courses by an achievement test, you could have elected a course from among some forty open to freshmen, including elementary geophysics, history of science, university orchestra, etching and engraving, introduction to the study of religion, systematic sociological theories or—if you desired a commission in the Naval Officer Reserve Corps—naval history and sea power to 1815. Depending on your predilection you could have attended morning prayers at 8:40, a Roman Catholic mass at noon, Episcopal Eucharist on Wednesday evening, or at anytime stopped by the office of the Counselor to Jewish Students. Athletics, however, would have replaced religion as a compulsory exercise: you would have been expected to participate in one of nine team sports and one of eight individual or combative sports in physical education.

The process by which Caesar's *Commentaries* and Aesop's *Fables* have been superseded by Machiavelli, Dostoyevsky, and the rest has involved several steps, as illustrated by the introduction of the modern European languages, the experimental sciences, historiography and the behavioral sciences, the performing arts, the new

28

technologies, and physical education during the nineteenth and into the twentieth centuries. At first, the new knowledge is excluded by the colleges, although it is taught elsewhere. Anyone interested in it must go elsewhere—to a private tutor, or, as Americans did throughout the nineteenth century, to Europe. Then, as a result often of student interest, it is offered informally by an adjunct instructor, often for extra fees with no credit and "at such hours as will not interfere with the regular studies." Later, the special charges are reduced and students can earn partial credit for it in comparison to the same work in prescribed subjects. Finally it is admitted into the upper levels of the curriculum with permission that it may be substituted for certain limited work. Eventually it becomes accepted for lower classmen and may finally become required for them. Ultimately it may be adopted by the lower schools and largely squeezed out of the colleges into preparatory work.

Beyond this natural "percolating" process, the major device for adding more knowledge has been the elective principle. Rather than directly substituting the new for the old, the new is merely added—either as an elective course that may be taken in lieu of the old, or as a course in a new parallel degree program like the Bachelor of Science. Most educational "innovations" are introduced in this fashion. Conflicts are avoided by beginning separately and then only slowly allowing the new to be substituted for the old. Thus in 1826 George Ticknor obtained the concession that freshmen at Harvard might elect a modern language in place of half the required Greek and Latin. In 1838, the study of Hebrew first came to Wesleyan in the form of a Methodist minister on inactive service—William M. Willett. He was given a minimal appointment without pay and allowed to teach Hebrew to any students who wished to elect it for a small fee. In 1847, Yale tolerated the sciences by allowing Benjamin Silliman, Jr., and John Pitkin Norton to use a vacant house owned by the college for their teaching of chemistry, on the condition that they pay Yale $150 a year rent, that the new program would receive no financial support from the university, and that its courses would not ordinarily be open to Yale College students. From 1870 to 1940 at Yale, moreover, the curriculum received "seven rather substantial reorganizations," according to Yale's historian, George W. Pierson, "to say nothing of a long series of minor adjustments and experiments."[18] The first optional courses or substitutes were admitted in 1876; the upperclassmen obtained permission for almost completely free electives by 1893, and freshmen won similar options early in this century. And as a final example, by the end of the nineteenth century even pedagogy entered Harvard and Columbia, where it was offered as noncredit courses by Paul Hanus and Nicholas Murray Butler, encouraged by Presidents Eliot and Barnard.

In this way, knowledge that is extracurricular in one age becomes curricular in a later era. What is first offered at one level eventually moves down to lower levels unless it is retained for specialists (as the diagnosis of disease has been preserved for medical practitioners) in protected enclaves like the professional schools. Similarly, what is originally offered in marginal institutions is accepted into the colleges and universities often through the addition of a separate administrative unit. Thus science and engineering entered the classical colleges through parallel units such as the Lawrence and Sheffield Scientific Schools at Harvard and Yale. Women were integrated into the student body after being segregated in separate colleges like Vassar and Mount Holyoke. Adults joined the ranks of students when extension programs became accepted educational activities. Topical courses of the "free universities" that sprouted after the Berkeley revolt are being incorporated into the very institutions that originally spawned them by spurning them. And technological programs are continually adopted by academic institutions from proprietary schools (the current example being computer programming) thus offering education at lower prices for the students and at the same time forcing the proprietary institutions and marginal private colleges to spearhead still newer nonacademic programs in order to survive.

Academic accretion, in short, proceeds through borrowing,

[18] George W. Pierson, "The Elective System and the Difficulties of College Planning, 1870–1940," *The Journal of General Education, 4, 3,* April 1950, 168.

adopting, and augmenting educational ideas among institutions. Thus the modern American multiversities have grown by absorbing one by one the multitude of services formerly performed by specialized institutions. They have grafted onto the undergraduate college the forms and functions of the technical institute, the graduate school, the research bureau, the independent professional school, the experiment station, the Chautauqua, lyceum, correspondence school, boarding house, finishing school, encounter group, and museum.

At the same time, other knowledge is abandoned through attrition. Some ceases to be necessary for most students, like navigation and surveying. Some is carried into the lower schools by college graduates who teach their own students what they themselves learned in college, thereby forcing the colleges to adapt to new students who arrive as freshmen already versed in college level mathematics, science, and English. Some is consolidated and synthesized into principles and comprehensive knowledge. Thus out of discrete programs in business schools, colleges of education, and departments of political science, for example, comes the development of a field of administration. From ethnographies of cultures and people ethnology emerges as the study of culture. From links of the biological sciences with chemical and physical research comes new molecular knowledge, just as ecology links the biological and social sciences.

This process of synthesis permits education to be concentrated. It leads to suggestions such as Fritz Machlup's that "what is now taught in twelve years can just as well, or better, be taught in nine years or ten; and what is now taught in ten years can be taught in eight."[19] Indeed, the synthesis of knowledge into generalizations and theory constitutes the most important part of academic reform. Just as in law, where the mere addition or subtraction of elements does not in itself constitute invention, so in education the mere accretion and attrition of knowledge—the simple expansion and discarding of information without its reorganization or synthesis—does not constitute academic reform. The discipline of the philosophy of science does not germinate easily if philosophy and

[19] *The Production and Distribution of Knowledge in the United States.* Princeton: Princeton University Press, 1962, p. 129.

science remain isolated from each other, and having both a law school and a sociology department does not necessarily guarantee the creation of courses in the sociology of law.

Theoretically, these processes of academic accretion, attrition, and synthesis should be continuous. Since educational institutions operate on annual cycles, academic change should be evident in each cycle as year by year the elements of the educational program are eroded and replaced by others. And overall within higher education this is what happens. But it is clear that the flow of academic change on a departmental, institutional, and even a regional basis is not continuous, and nationally over time it is not constant. The process of accretion and attrition is not always gradual: instead it is impeded at one spot, deflected at another, and dammed completely for decades elsewhere. At one period in one area it flows swiftly; at another, slowly if at all; and occasionally, after periods of quiescence, there occur the "shocks of drastic adjustment" such as those that concerned the Muscatine committee at Berkeley.

But why is it that academic reform is not continuous in all institutions at all times? Why do some colleges seem to suffer repeatedly from what one disgruntled professor with whom we spoke diagnosed as "curricular constipation"? What are the restraints that limit the continuity of change and precipitate infrequent and drastic reform? What part do environmental pressures or organizational features play in the process?

The curriculum changes—that is clear. But why it changes is the basic problem of this book. From reviewing the history of higher education as it has been analyzed up to now, certain causes stand out as crucial.

Why aren't today's students studying Caesar's *Commentaries,* Aesop's *Fables,* or Quackenbow's *Course of Composition and Rhetoric?* Why are they not required to attend morning chapel and evening prayers? One reason is that the world has changed, and with it, the market for a gentleman's schooling in Caesar, Quackenbow, and Scripture. To put it bluntly, such schooling has no market. Nobody is willing to buy it. Few students would enroll in it, and fewer benefactors would underwrite it. In the sociologists' term, it is not functional—it is not useful either for work or even for the ornamental purpose of conspicuous consumption. Quackenbow carries little status today over cocktails or with a date from Vassar.

Without a market, an educational institution cannot survive. Indeed no organization—a family, a grocery store, a university—can exist without support, without the willing volunteer energy of its members or outside financial underwriting. And when this support lapses, the organization disintegrates—its members separating or merging with another group—or it finds other support, not infrequently by altering its purposes in order to preserve its structure. As Herbert Simon has noted, "organizational objectives are constantly adapted to conform to the changing values of customers, or to secure new groups of customers, in place of customers who have dropped away."[20] When Greek will not sell, French and German get a try. And when women's colleges cannot survive, they try co-education. ". . . Our colleges are not filled because we do not furnish the education desired by the people," Francis Wayland told the members of the Corporation of Brown University on March 28, 1850, in introducing his landmark proposals for reform of American higher education. As author of America's first leading textbook on political economy, he couched his rationale in clear economic terms:

> We have produced an article for which the demand is diminishing. We sell it at less than cost, and the deficiency is made up by charity. We give it away, and still the demand diminishes. Is it not time to inquire whether we cannot furnish an article for which the demand will be, at least, somewhat more remunerative? . . . We must carefully survey the wants of the various classes of the community in our vicinity, and adapt our courses of instruction, not for the benefit of one class, but for the benefit of all classes.[21]

[20] Herbert Simon, *Administrative Behavior*. New York: Macmillan, 1957, p. 114.

[21] *Report to the Corporation of Brown University on Changes in the System of Collegiate Education*. Providence: George H. Whitney, 1850, pp. 34, 50.

Wayland's argument illustrates a fundamental fact. As the resources in a society dry up for one type of education, most educational institutions try to accommodate themselves to new sources of support. Indeed, the flow of resources—their extent, direction, and limitation—inevitably is the prime determinant of academic change. The material and attitudinal resources that are available to colleges and universities, or that they can make available to themselves, will determine their program.

Academics do not enjoy this fact. We like to think of ourselves as autonomous. Like most people, we prefer that our livelihood and specialty be ours alone to control. It is somehow threatening and almost unprofessional to view ourselves and our careers as influenced by outside pressure. But the fact seems clear: education is not the tail that wags the dog of society, and society determines the direction that education will follow. The historians of education, at least, have recognized this impact of social resources. ". . . The revolution in the curriculum," Willis Rudy has observed in his analysis of American college programs, "was produced by a revolution in American life."[22] "The promise of numbers, influence, and respectability could not seriously be ignored or resisted in high places," Laurence R. Veysey concludes in his review of the emergence of American universities between 1865 and 1910.[23] And Robert F. Byrnes, chairman of the history department at Indiana University, has stated:

> . . . we should not be surprised if the curriculum and everything about a college is buffeted by forces outside the college to a greater degree than it influences or creates these forces. Indeed, if we review the relatively few changes in curriculums over the past 30 years, we must admit that these revisions have been produced because of pressures from the outside. The college follows, it does not lead. The curriculum reflects the so-

[22] *The Evolving Liberal Arts Curriculum: A Historical Review of Basic Themes.* New York: Institute of Higher Education, Teachers College, Columbia University, 1960, p. 11.
[23] *The Emergence of the American University.* Chicago: The University of Chicago Press, 1965, p. 439.

ciety in which the institution is based; it does not significantly affect or change that society.[24]

Thus the rate of educational change varies with that of social change. A stable, tight-knit community such as the Massachusetts Bay Colony in the seventeenth century or even an isolated farming community today tolerates little educational deviance; but a transitional society such as urban America expects rapid academic acceleration. The effects of nineteenth-century industrialism have reverberated throughout American social life and into the colleges. Each of our involvements in war has wrenched and remolded the educational system. And the continuing struggles between conflicting interest groups within society has been played out across many a college campus.

For example, the resources available to American education are increasingly national, secular, and rationalistic in aim rather than local, parochial, and spiritual. Until the past century, American higher education was ecclesiastically controlled. Denominational money underwrote most institutions and church bodies prescribed their programs. Divinity and revelation were then considered immutable and inviolately true, while natural philosophy dealt with "base" and "ruin'd" nature. But the groundswell of western society has been toward greater power over life and nature not through revelation but through comprehension, and this strain toward reliable knowledge has been institutionalized in the process of science and the system of education. After the Civil War, Cornell and then Johns Hopkins could open as secular or nonreligious institutions; and since then, cognition has replaced piety as the dominant value of academia.

Secularism has expanded as funds have slowly arrived from

[24] "Effective Teaching, Our First Need," *The Challenge of Curricular Change*. New York: College Entrance Examination Board, 1965, pp. 72–73. See, in addition, Freeman Butts, *The College Charts Its Course: Historical Conceptions and Current Proposals*. New York: McGraw-Hill, 1939, p. 86ff., and W. H. Cowley's various taxonomic analyses of American higher education, such as his "An Overview of American Colleges and Universities," duplicated, Stanford University, 1960.

noneclesiastical sources—first from state and federal governments and private philanthropists and financiers and more recently from corporations and foundations. They have supported intelligence primarily as the solution to utilitarian problems and as the source of social power, and have been less interested in human experience that is not knowledgeable—poesis, aesthetics, mysticism, "being." Employers want productivity; the schools want knowledgeable teachers; people want to understand themselves and their environment. And thus predictable knowledge expands. Civilization calls for it.

Through Biblical and Greek and Roman "antiquities," the colonial literary colleges like King's College taught the wisdom and social understanding of the ancients to the civil servants of colonial society and then of the new United States—its statesmen, lawyers, ministers, and schoolteachers. But to understand the new nation and its polity, out of the broad study of ancient languages and authors, the colleges adopted history as a discipline; and Jared Sparks assumed the first professorship in the field at Harvard in 1839.

Industrialism demanded technological and financial experts, and the colleges cautiously acquiesced. In 1847, Harvard had planned to open graduate work in arts and sciences, but moved instead to open its Lawrence Scientific School when Abbott Lawrence provided $50,000 for it. And Yale in 1860 named its scientific program after Joseph Sheffield, following his $100,000 gift of a building and endowment.

And as the nineteenth century grew rife with economic and political issues—slavery, bimetallism, the single tax, socialism, anarchy, unionism—the field of economics developed as an ideological study. Boston businessmen made it clear that Harvard should correctly teach the facts of profits, rent, investments, protectionism, capitalism, and the control of labor; and they put up the money for Charles F. Dunbar, the editor of the *Boston Daily Advertiser,* to become in 1871 the first full-time professor of political economy in America.[25]

[25] Michael J. L. O'Connor's dissertation on the *Origins of Academic*

From a few centers, the new knowledge spread. In 1876, thirty-eight American colleges were offering at least one course in political economy, although only three of them—Harvard, Yale, and Middlebury—offered more than one. But by 1892, at least sixty-six institutions had at least one course; and five universities were offering more than ten courses each.[26] In 1889, only four institutions were offering sociology by name. But by 1901, over a hundred colleges and universities were offering a total of nearly four hundred courses in the field; and by 1909, more than three hundred were offering a total of over a thousand.[27]

By the twentieth century, the denominational colleges were in such competition with the public state universities and land-grant colleges—which offered practical studies as well as classical education—that they were forced to alter their programs by admitting subjects that were most attractive to students and least intolerable to the faculty. Chief among these, of course, was pedagogy. With the growth of the public high schools, one liberal arts college after another disdainfully assumed the function of teacher education; and of necessity rather than desire, many of them in reality became by mid-century private teacher-training institutions.

During the twentieth century, the states and the philanthropic foundations have underwritten the major innovations in higher education. The foundations have supported the development of new professional specialties, championed the performing arts in

---

Economics in the United States (New York: Columbia University Press, 1944) relates the entire history from the John Alford bequest of 1789 for a chair in ethics and politics at Harvard. O'Connor observes: "Political economy offered a field where natural religion and pecuniary values could be adjusted. Therein the ethical and humanitarian ideas of the minister could be shown to be at one with the practical needs of the accumulator of capital. The clerical textbooks that were actually produced did deal at length with the idea that moral purposes were in harmony with those of the merchant capitalists, and, indeed, with those of all society" (p. 106).

[26] J. Laurence Laughlin, "The Study of Political Economy in the United States," *The Journal of Political Economy, 1,* 1892–93, 1–12, 143–151.

[27] L. L. Bernard, "United States," *Encyclopedia of the Social Sciences,* Vol. 1. New York: Macmillan, 1930, p. 341.

the curriculum, and—primarily through the American Council of Learned Societies and the Social Science Research Council—underwritten new academic disciplines. Linguistics, as one example, reached the status of a specialty in 1924, when the Linguistics Society of America came into being. The Carnegie Corporation provided the financial assistance, and, as the discipline developed in the 1930s, the American Council of Learned Societies supported its annual Linguistics Institutes. During World War II, linguistics received its largest impetus from the federal government. After the war, the Social Science Research Council helped organize the new area of "psycholinguistics" with a seminar at Cornell in 1951; in 1958, the American Council of Learned Societies and the Modern Language Association played a major role in obtaining support for linguistics in the National Defense Education Act; and in 1963, the National Science Foundation aided in founding the Social Science Research Council's committee on "sociolinguistics."

During the past decade, the National Science Foundation has been stimulating change in college curricula in mathematics, physics, and other sciences, as well as underwriting a rapid expansion of oceanographic studies. In 1967, the Ford Foundation poured $5 million into programs of research and training in ecology at eight universities, and these programs will ultimately begin to affect most college curricula in the sciences.

From these historical examples, the significance of resources in determining academic change may be already evident. But the recent innovations mentioned earlier in this chapter as examples of accretion offer similar testimony. Of all of them, only MIT's freshman seminars began without outside financing. Harold Guetzkow's development of inter-nation simulation was supported by the Carnegie Corporation, the Air Force Office of Scientific Research, the Navy Purchasing Office, the Office of Naval Research, and the United States Office of Education. Suicidology has been inaugurated with National Institute of Mental Health support; the Center for the Study of Violence at Brandeis came into being through a gift of Samuel Lemberg and project support from the Ford Foundation and the National Institute of Mental Health; and Harvard's freshman seminars were stimulated by a gift from an anonymous benefactor who was interested in helping freshmen and who turned out to be Edwin H. Land himself. Even San Francisco State's experimental college was not financed through the regular college budget but through student funds allocated by the Student Association.

All of these examples illustrate the impact of new sources of support. New courses are offered, new curricula developed, new institutions are established because of changes in society at large and because individuals and groups are willing to be convinced to finance them. But more specifically, it also appears that the accretion of these new tasks occurs most easily when new resources are limited directly to these projects. Endowments and unrestricted income are almost invariably used by most institutions to maintain and expand their existing functions and programs rather than to add distinctive new activities. This fact helps explain the continual tension between donors who wish to specify the uses of their support and institutions that naturally desire unrestricted gifts.

In short, the first key to academic reform is that of resources: an existing program will continue to exist as long as it can find support. A new program will be tolerated if it costs no money or it brings its own support. It will be resisted if the new funds it requires could be used for the expansion of existing programs. And it will be actively opposed and accepted only under duress if existing resources must be divided to include it.[28]

This tendency is the fundamental reason why the source of

[28] The roots of this generalization have been noted by such observers as Edmund Day, the president of Cornell, 1937–1949. "From time to time," he wrote in 1946, "new departments have to be created, new schools and colleges constituted, major realignments or readjustments initiated in existing departments or divisions. Generally speaking, the impulses which lead to these innovations do not come from the professional staff. Quite naturally, the organization as it stands is likely to view with skepticism any major additions to program which may set up fresh competition for available funds. It is fair to say that, by and large, academic organization is resistant to change. The *status quo* tends to root deeply in academic soil." ("The Role of Administration in Higher Education," *The Journal of Higher Education, 17,* 7, October 1946, 342).

academic change has always been and continues to be predominantly outside of the educational system, for the resources that support the system overwhelmingly come from outside the institutions themselves. The surrounding society and its members create educational institutions: they nurture and finance them; and while educators work at molding the wishes of their benefactors about education, the educational enterprises of any society are inevitably molded to the wishes of their patrons.

An unconventional institution such as Antioch or Bennington can survive as long as it can attract support from some source or other for an off-beat program. (Thus a diversity of institutions stems from diverse sources of support.) On the other hand, a conventional college may find that to compete successfully with others, it must deviate from them just enough to attract new clientele without jeopardizing its existing base of support. In the United States since 1950, despite the rapid growth of new colleges, an average of more than five colleges a year have gone out of existence and four a year have merged with other institutions. Some that might have followed them over the brink of collapse have been saved from extinction by gaining support for a transformed program and others have been able to keep their program intact by finding new support—chiefly by becoming public or by obtaining more state and federal aid.

If, in sum, the flow of resources is the underlying determinant of academic reform, what is the proximate mechanism by which reform occurs? That is, how is change implemented? The answer seems to lie primarily with individual advocates and with new blood through the process of turnover among personnel.

Each new addition to the curriculum—the modern European languages, the sciences, the creative arts, and the practical and technological arts ranging from agriculture to television broadcasting—has been regarded with indifference or attacked with antagonism by many academics. In every case, the new knowledge has been championed instead primarily by outsiders—by students, citizens, legislators, philanthropists, and, in recent decades, foundation officials—all aided by a nucleus of educators whose interests were outside of or marginal to the existing curriculum.

Processes of Reform

Thus the extensive reform of American colleges during the nineteenth century, while stemming from and financed by the dramatic social and economic revolution of American society, was implemented by two streams of newcomers into American higher education: on the one hand, the educators sympathetic to utilitarian education, like Francis Wayland or Jonathan Baldwin Turner, who tried to push mechanical and agricultural education into the classical colleges for the benefit of the working classes, and, on the other hand, the scholars—either European by birth, like Louis Agassiz, or teutonized by European models, like George Ticknor—who brought new concepts of the university across the Atlantic to America. These men, the new technologists, scientists, and scholars, were what the social scientists term "marginal" men: their experience outside the classical college made them discontented with its limitations and provinciality. Joseph Gusfield and David Riesman have observed the influence of such advocates in these words:

> On the margins of the disciplines are those who have been unable to internalize the codes of their occupational surroundings or who have not been satisfied with them. It is from these men that there comes the willingness to take risks and the rebelliousness from which innovation is possible, sometimes in research, and quite generally in educational reform.[29]

These advocates of new knowledge—the pioneers in new fields, the evangelists of learning—look for means with which to teach and explore and for students to win and inspire. As Terry Clark has pointed out in his analysis of the development of disciplines, they want an organizational home that will perpetuate their vision, afford it protection and prestige, and serve as a base to train recruits; and they seek this home in the university.[30]

Behind every such advocate necessarily stands a patron or a group of supporters, willing to be convinced of the benefits of the

[29] Joseph Gusfield and David Riesman, "Faculty Culture and Academic Careers: Some Sources of Innovation in Higher Education," *Sociology of Education, 37,* 4, summer 1964, 305.

[30] Terry Clark, "Institutionalization of Innovations in Higher Education: Four Conceptual Models," *Administrative Science Quarterly, 13,* 1, June 1968, 1–25.

new endeavor. Thus America's first scientist, Isaac Greenwood, went to London to prepare for the ministry in 1724, three years after graduating from Harvard. There he attended the scientific lectures of J. T. Pesaguliers, and was so enthralled with the Newtonian ideas he heard that he was able to convince Thomas Hollis, a London merchant, to give Harvard £1,200 sterling for a Chair of Mathematics and Natural Philosophy—a chair which Greenwood thereupon occupied until his dismissal for drunkenness ten years later.[31] During the nineteenth century at Harvard, George Ticknor's elective proposals succeeded as adequately as they did because of his support among the laymen on the Harvard Corporation. President Eliot's reorganizations of the university had similar backing from the corporation. And psychology under William James entered Harvard's curriculum in 1876 only after much nudging from the Board of Overseers.[32]

Throughout the history of American intellectual life, in fact, the same pattern of support reappears. Without the influence, for example, of Samuel P. Ruggles, a trustee of Columbia, and of President Henry Barnard, J. W. Burgess would not have succeeded in reforming Columbia into a university. Burgess came to Columbia from Amherst in 1876 with the hope of offering to seniors elective courses on weekday afternoons in political and constitutional history and in the economic and social sciences; but the faculty voted down the idea of afternoon electives as a dangerous innovation. He incurred the displeasure of Columbia's librarian, who kept the collection open only an hour and a half a day five days a week, and so he got permission from the trustees for a separate library, librarian, and appropriations sufficient to keep the new facility open all day and evening six days a week. Concluding that only a separate school of political science would permit the social sciences the freedom they deserved, he persuaded the trustees to agree to a new unit in 1881 and to staff it with himself, a former student from Amherst, and

[31] See Theodore Homberger, *Scientific Thought in the American Colleges, 1638–1800.* Austin: The University of Texas Press, 1946.

[32] See Paul Buck (ed.), *Social Sciences At Harvard, 1860–1920: From Inculcation to the Open Mind.* Cambridge: Harvard University Press, 1965, pp. 178–185.

two students then studying in Europe. "And now, with the founding of this faculty of Political Science in Columbia College," he later reminisced, "a new theory of knowledge and progress and education was thrust into this peaceful and contented institution, which had not for many years given birth to any new idea, which, in fact, was inclined to regard new ideas as impious departures from established truth."[33]

Elsewhere, without Glenn Frank's insistence as the new president of the University of Wisconsin, Alexander Meiklejohn would not have been hired as a professor of philosophy, nor named to a four-member University Commission that recommended the implementation of his theory for an experimental college, nor operated the Experimental College until its demise in 1932 from financial problems and faculty antipathy. At Antioch, Arthur Morgan's innovations would not have succeeded without the continuing financial support of Charles Kettering. At Swarthmore, Frank Aydelotte's program would have foundered in 1928 except for $4 million of backing from the General Education Board. And most of the former normal schools would today still be only teachers colleges if some of their professors and administrators together with their governing boards and state legislatures had not fought the normal school advocates and pushed them into multipurpose status.

Conversely, recall that Johns Hopkins was crippled irrevocably in its leadership of American universities when in 1887 the Baltimore and Ohio Railroad passed its dividend, since the university's total endowment consisted of 15,000 shares of B&O stock. G. Stanley Hall's great vision for Clark University in 1889 faded when Jonas Clark withdrew his support after three years. Even Yale's academic conservatism during the past century has been attributed in part to President Noah Porter's deficiencies in fund-raising and Yale's subsequent poverty in comparison with Harvard.[34]

[33] J. W. Burgess, *Reminiscences of An American Scholar: The Beginnings of Columbia College.* New York: Columbia University Press, 1934, p. 203.

[34] See George W. Pierson, "The Elective System and the Difficulties of College Planning, 1870–1940," *The Journal of General Education,* 4, 3, April 1950, 169.

Dynamics of Academic Reform

In short, not only must the necessary resources be available for reform, but an advocate must succeed in gaining access to them. And out of this competition among advocates for support of their enterprises evolves the pattern of higher education within society.

Another important fact may already be apparent: the advocate of academic change generally comes from without instead of from within an institution. "The quickest way of changing an institution is to change its leadership," James A. Perkins and his associates on the New York State Regents Advisory Committee on Educational Leadership recently observed.[35] Their rationale seems well documented: the most common mechanism of academic change appears to be that of the turnover of personnel—the replacement of institutional leaders and members by newcomers from other institutions and from outside the educational system.

The significance of new blood for change within organizations has long been known. Political theorists attribute at least part of the adaptability—and thus the long life—of American government to the limited terms of office of elected officials and the opportunities that the Constitution thus affords the voting citizens to "kick the bums out." Conversely the inflexibiliy of bureaucracy is in part due to the low level of rotation that is common under civil service.[36]

Even in the sciences—supposedly as open as any professional field to change of ideas on the basis of evidence—reform has depended on the passage of time. Bernard Barber has examined this old-guard phenomenon within the sciences, and reports that major innovators such as Lavoisier, Helmholtz, and Lister could not ex-

---

[35] The New York State Regents Advisory Committee on Educational Leadership, *Leadership for Education: A Final Report*. Albany: The Board of Regents of the University of the State of New York, 1968, p. 4.

[36] For example, see Arthur M. Schlesinger, Jr.'s animadversions on the vested interests and cozy alliances of the "permanent government" in the executive branch of the federal government in his *A Thousand Days*. New York: Houghton Mifflin, 1965, pp. 680–682. Incidentally, in regard to the importance of turnover, the most significant legislation ever passed affecting higher education—the Land-Grant College Act—was approved in 1862 by President Lincoln, whereas President Buchanan had previously vetoed it.

pect acceptance of their ideas from their colleagues. Instead, they looked for approval only from the younger generation of scientists. He cites Max Planck's sour observation:

> A new scientific truth does not triumph by convincing its opponents and making them see the light, but rather because its opponents eventually die, and a new generation grows up that is familiar with it.[37]

And he quotes Hans Zinsser's remark:

> That academies and learned societies—commonly dominated by the older foo-foos of any profession—are slow to react to new ideas is in the nature of things.[38]

Such observations as these simply illustrate the common fact that changes in the operation of a system or an organization are influenced by changes in its membership. New members of an institution will naturally tend to alter the organization unless they deliberately avoid or are restrained from doing so, simply because newcomers disrupt tradition by being unaware of it. (Thus the members of any group who wish to preserve the status quo generally resist the recruitment of new leaders or members from outside. Succession from among insiders, for better or worse, intensifies existing norms and isolates the group from external influence.) Inbreeding protects against "barbarians"—whether the barbarians be scientists, Methodists, shaggy hippies, or hotshot Ivy Leaguers.

Unlike some other organizations, colleges and universities are almost completely dependent on turnover of personnel to accomplish major reforms. As mentioned earlier, the ideology of the academic profession treats the professor as an independent professional. Under this ideology, once a professor has joined a college

[37] Max Planck, *Scientific Autobiography,* Frank Gaynor, translator. New York: Philosophical Library, 1949, p. 33, quoted in Bernard Barber, "Resistance by Scientists to Scientific Discovery," *Scientific Manpower 1960.* Washington, D.C.: National Science Foundation, May, 1961, p. 38.

[38] Hans Zinsser, *As I Remember Him: The Biography of R. S.* Boston: Little, Brown, 1940, p. 105, quoted by Bernard Barber, *op. cit.,* p. 46.

faculty, and particularly after he achieves tenure, his colleagues have little power beyond persuasion to affect his attitudes and behavior regarding his responsibilities; and they make little effort at persuasion because of the norm of professional courtesy. ("You tend to your students, and I'll tend to mine.") Thus the process of academic reform occurs of necessity through change *of* persons—the replacement and rotation of individuals—rather than through change *in* persons, such as changes in their attitudes and skills. Outside of higher education, most analysts of social and organizational change, be it in business and industry, race relations, or modernization in developing countries, emphasize the importance of attitude change in the reorganization process. Even in the lower schools, they recognize that curriculum change comes about, as Gordon Mackenzie observes, by either "getting new teachers into the classroom, or changing those who are there."[39] But in contrast, higher education operates under a philosophy opposed to "changing those who are there." The faculty will not be changed. And thus, while the major function of higher education and of the total educational system can be viewed as that of assisting in behavior change, the personnel of colleges and universities consider themselves exempt from this process. Requiring changes in students is legitimate; expecting them of the professor is illegitimate: it smacks of coercion and a violation of his academic freedom.

Take one example. How does the art of metal sculpture, such as the shaping of steel, enter the program of an art department that has been traditionally oriented to clay, wood, and stone sculpture? If, in fact, it enters the curriculum at all, two means are available: a member of the department faculty may pick up the new techniques himself and begin to teach them, or a new instructor brings them with him by chance or by design from outside. The second procedure, the arrival of the outsider, appears to be most common. Artists are generally not expected to work in all media or to change their repertoire, just as scientists are not expected to

[39] Gordon Mackenzie, "Curricular Change: Participants, Power, and Processes," in Matthew Miles (ed.), *Innovation in Education.* New York: Bureau of Publications, Teachers College, Columbia University, 1964, p. 417.

shift their topics and styles of research or composers to alter their approach to music. A composer may come to be regarded in mid-career as old-fashioned, but typically we respect his right to choose his individual style of composition. The professor is an independent professional in the same sense: his style, techniques, and concerns are his alone.

Changes in curricula and teaching thus cannot easily be imposed; instead they must be individualistic and consensual. In addition, few institutions conduct extensive orientation for new faculty members or provide any in-service education for them beyond sabbaticals and leaves of absence. For all these reasons, the turnover of personnel through the slow process of selection, replacement, retirement, and rotation of members is more central to the process of academic reform than to change in most other organizations. As the president of one college ruefully admitted, "The only way I could change the music department was to change the faculty."

Earlier we mentioned the revolution that the young American scholars wrought in collegiate life throughout the nineteenth century upon their return from European universities. Other examples also illustrate the significance of new blood. Charles W. Eliot, in his first year as president of Harvard, looked not to teachers of law for a dean to reform the Harvard Law School and, through it, legal education nationally, but instead brought in Christopher Columbus Langdell from private practice in New York City. Daniel Coit Gilman at Johns Hopkins in 1876 brought John S. Billings from the Army Surgeon General's office—not someone from another medical school—to help plan a revolutionary medical school and hospital. The immigration to the United States of Europeans during the oppressive 1930s stimulated a ferment of new ideas that continues to this day. Among its leaders were such scholars as Abraham Wald in statistics, Werner Winter in linguistics, Walter Gropius in design, Paul Lazarsfeld in sociology, and Albert Einstein in physics. The University of Iowa's famed creative writing workshop stems from Paul Engle, who returned to the United States from Oxford in 1937, and was offered $2,500 by George Stoddard, then dean of the graduate school, to teach writing. And many of the great changes in college programs after World War II appear to have been stimulated not only by the disruption of tradition during the war but also by the resulting circulation of faculty members and administrators from one institution to another. At Wesleyan University in Connecticut, for example, Victor Butterfield became president in 1943 and set out to recruit professors such as Nathan Pusey, who shared his vision of the institution. By the postwar period he had brought in fifty-four of the seventy-five members then on the faculty; and together they set in motion Wesleyan's notable transformation these past two decades.

In short, the newcomer seems crucial for academic change. He may come from outside higher education altogether. He may be exploring problems regardless of departmental and disciplinary boundaries. He may represent different values, different goals, a different culture than his predecessors. The recruitment of such individuals as catalysts of change accounts for much of the process of reform. One result of this fact is a generally higher level of academic innovation at institutions that are expanding in contrast to those staying the same size. Expansion permits new programs and the hiring of new faculty at a rate faster than replacement. "We were growing," a trustee of a particularly dynamic state college remarked to us, "and we couldn't have changed so easily otherwise. We set up new committees and programs, rather than having to substitute them for old ones." And in addition, having a high proportion of newcomers, expanding institutions often exhibit the euphoria of success and high morale that the stable institution may lack and that the declining institution desperately needs. With growth comes the possibility of perquisites—and to the professor a chance to teach his own specialty.

Finally, it is evident that colleges and universities differ among themselves not only in their rate of growth but in their tolerance for outsiders and new blood. Just as departments vary in their demands for disciplinary orthodoxy, institutions vary in their support for advocates of change. Some, at certain times, will recruit faculty and staff from outside the traditional limits of the disciplines or even of higher education at large; some will tolerate unusual and unorthodox educational ideas and techniques; some will actively encourage and evoke the reconsideration of tradition and taboo; while others are less able or willing to do so. In short, some are more open and responsive to the possibility of reform than others.

Thus the evidence to date from historians, observers of academic life, and the reformers themselves points to three dominant sources of change in higher education: (1) the resources available for it, (2) the advocates interested in it, and (3) the openness of the system to them. In every case of academic change, these factors together appear to determine its outcome.

But people who are concerned about academic reform— faculty members, administrators, trustees, and students interested in influencing educational policy ask about the importance of specific factors. How vital is presidential leadership? How effective is student pressure? How significant is the turnover of faculty? What arrangements can best facilitate change? Does one kind of administrative structure generate more reform than another? And of all these factors, are any more critical than others in assuring *continual* responsiveness and flexibility and self-renewal?

We ourselves have opinions about these issues, just as most everyone does. But to speak of these questions on the basis of empirical evidence as well as the conclusions of history and scattered observation, the Institute of Higher Education undertook to study the dynamics of academic change in a variety of colleges and universities during the past half-decade. Relying on all the evidence that the history of higher education provides and that this chapter has summarized, we surveyed the changes that have been made in the programs of over a hundred institutions and we then sought to account for these changes. The next several chapters present our findings. Chapter Three begins by describing the changes themselves; Chapter Four examines the causes of these changes as perceived by the people involved in them; Chapter Five identifies the sources of the changes as we perceived them; and Chapter Six extracts from all of this information our conclusions about the process of academic reform at large.

49

CHAPTER III

Changes in Curriculum

*Change does not neces-
sarily assure progress, but
progress implacably re-
quires change.*[1]

Henry Steele Commager

[1] "Change in History," *Freedom and Order: A Commentary on the American Political Scene.* New York: Braziller, 1966, p. 244.

50

Our concern with academic reform goes beyond an interest in its history, illuminating though the past is. We seek to know the sources of change in order to help affect the future; and to this end we have analyzed empirically the changes that have been occurring in American higher education in the past few years. Dramatic transformations of colleges and universities were wrought after World War II, but what has actually taken place within their programs in the past few years? How is higher education different today from what it was, say, five years ago? And where have the most changes occurred? This chapter reports what we have found. It describes the developments that have taken place in the educational program between 1962 and 1967, and it serves as an introduction to an analysis in later chapters of the reasons for these developments.

To begin with, it should be noted that rapid shifts have been taking place in the past several years within the extracurriculum—that is, the program which is not required of students in order for them to graduate. College students have become far more politically and socially active since the civil rights movement began to attract national consciousness after the lunchroom sit-ins in Greensboro, North Carolina, in 1960. On the picket line, at the negotiating table, and over coffee in the union, many undergraduates have come to perceive themselves and their professors far differently than did their predecessors a decade ago. Their attitudes, activities, and culture appear to be changing radically.

The data which follow, however, do not emphasize these changes in the extracurriculum—despite the evidence that the most significant and vital educational experiences of students often take place outside the classroom. As we mentioned earlier, the major problem of academic reform from our perspective lies within the classroom and the curriculum, where the dynamics of change are particularly restricted. The most critical issues of all, we sense, involve what is required of students and what is open to them: the formal institutional expectations and options for the students. Here is where the accusations of moving the graveyard point and where the difficulties of reform are greatest.

51

In addition, for a study such as this, accurate data are more difficult to obtain on changes in the informal educational program than on those in the formal curriculum. We needed comparative data over a period of at least half a decade in order to measure the changes that were taking place, and the facts about student life even five years ago are now fugitive: students are themselves seldom historians, and the reminiscent comparisons by alumni of yesteryear with today are colorful but suspect. While the morgues of campus newspapers might be a major source of information for comparing what has been occurring on campus, even more readily available are the historical remains of the formal curriculum, preserved in the official publications and archives of the institution. For these several reasons, we have focused on changes in five fundamental expectations and options within higher education:

1. The courses offered to students, such as "Natural Sciences 115: Cosmography."

2. The programs in which students can major or concentrate their study, such as American studies or medical technology.

3. The requirements that students must meet to earn a degree—for example, the necessity for two years of a foreign language, or a year's work in humanities, or a grade-point average of "C."

4. The requirements for majoring in a program—for instance, the courses that a student must take in a particular field, such as economics or history or sociology courses for a major in political science.

5. Regulations regarding the curriculum, such as attendance, tardiness, and conduct.

The details of how this information was gathered by the staff of the Institute of Higher Education appear in Appendix B. In brief, we began by selecting at random and on a stratified basis 110 institutions from among all of the accredited four-year colleges and universities in the contiguous United States. (We stratified this sample by deliberately oversampling the independent institutions and those that offer the doctor's degree in order to make sure we studied enough of them, and, as Appendix B indicates, the 110 institutions that we happened to select do not seem to be unrepresentative of the types of institution we hoped to study.) Next, although we were particularly concerned about reform in the four-year colleges and universities, we randomly selected eleven two-year colleges to compare with the senior institutions. Then we attempted to determine from the documents of all of these institutions, such as their bulletins and catalogs, the amount of change that had occurred between 1962 and 1967 in the five measures of the curriculum that we listed above. We were curious, of course, about the new courses and new programs that the institutions were offering during these years of expansion in higher education; but we were far more concerned with those that they had discarded or revamped. As we said before, academic reform is a process that involves synthesis and attrition as well as accretion; and our interest lies in reform, not merely in expansion. The expansion of knowledge and the broadening of the undergraduate curriculum that we described in the last chapter occur almost continually in American higher education as new ideas, new courses, and new disciplines are added to the curriculum. But more important to us than this expansion is the reform of the curriculum. From our perspective, it is the primary measure of institutional vitality of a college or university. Hence we looked for changes in the content of courses and programs—not, as an illustration, in whether they were taught by seminar or closed-circuit television but instead, in the concepts that they contained. Were courses in a language department, for instance, based on recent developments in linguistic science? Or had introductory sociology moved beyond William Graham Sumner and Lester Ward?

Our view about the importance of such changes was expressed perfectly by the president of a women's college whom we interviewed when he said to us:

> The most important and significant change, although largely unnoticed, is the recasting of the body of knowledge, course by course, department by department, year by year, whereby professors don't use their last year's notes.

Thus we went beyond an analysis of curricular accretion to assess the amount of reform in each of the five measures we used. By comparing the description of each course offered in 1962 and in 1967 by a sampling of departments at each institution, we attempted to learn how many courses had remained substantially unchanged during these five years and how many of them had been added, dropped, or significantly altered. Similarly, we analyzed the number of major programs that had been added and dropped at each institution and the changes that had been made in its degree requirements, in majoring requirements, and in student regulations. The method of this analysis can be found in the appendix, but one point needs emphasis here: we deliberately did not evaluate these changes as either good or bad. We have quite definite opinions, of course, about the direction of these changes in higher education; but for the purpose of understanding the sources of change, the extent of the change is more important than an evaluation of the change. In other words, the dynamics involved in academic reform do not vary in terms of our own personal predilections about each change. Moreover, in education, what is one man's reform may be another man's relapse. Thus, although our biases have probably crept into the description which follows, our analysis that led to this description was as objective as we could make it.

Turning to the findings themselves, here is what was happening in American colleges and universities during the past half-decade, first in their courses, then in their major programs, and finally in their several requirements.

The synthesis and reorganization of knowledge within each course seems to us to be the most important indicator of academic ferment in higher education—of intellectual creativity rather than ritualism, of academic exploration rather than canned recitation, of the winnowing and sifting of knowledge beyond mere accretion. By 1967, the 110 institutions that we surveyed had reorganized or substituted, on the average, one out of every five courses that they had offered in 1962. Their rate of course reform, according to our measure, was slightly over 4.4 per cent a year.[2] Some portions of

[2] Our method for reaching this figure was as follows: We examined on the average four departments at each institution in our sample, and in

the curriculum were admittedly far more stable than this, while other portions were being transformed far more rapidly. But theoretically, at least, this means that the content of the undergraduate curriculum is being reconstituted completely at least every twenty-two years.

Out of our sample of 426 departments, we found four of them that appeared to have completely reorganized their undergraduate courses. One was a small statistics department at a major university; two were departments of theology at two Roman Catholic institutions; and the other was the philosophy department at one of these same Catholic institutions. The effects of recent ferment in Catholic thinking since the Second Vatican Council seemed clear here. For example, at one of the two, instead of a theology program centered on the life of Christ and consisting of courses on "Christology," "Christian Awareness," "Christ's Life Communicated to the Church," and "Christ our High Priest," the department is now offering courses on Pauline theology, the layman in the twentieth century, the Church and Vatican II, introduction to modern atheism, and introduction to Protestant theology. At the other extreme, it seemed that seventy-three of the 426 departments had not indicated any change at all in their existing courses, although there were undoubtedly some changes of content that found no expression in the printed catalog.

Comparing the fields of knowledge within the curriculum, all four major areas—the humanities, the social sciences, natural

---

1962–63 these 426 departments offered a total of 10,015 courses primarily for undergraduates. Our measure of course reform was the proportion of courses that were *dropped* between 1962 and 1967 at departments that during this same period *increased* their total course offerings and the proportion of courses that were *added* at departments that during this same period *decreased* their number of courses. We considered a course dropped and another one added, as Appendix B illustrates, if the description of its content changed substantially during those five years. There were 2,195 such courses, according to our calculations, that were not explained by the simple trends of departmental expansion or contraction, giving a five-year total rate of 21.9 per cent and an annual rate of 4.4 per cent. Taking the mean of the departmental means gives a five-year rate of 22.6 per cent, as Table 1 indicates. Taking the mean of the institutional means gives a rate of 23.2 per cent, as Table 2 illustrates.

sciences, and vocations—show almost identical rates of course reform. But among particular subjects, considerable differences occur,
as Table 1 shows. Despite the small number of cases for some fields,
these differences give some indication of the ferment that appears
to be taking place in portions of the undergraduate program. The
most radically reorganized disciplines during the past half decade
seem to be religion and mathematics (where at least one out of
every three courses was reformed during the past five years), followed by engineering, philosophy, and speech (where over 30 per
cent of the courses were reorganized). The most static fields appear
to be physics and geology, where 12.8 and 9.2 per cent respectively
of their courses were reorganized.

In Chapter Five we examine in greater detail some of the
correlates of these differences in the amount of reform occurring in
the various departments, but here may be the point to indicate that
all of the 110 institutions gave at least some indication of vitality in
terms of course reform. In other words, none of the institutions was
completely devoid of any indication of reform in all of the four departments that we happened to examine. Five of the 110 institutions failed to indicate any reform in three out of the four departments, and ten more showed no life—no course changes—in two of
the four. But none was completely dormant.

In terms of institutional level and type, the independent colleges tend to score the highest of all, with the religious colleges second, as Table 2 indicates. (Significantly, the independent colleges
were expanding their course offerings during the past half decade
the least of all of the six types.) While exceptions exist, the poorest
showing in terms of course reform among the six types of institutions appears among the independent and denominational universities—several of which are large, urban, and service-oriented institutions. The small sample of eleven junior colleges that we compared
with the senior institutions tended on the average to change their
course offerings far less: their rate of course reform was only 8 per
cent over the five-year period, in contrast to the senior institution
average of over 20 per cent.[3]

[3] Not all of the eleven, it should be emphasized, appeared so static.

Changes in Curriculum

Table 1

Undergraduate Course Reform, 1962–1967

Area	Number of Departments Sampled	Average Per Cent of Course Reform
Humanities	111	22.8
English and related fields	21	19.2
Languages except English	31	17.9
Music and Art	26	20.1
Philosophy	12	30.5
Religion (including two vocational departments of Theology)	8	35.9
Speech, Drama, and Journalism	13	30.4
Social Sciences	107	23.6
Anthropology and Sociology	19	25.1
Economics	15	20.2
Geography	5	21.8
Government and Political Science	19	28.8
History	18	21.8
Psychology	23	20.9
Social Studies	8	27.6
Natural Sciences	107	22.3
Biological Sciences	29	24.1
Chemistry	19	20.9
Geology	9	9.2
Mathematics	25	35.2
Natural Science or Physical Science	5	13.5
Physics and Astronomy	20	12.8
Vocations	101	21.5
Business and related fields	20	27.7
Education	40	18.1
Engineering	13	32.9
Health and Physical Education	10	20.0
Helping Professions, including Home Economics, Library Service, and Nursing	18	14.7
Total	426	22.6

Table 2

COURSE REFORM IN VARIOUS INSTITUTIONS

Level and Type of Institution	Number of Institutions	Average Per Cent of Course Reform
Four- and Five-Year Colleges:		
Public	24	21.7
Independent	15	30.1
Religious	30	26.3
Doctoral-Level Institutions:		
Public	16	21.4
Independent	14	18.6
Religious	11	18.2
Total Senior Colleges and Universities	110	23.2
Two-Year Institutions	11	8.0

At the same time that these reforms were being made in courses, the whole curriculum was expanding. The institutions were dropping courses at the rate of 5 per cent a year but they were introducing new ones at an annual rate of over 9 per cent. Thus over the past five years, the undergraduate curriculum simply within existing departments—not counting new departments—grew by 20.4 per cent. The state colleges were burgeoning. One of them in our sample increased the number of its undergraduate courses by 53 per cent. But as a group, the universities were expanding their courses more consistently than the total group of undergraduate colleges of all types.

Complaints about rampant course proliferation and pleas to prune the undergraduate curriculum appear to have had only a slight impact on the tide of new knowledge and specialization that

---

While several did nothing but expand, one—a private New England women's junior college that did not expand—had made major revisions in several departments and over the five years had a course reform rate of 28.6 per cent.

has been sweeping through higher education with the expansion of the student body and the growth of the faculty ranks. Courses that were formerly one semester in length have grown to two semesters; independent study has been added in many departments; and more specializations within departments have become available to undergraduates.

This expansion has come particularly at the upper levels: departments which expanded their courses only in the junior and senior years were more than three times as numerous as those which introduced more courses for freshmen and sophomores. Thus a student of Russian at one state college could now enroll in separate courses in Chekov, Pushkin, and Gorky. Elsewhere Milton and Chaucer now each have their own courses. At one college, basketball coaching and football coaching are now separated. At a state university the study of guitar has been admitted to the music department. At other institutions, photography by either motion picture or still camera is entering the arts curriculum. Computer technology, techniques, and theory are being incorporated particularly into mathematics and business. Statistics is entering the course lists of the remotest mathematics departments. Political science is becoming international in scope. Genetics, ecology, oceanography, and marine biology are being introduced into the biological science programs. Geography is incorporating urban studies. Physics and chemistry are allowing undergraduates to undertake independent research. And in history, more and more courses are appearing on specific areas—Canada, Cuba, India, China, Latin America, the Near East. Thus through accretion, knowledge from the graduate schools is percolating rapidly into undergraduate courses.

As part of the percolation process, the departments—and particularly psychology, chemistry, and mathematics—have been sloughing off their introductory courses that are no longer needed because of the continuing sophistication of secondary school students. "Man and society," for example, has increasingly become part of general education at the high school level rather than at the college level. Similarly the colleges have been abandoning introductory courses on marriage and the family in their sociology departments, cat anatomy in biology, personality in psychology, and photography in the physics department.

Within the vocational fields, course attrition has been particularly heavy among methods courses at some education departments. And throughout the curriculum, departments appeared to be dropping their service offerings and narrowing their focus. "Mathematics in agriculture" and "mathematics and life insurance" were eliminated at one state university; "zoology for teachers" disappeared at another; elsewhere a psychology department abandoned "methods of personnel selection"; a noted engineering department dropped its courses in economics, law, and ethics; and a respected independent college eliminated "art and society."

This apparent trend toward a more academic focus of the departments is particularly evident in the vocational fields, where specifically practical courses are being replaced by cognitive theory. "Television and radio announcing" departed from the speech department of a state college; "motion study and job simplification" disappeared at a business school; "lettering" was succeeded in an art department by "design"; the remains of "social welfare and social work" were eradicated at one sociology department; and at another, "introduction to social work" was replaced by "great social thinkers." A biological science department shifted from "forest science" and "ornithology" to courses on animal behavior, marine biology, and mechanics of organic evolution; an economics department at an independent university dropped courses on social security, public utilities, economics of industrial location, and urban land economics, and substituted courses in macroeconomics, mathematical economics, and economic growth and development. In marketing at a denominational university, "credit and collection," "essentials of salesmanship," and "retail merchandising" disappeared in favor of "consumer motivation and research" and "new product development." And in the religion department at another denominational university, the emphasis shifted away from the techniques of running a church and toward the theology and religion that are taught by the church.

Changes in Curriculum

In this way, institutions of higher education are becoming more like each other. Some observers, such as David Riesman, have commented on this process of academic "isomorphism" whereby all institutions come to resemble each other.[4] For example, Martin Meyerson foresees the prospect of their thus all becoming "as bland and uninspired as turnpike restaurants,"[5] and Warren Bryan Martin notes that even supposedly diverse institutions are caught in what he calls a "one-model box."[6] The most common examples of this trend are the formerly distinctive institutions such as technical institutes and teachers colleges that are becoming multifunctional by adopting general college programs. But the process is evident in other ways, too. The state colleges, for example, are giving up their traditional local orientation. Rather than emphasizing the history and geography of their state, which at one time was mandatory in order to produce properly-oriented schoolteachers, their social studies departments are becoming as international in scope as those of the state universities and the private colleges. Their art departments are de-emphasizing art appreciation and incorporating art history along with practice. Their language departments are moving toward the traditional university emphasis on foreign literature as well as foreign language—despite recommendations by the Modern Language Association. And their biology courses are less frequently "biology teaching" for secondary school teachers and instead are biology for biologists.

Similarly the southern colleges are becoming less regional. "The sociology of the South," for instance, is disappearing. Catholic colleges are becoming less ideological and parochial. "Social encyclicals" disappeared at one, and at another a focus in political science on the "systematic philosophy of the state" and the origins and

[4] Riesman's discussion of the concept appears in his *Constraint and Variety in American Education*. Lincoln: University of Nebraska Press, 1956, pp. 35–43.

[5] "The Ethos of the American College Student: Beyond the Protests," *Daedalus*, 95, Summer 1966, 737. Reprinted in Robert S. Morison (ed.), *The Contemporary University: USA*. Boston: Houghton Mifflin, 1966.

[6] Warren Bryan Martin, *Conformity*. San Francisco: Jossey-Bass, 1969.

theory of sovereignty has been modified through courses in political behavior and civil liberties. At almost all institutions, in fact, knowledge is being synthesized and broadened, moving away from the specific to the conceptual and theoretical. In literature and philosophy, for example, despite the additional courses in Chekov or Milton, a shift seems underway from the study of individual authors toward the study of particular periods. At an eastern state university courses on tractors, crop processing mechanisms, and design of farm electrical equipment were supplanted by "electrical power and machinery" and "engineering concepts and design." Elsewhere, "educational psychology" was succeeded by "the psychology of learning," and in an aerospace engineering department, "aircraft production" was succeeded by "aeroelasticity."

Moreover, the skills desired were becoming the skills of analysis and research rather than application. A course in interviewing techniques was introduced at a predominantly Negro state college, while "research methods in political science" came to a New York state university campus. Perhaps most symbolically, at a music academy where students are preparing for professional careers, the physical science course that had been required in 1962 was "sound and acoustics"; but by 1967 this relatively specific course was replaced by "the history and philosophy of science." And surprisingly, as part of this national trend, courses on the Negro and race relations were being dropped by several institutions between 1962 and 1967—replaced at one western state university by (of all things) the study of ancient civilizations.

This trend toward abstraction has been taking its toll particularly in physical education. Requirements in health and physical activities were declining, and one college abandoned the field altogether, leaving to its recreation director the task of renting bicycles to any students who wanted exercise. One exception to this abstract trend, however, was the field of religion, which seemed increasingly involved in social life and social problems. Thus one religion department dropped "Christian biography" for "religion in American culture." Another exception was in the arts, where personal artistic expression was continuing to coexist with art history, philosophy, and criticism.

A few institutions—and, in fact, several of the most dynamic —seemed to be going against the specialist and abstract trend. At one such college in Massachusetts, a communications department introduced a course on the relation of communication media to government and society. At another such college in Missouri, the behavioral science department broke the boundaries between psychology, sociology, and the institution's urban environment by tackling courses on the technopolitan society and culturally regressive groups, rehabilitation and cultural deprivation, political participation in lower income groups, inner city problems, the freedom revolution, and community reorganization.

But, in summary, the dominant trend in course expansion and reform during the period from 1962 to 1967 was away from service and away from the consideration of the significance, function, and utility of the disciplines. For better or worse, academic fashion and academic respectability pointed instead toward the analysis of disciplinary issues for their own sake and for the sake of knowledge itself.

Turning from the content of courses to the options open to students for majoring, the 110 institutions offered a total of over 2,400 majors in 1962, ranging from one prescribed program for all of the students at a theological seminary to over seventy majors at two midwestern land-grant universities. The colleges in our sample were offering an average of seventeen majors, while the doctoral-level institutions were offering their undergraduates an average of over thirty. Among all 110 senior institutions, as well as among the eleven junior colleges, in 1962 undergraduates had an average of twenty-two options from which they could choose a field of concentration, but by 1967 they had nearly twenty-five to choose from, and of these, four were new during the intervening five years. In other words, for every twenty majors that these colleges and universities offered in 1962, by 1967 they had on the average introduced four and dropped between one and two. In percentage terms, they were adding new programs at a rate of 4 per cent a year and dropping old ones at 1.5 per cent a year.

Not all the institutions were expanding the number of their undergraduate programs, but seventy-six of the 110 did so, and averaged an increase of 15 per cent. As might be expected, the greatest expansion of opportunities was occurring at the state colleges. Several of these former normal schools had been restricted to a handful of programs in elementary and secondary education, but by the mid-sixties they were beginning to offer subject-matter majors. One of them, with a total of twelve programs in 1962, added twenty-one more majors by 1967.

Among the 110 institutions, more change occurred in the vocational fields than anywhere else, with new programs being created primarily to serve new occupations. Their undergraduate students could enroll in a total of 115 new occupational programs —among them agricultural climatology, computer science, family service, international service, scientific writing, transportation engineering, urban planning, and wildlife management. Most common of all were new majors in specialized fields of teaching, such as education for the handicapped, the retarded, or the mentally disturbed.

Beyond these occupational majors, the greatest growth occurred in the social sciences and foreign languages. Psychology for the first time became a separate undergraduate concentration at thirteen of the 110 institutions during the half-decade; political science became separate at twelve, and sociology at ten. Eleven institutions commenced a program in Spanish; ten began one in German; eight introduced Russian; five added French; three, Italian; and one each organized a major in Slavic, Arabic, or African languages.

Among the natural sciences, seven institutions added physics to their list and seven more added biological sciences. Even at the liberal arts colleges, where the scarcity of scientists had raised fears that science would have to be abandoned in lieu of the humanities, no such trend was evident: two liberal arts colleges did close their physics majors, but six others established one. More significantly, however, most of the new specialties for undergraduates in the sciences are being introduced only at the universities. Astronomy, biochemistry, ecology, genetics, and mineralogy all opened as undergraduate majors among the forty-one universities in our sample, while only physics, chemistry, geology, and biology were finding their way into the colleges.

The disciplinary majors continued to splinter, with specialties emerging along the same path in the colleges that they had followed earlier in the universities. "History and government" finally separated at one college, "speech and drama" split at another, "classics" divided into Greek and Latin, and "romance languages" broke into separate European tongues. Thus philosophy is rarely still considered a part of theology, or social work part of sociology, or psychology part of the education department. And as the institutions expand, separate schools are being organized: a college of fine arts divorces itself from arts and letters at one state university, while colleges of business and of education expand out of the liberal arts college of another.

At least some synthesis has been taking place, however. Three institutions witnessed the merger of botany and zoology into biology. Four others organized new joint majors, including economics and sociology, history and social science, and physics and biological sciences. Occasionally completely new interdisciplinary programs have been accepted—the most common being one or another of the "area studies." For example, seven institutions added American studies as a major (while, interestingly enough, four others dropped it). Four universities added Asian studies; and one each organized Latin American, Russian, African-Middle-Eastern, and medieval studies as majors. At four institutions, linguistics was at last coming into its own by separating itself from its parental disciplines. At one of these institutions—a state college—its birth was being guided by a coordinating committee including faculty members not only from English, modern languages, and speech, but also from mathematics, philosophy, anthropology, sociology, and theater.

Besides the seventy-three colleges and universities that expanded their number of majors, ten of the 110 institutions made no changes at all in their major offerings during the five years. Eight others did not change their overall total, but replaced one or more fields of concentration with others. And the remaining sixteen—the majority of them private institutions rather than public—cut back their options.

The rate of replacement for all 110 institutions and for the two-year colleges as well was between 7 and 8 per cent over the five years, or one program dropped and another added for every fifteen in the curriculum. The bulk of those dropped were in the occupations, where fifty-two separate programs among the 110 institutions were phased out. Particularly hard hit were what can best be termed the "arcadian" subjects, such as home economics, dairy industry, foods and nutrition, and rural sociology. In addition, the nonacademic vocations, such as secretarial science, marketing, advertising design, and interior decoration, were being abandoned to limbo or to other institutions; and what used to be called the preprofessional curricula were ebbing in favor of the disciplines. One institution that had dropped its preprofessional programs justified its new policy with the statement that "preparation for professional study is best advanced through one of the liberal arts programs."

This statement summarizes remarkably well the trend that has been occurring in undergraduate majors between 1962 and 1967. They are increasingly "preparation for professional study," limited to one of the traditional "liberal arts programs." Certainly greater opportunities now exist for undergraduates to select their own particular field of specialization: at the universities, specialties that a decade ago were graduate-level programs have become undergraduate majors, while majors formerly available to undergraduates only at the universities have now spread throughout the colleges. This growth, however, has taken place in the occupational fields and the traditional disciplines; efforts at breaking departmental boundaries and creating area-centered, period-centered, problem-centered, or tailor-made individualized programs have been scattered and infrequent. For instance, only fifteen of the 110 institutions offered a sufficient number of interdisciplinary programs to comprise at least 10 per cent of their undergraduate options, and only three of these—all three of them prestigious private institutions—clearly indicated that students could design their own major programs with the advice and consent of their adviser. The concept of a major organized around student interests and concerns rather than around disciplinary or occupational criteria thus remains generally dormant.

The trend toward academic standardization seems equally evident from changes in curricular requirements and regulations. During the past five years, many formerly struggling institutions have had the opportunity—thanks to the supply of students—to move toward academic respectability. They have been instituting general requirements for all students, leaving to other institutions (and apparently primarily to the community colleges) the task of educating students uninterested in these requirements. Former vocational colleges have at last embraced general education. For a bachelor's degree the tiny teachers colleges, technological schools, and Bible colleges are now enforcing a common standard that consists of required foreign language, humanities, and the sciences. And more state universities are imposing these requirements on all of their students and not simply on those in the liberal arts.

Higher levels of competence are being expected as well. Students at one university can no longer use the introductory mathematics course to satisfy the mathematics requirement for graduation. At a women's college, students in German are no longer permitted to count toward the major a course of German literature in translation. The colleges have had the opportunity to be more strict in enforcing rigorous standards of achievement and have tended to take advantage of it: Eight of the sample raised their required grade-point average while only three of them—all of them already highly selective—reduced theirs.

Among the majority of institutions, general education has suffered from the centrifugal force of the expansion of knowledge. We found no attempts at integrative, comprehensive, systematic overview programs of general education comparable to those introduced after World War II. The attempt at *Weltanschauung* has passed, possibly from a lack of both faculty interest and faculty

67

competence. At several religious universities, even the weekly assembly program—the last remnant of their former chapel requirement—has ended, while at two of the colleges it remains the one integrating experience still left in the program. A few state colleges are adding comprehensive examinations for their seniors, but more institutions are abandoning them than adopting them. Instead, the disciplinary specialties have triumphed.

Several institutions have cut back their distribution requirements in general education, and even on those campuses where general education has not declined, it has reverted from a series of prescribed courses to groups of options. Abandoning the chow-line approach to general education whereby all students took the same courses, and unprepared to adopt a cafeteria philosophy of completely free selection, the colleges appear to be compromising on a long-established plan that might best be called the "Chinese restaurant" approach to general culture in which undergraduates "Select two from Group A and two from Group B."

A few institutions are increasing requirements in the hard sciences, but far more often, they are requiring students to select one or two courses in the creative arts. This seems particularly true at several Catholic colleges, which shifted some of their emphasis in general education from theology, philosophy, and literature into the arts and the social sciences. The one area of general education suffering a decline appears to be physical education, where requirements are being reduced. And although by the end of our study, efforts had yet to gain momentum to push ROTC completely out of the curriculum and into the extracurriculum, several state universities during the half-decade made it elective rather than required.

In sum, general education is being "disciplined." The most noteworthy example of this trend has been the fate of Daniel Bell's proposals for strengthening Columbia College's required program, which fell on fallow ground among the satrapies of Columbia's departments. The only evidence of a general countervailing movement lies in the several institutions that introduced a January term between semesters—a month of study that might retain a broader focus than the typical departmental course. The trend, however, has been away from "education for breadth." General education has always been primarily a reaction to cultural crisis—as its major institutional origins in the United States after World War I, in the Great Depression, and after World War II illustrate—and apparently the five years from 1962 to 1967 did not seem to many academicians culturally critical enough to demand new programs of general education for all students.

While these shifts have been occurring in general education, two related trends appeared in the requirements governing specialization and majoring. On the one hand, more attention is being devoted to the major. By and large, the proportion of time that students devote to their major field and closely related courses has increased over the past five years. A few departments reduced the number of hours they required, but more—particularly, for some reason, the history departments—extended them. Some fields were recommending earlier specialization, particularly since they were expecting more work by their students in neighboring fields. In psychology, statistics was increasingly required; in English, a foreign language; in chemistry, mathematics and physics; and in biology, chemistry, mathematics, and physics.

On the other hand, along with greater concentration has come greater freedom within the major. Students can now choose far more courses from within their field to form their major program than they could earlier, when most of the courses were prescribed. At some colleges, there now exist twice as many opportunities for electing courses in the major field as a half-decade ago. For example, at one university, only one-third of the hours in zoology were elective in 1962; now two-thirds of them are. And at one Catholic university, in order to major in economics students need to take only six credits of Latin now as opposed to eight credits five years ago. The only exception to this increased flexibility appeared at several state colleges, which are moving into university status and appear to be tightening up requirements by increasing the prescription of their programs.

As for differences among the disciplines, the greatest change in requirements for students majoring in each field has come in anthropology and sociology, business, mathematics, and the performing arts, where over a third of the departments that we surveyed appear to have made moderate to major changes in their requirements. The fewest changes are evident in physics, where only one out of eighteen departments showed comparable evidence of change, and eight showed none at all.

In terms of differences among institutions, over a fourth of the 110 in our sample appear to have made no changes in their degree requirements during the past half-decade, and only seven made substantial alterations—one of them a college which dropped its distribution requirements entirely in favor of personal advisement and an individualized curriculum for each of its students. Whether it was a function of the small size of the colleges, their freedom from the graduate schools, or their need to compete with the universities for students, the colleges in our sample altered their demands somewhat more on the average than did the universities, and the religious colleges as a group changed the most of all.

Turning finally to the regulations governing students in the classroom and on the campus, it is clear that while the mass media have been titillating the public with reports of avant-garde developments at a select number of institutions regarding open parietal hours and coeducational dormitories, most institutions across the nation have tended to remain protective and sheltering and are only cautiously loosening their parental restraints.

During the years from 1962 to 1967 students were increasingly involved in institutional governance, and on more and more campuses they were evaluating the curriculum and establishing their own judicial system. But above all, they became more free to decide about attending class. More institutions changed their regulations on attendance than on any other issue, with at least twelve of the 110 moving to hold students responsible for their own achievement rather than for attendance. Moreover, no longer at one state university is a professor expected to report three consecutive absences of a student to his dean; at a Catholic women's college, three tardinesses no longer count as an absence; at a Catholic university, students are now "encouraged," rather than required, to attend weekly mass; and at other colleges, only freshmen or freshmen and sophomores are still required to attend convocation. This emancipation of the upperclassmen is not entirely the result of a change in educational philosophy, however. Occasionally it has been the expedient solution to the problem of a large student body and a small auditorium, the lack of closed-circuit TV, or the dilemma of split convocation sessions or alternate-day attendance.

These changes in curricular regulations have been paralleled by an easing of out-of-class regulations. Off-campus housing is now possible, particularly when all the college-owned facilities are filled. Curfews are being extended or abolished. Key privileges are being expanded. The institutions are less in league with parents: at one denominational college, freshmen grades are now sent home only twice a year rather than four times. At another college, a student's "entering into matrimony" would have resulted in automatic suspension five years ago, but now it is tolerated upon written permission of his family. Still another had made at least a slight concession to modernity: while continuing to be "strictly opposed" to profanity and other vices, it no longer "strictly prohibited" them.

Most of these trends in expectations and options for undergraduates over these five years point toward specialized technical competence as the basic goal of the institutions for their students—that is, a more highly skilled proficiency of a more intense and narrow nature. By the end of their senior year, for example, students are expected more and more to demonstrate some professional competence and achievement, whether through performance in music, a senior show in art, or high scores on the Graduate Record Examinations.

At the most prestigious institutions which head the academic procession, this pressure appears less direct. Having already recruited able young specialists, they appear to be relaxing their requirements: they are tending to permit freshmen greater opportunity for selection of upper division courses, to allow pass-fail grading in order to encourage greater exploration of the curriculum, and to permit a student to fail several courses and nonetheless graduate.

71

And throughout the system, institutional control over nonacademic performance is easing, as colleges slowly relinquish their watchdog role over student life. A student's opportunities for choice are expanding considerably—at least within the traditional academic fields, if not in interdisciplinary or action programs. But the diversity of aims of the institution has been shrinking toward a common academic model of abstract knowledge, bringing with it hints of the chill malaise of pedantry. Students, it seems, are expected to decide on one focus of study and then excel in it. Technical proficiency is demanded, and the image of the technocrat appears to be emerging as the academic ideal.[7]

---

[7] This orientation that we sense developing is also noted by Edward Gross and Paul V. Grambsch in their study of perceived and preferred goals among administrators and faculty members at sixty-eight universities. (*University Goals and Academic Power.* Washington, D.C.: American Council on Education, 1968, p. 109.) Paul L. Dressel and Frances H. DeLisle have surveyed 322 colleges and universities to analyze the changes in their curricula between 1957 and 1967. They found some of the same trends that we note here, and they conclude: "The trends substantiated by this study are not great in number and less extensive in nature than one might have expected considering the curricular ferment of the past decade. . . . Despite all of the talk about innovation, undergraduate curricular requirements, as a whole, have changed remarkably little in ten years. In many cases, the most that could be said of a particular institution was that its curriculum has been renovated—that is, requirements were restated in terms of new patterns of organization and course offerings and updated to recognize the rights of newer disciplines to a place in the sun. One suspects that, in some cases, this latter consideration rather than a real concern for flexibility may have motivated a move from specific course or discipline requirements to broader distribution requirements. In many cases, the minor changes in requirements, amounting to no more than a reshuffling of credits, can only be characterized as tinkering, although one can imagine faculties spending many hours on these pointless decisions." (*Undergraduate Curriculum Trends.* Washington, D.C.: American Council on Education, 1969, pp. 74, 75.)

~~~~~~~~~~~~~~~~~~~~~~~~~~~~~~~~~~

CHAPTER IV

Agents of Change

~~~~~~~~~~~~~~~~~~~~~~~~~~~~~~~~~~

We have a tendency toward stagnation here.

A professor at one of the colleges in our sample

The history of American colleges and universities, as Chapter Two indicated, seems to point to three dominant sources of change in higher education: the resources available for change, the advocates interested in change, and the openness of academic institutions to advocacy. But what about the recent changes just described in Chapter Three? Did they stem from the factors that have seemed to be important historically? And what do the men and women who have been involved in these recent changes perceive as their cause? What additional perspective do they have about the sources of reform? Do they sense that other factors are more important? If so, which ones?

To answer these questions, we sought the opinions of several members of each of the institutions in our sample. We did not end our study with this poll of opinions about the roots of academic change. Beyond these impressionistic data, we also sought hard facts about the correlates of change, as Chapter Five shows. But since the attitudes of faculty members and administrators are so crucial to the process of academic reform, this chapter analyzes their views from their own vantage points about the sources of reform.

These opinions were collected as part of the process of gathering together all the information that we judged might bear an important relation to the changes that we had measured at each institution. Some information, of course, could be obtained from institutional records and published data; but some was available only from members of the institution—such facts, for example, as the steps that are involved in deciding on a new program or the attitude of the president toward involving students in curricular decisions. The process by which these facts and opinions were collected is described in detail in Appendix C; but in brief it involved one of the first extensive series of telephone interviews that has been undertaken with college administrators and professors. Our goal was 330 interviews—three at each institution: one with an administrator, another with a department head, and a third with a professor. We succeeded in interviewing 234 of the men and women we had hoped to contact, or 71 per cent in all, with better success among administrators than among department chairmen and professors and at universities than at undergraduate colleges.

The telephone interviews were conducted by some ten members of the staff of the Institute of Higher Education—most of them graduate students at Teachers College. After completing a call, the staff member dictated the most important comments onto tape and completed an interview form for later analysis. From the responses to several of the questions as transcribed by the interviewers, this chapter summarizes the attitudes of academics toward, first, the sources of initiative for change and the leadership of change, and second, the influences for and against change and the obstacles to it.

Regarding initiative for change, the administrators and faculty members with whom we spoke tend to see themselves as the instigators of academic change. We began by asking each of them this question: "As you can imagine, we are particularly interested in the ways that changes have come about in the programs of American colleges and universities. Where has the initiative come from for recent changes in the program of *your* institution?" Table 3 outlines the differences of perception among administrators, department chairmen, and professors on this issue. Notice how much more frequently the administrators name administrators as the initiators of change (45 per cent of the time) than do the department chairmen or the professors (29 per cent for each of them). Similarly, note how much more often the chairmen identify chairmen than do administrators or professors (15 per cent of the time in comparison with 4 and 7 per cent respectively). And finally, observe how much higher professors rate themselves than do the administrators (43 per cent in contrast to 29 per cent).

Combined, these three groups of respondents claim 80 per cent of the initiative themselves. If we had asked students or trustees or other groups the same question, we suspect that they, too, would rate themselves more highly than our respondents did, rather than accounting for only the 19 per cent assigned them by our respondents.

We had not expected that the answers to this general question would pattern themselves so closely to our respondents' own roles. The men and women with whom we spoke did not seem self-important or egotistical. Instead, in our conversations they were if

75

Table 3

INITIATORS OF CURRICULAR CHANGE

Group Identified as the Initiator (Per Cent)

Respondents	Adminis-trators	Department Chairmen	Faculty Members	Commit-tees	Students	Trustees	Outsiders	Total
Administrators	45.4	4.2	28.9	2.5	6.7	4.2	8.4	100.0
Department Chairmen	29.1	15.5	41.0	5.5	5.5	0.9	2.7	100.0
Professors	28.9	7.2	43.5	1.2	9.6	2.4	7.2	100.0
All Respondents	35.2	9.0	36.8	3.2	7.1	2.6	6.1	100.0

anything generally modest, as well as delightfully open, relaxed, and thoughtful. But apparently, like the taxpayer who suspects on April 15 that he is the main support of the United States government, and like many of us who tend to see ourselves in the best light, they tend to see themselves as the prime source of curricular improvement. Not only do administrators and faculty members have mirror images of themselves as the instigators of reform, but their high evaluation of themselves tends to affect their opinions of each other —generally for the worse.

As an illustration, at one private college, a professor who had just resigned his position claimed that the individual professors were left entirely on their own to initiate reform. "The administration isn't progressive enough. . . . There's no leadership at the dean's level. There hasn't been any change." The chairman of one of the science departments, however, saw the changes stemming from the Educational Policies Committee—which he had chaired for eight years and which was composed half of department chairmen. And the president sensed that reform stemmed from his office:

> The administration is very flexible. They're far more flexible than the senior faculty. The faculty are naturally reluctant to change. But the junior faculty—they come in and they want to change everything. They're not very influential, however. Lots of the changes they want to make are not appropriate.[1]

In terms of the *causes* of change, our respondents tended to attribute the reasons for the change to the most immediate and

[1] In this way, our respondents appear to differ from the faculty members and administrators at some institutions that Richard I. Evans visited in his study of the adoption of classroom television in college teaching. "In several cases in our sample," he writes, "the administrative and the faculty segment both felt that the other was responsible for initiating innovation; as a result the rather humorous picture presents itself of two people listening on the same telephone line with neither of them saying anything." (Richard I. Evans in collaboration with Peter K. Leppmann, *Resistance to Innovation in Higher Education: A Social Psychological Exploration Focused on Television and the Establishment*. San Francisco: Jossey-Bass, 1968, p. 132.) The difference may lie in the fact that we asked not about responsibility but about actual initiative.

proximate influence of all—and in particular, to their own attitudes and those of their associates. In the interviews, we asked them to tell us about some recent alteration in the program of the institution, the reasons for this change, the individuals involved in it both inside and outside the institution, and any obstacles that impeded it.

A few respondents, such as the professor mentioned above, disgustedly could think of no significant changes to report, while a few had difficulty in recalling anything recent. One university vice-president reported the introduction of general education courses that took place twenty-two years previously, in 1946. But the other respondents reported some 220 examples, ranging from the rewriting of a university handbook and the adoption of a new textbook in a freshman course in business administration to the decision to merge the institution with another.

Of all of these examples, expansion of the program led the way. We received more illustrations of new undergraduate majors than any other (forty-seven of them), followed by enlarged, expanded, or strengthened programs (thirty-six), and the addition of a particular course (twenty-five). Only six involved the elimination of a course or program, as the examples in Table 4 illustrate.

By and large, our respondents attributed these changes to relatively personal and local causes rather than to broad trends or external forces. Just as the infantryman at the front line has a different perspective of the forces affecting the tides of war than the detached military analyst and historian, so educators on the front line of education have an immediate view of educational change.

Sixty of them—the largest single number, as Table 4 shows —spoke primarily of personal or institutional dissatisfaction with the program as the reason for the development: their feeling of a need to keep the institution abreast of the times, for example, or to adapt it to a changing environment, or to make the program more relevant to present conditions by updating it. Fifty-three others talked in terms of a desire to provide particular opportunities for students—to allow more specialization or require less specialization of them, to offer foreign study or interdisciplinary work to them, to meet the needs of exceptional students. A total of over sixty attributed the development simply to the interest of one or another person or agency—such as the particular professors or students or administrators or outsiders. And fourteen mentioned the necessity of training manpower in particular fields.

In short, these are the proximate reasons for change. Supporting these personal dissatisfactions and interests of individual administrators and faculty members have been the demographic and ideological shifts in American life which have led to the expansion of enrollments at the institutions and the increased financial resources available to higher education. These trends have allowed some of these individuals to be employed and permitted their departments and programs to be created. In other words, personal motivation dominates the thinking of the participants themselves. As most of us tend to do, they tend to think of causation in personal terms—not systemically.

Turning to the people who are seen as the leaders of change, a significant pattern emerges: some groups appear to be influential in initiating one type of development far more than another. In answer to the question, "With what person or group did the idea originate?" many groups were mentioned—among them students, faculty members, foundation officials, government agencies, trustees, administrative staff, and accrediting agencies. But note these differences among them: *Students* are seen as more influential in having courses added to the curriculum than in any other development. *Faculty members* are most influential in getting a program of study added to the curriculum. *Administrators* are most influential in getting requirements changed and in adding new units to the institution. And *trustees* and outside agencies are most influential in altering the entire status of the institution.

Beginning with the smallest of these changes—the alteration of a particular course and the addition of a course to the curriculum —and moving to the largest and most disruptive of them, our respondents' views of the origins of these changes run as follows:

Change in a Course. Students are seen as originating the idea for course changes more often than for any other type of change. Consider three examples:

Table 4

REASONS FOR CHANGE

Changes Reported (listed in terms of frequency)	Reasons									
	Dissatisfaction with the Present Program	Desire to Provide More Opportunities	Administrative Initiative	Faculty Initiative	Student Pressure	Outside Initiative	Manpower Needs of Region or Society	Resources Available	Other Reasons[a]	Total
Addition of a New Major or Program	6	11	2	8	2	4	6	6	2	47
Expansion of Curricular Offerings	8	14	2	2	3	1	2		4	36
Addition of a Course or Change in a Course	5	7		2	4	2	2		3	25
Addition of a New Unit to the College	6	5	5		1	1	3		3	24
Revision of Graduation Requirement	10	6	4	2	1					23

										Total
Curriculum Study	10	2	1	1	1				2	17
Calendar Change	5	5	3	1		1			2	17
Change of Institutional Status[b]	1	2	2			4	1		2	12
Reorganization of Personnel Structure	2	2	1	1					1	7
Dropping a Course or a Program	2							4		6
Total Reorganization of the Curriculum	2	1			1				1	5
Other Changes[c]	3		1			1				5
Total	60	53	21	18	14	14	14	6	24	224

[a] In order of frequency, the other reasons included a crisis situation (4), no one source or "just happened" (4), competition from other institutions (3), lack of resources (2), and miscellaneous (11).

[b] For example, a change from teachers college to multipurpose college or from religious college to independent status or a merger with another college.

[c] Other changes included the opening of new services to students (2), changes in admission requirements (2), and the creation of a new facility (1).

81

Dynamics of Academic Reform

The president of a religious college in Pennsylvania:
We had two courses introduced in the past two years at stu-
dents' request: one in data processing and one in linguistics.
They would not have been introduced otherwise.

*The chairman of the history department at an inde-
pendent university in the South:* We have gotten persistent inquiries about ancient history, so after a while we had funds
enough to bring in a man, so we brought him in in this area.
Right now we're getting more and more inquiries about English history so I suppose that will be our next appointment.

*An associate professor of English at another independ-
ent university:* There has been some student agitation this year
for changes in courses and it evoked a healthy and positive reaction from the administration, trustees, and faculty. The students organized a group of three hundred or so whose chief
concern was the inequality of opportunity given to the arts-
college students in comparison with engineering and business.
They wanted more courses with relevance, probably picking
up echoes from what was going on at other colleges. After the
students made their demands, the trustees set up a faculty and
trustee committee to look into the possibility of courses on
southeast Asia, poverty, and Negroes, etc. The whole thing has
moved harmoniously. There've been open meetings between
administrators and students, and concessions have been made
on both sides.

The stimulus for some courses seems to lie in other outside
influences. "We're trying to keep up with industry," said a professor
at a western university concerning the origins of new courses on
computers and numerical controls. And a southern college added a
linguistics course, according to the chairman of its English department, because the State Board of Education requires prospective
English teachers to take it.

Nonetheless, faculty members are seen as exerting the dominant role in originating course changes. That is, even though the
administrators and faculty members whom we interviewed see students as more influential in changing courses than in any other development, even here the students account for only 7 per cent of the
cases, in comparison to the faculty's 34 per cent.[2] One reason for

[2] The tabulations for this statement and the following one about the
perceived originators of change appear in the final table of Appendix C.

this discrepancy most likely lies in the tradition among academicians that a professor's course is, indeed, his course: He alone controls it. Observe some examples of this faculty initiative:

A mathematics professor at a state university: It's been felt in mathematics universally that many undergraduaes never found out what mathematics was all about. Students didn't learn until they were seniors or graduate students what mathematicians really *do*. We're adopting a new program to teach students what mathematicians do, so they will know. Next year we'll offer a two-quarter sophomore sequence on intermediate analysis—beyond calculus—following the Texas approach by proving theorems. The idea came from the influx of two Texans to the department about four years ago: Jim ———, a student of Moore, and James ———. They took the lead and the department curriculum committee made the decision.

An associate professor of physical education at a predominantly Negro state college: I thought it was necessary for us to establish relations with the outside realm. The physical education department was primarily for P.E. teachers and coaches, but other areas are now open, as recreation specialists and in hospitals and industry; and I can get them into jobs now that I couldn't before.

The chairman of a sociology department at a state university: The faculty of the department has tried to round out the offerings. We went through the catalogs of other universities and saw what they had that we didn't have.

The dean of home economics at a state university: The people in industrial engineering and distributive education desired a course in textiles. A survey of alumni showed that there was a need for a textile course in order to prepare students to work in the textile industry. Once this need was known, the faculty took the leadership in developing the course.

The academic dean of a religious college that prepares nuns for teaching, nursing, and social service: Our college has introduced an integrated science program. We had a study of our graduates, and the head of the science division found that our students needed a unifying course bringing together physics, chemistry, and biology. Our students need to be broadly educated, not simply in their discipline, since our graduates primarily go into teaching where they need breadth of knowledge. The students were unanimous in support of the course, although the humanities division objected to raising the course from five to fifteen credits.

A New Major.   Professors see themselves as more influential in originating new programs than in any other type of change—even more influential than in changes of courses, where they occasionally view students as important. Even the administrators admit that faculty members are responsible for a major share of the initiative for new majors—though, of course, not as much as are the administrators themselves. In all, professors and department chairmen are seen as originating the programs in just over half of the 166 cases reported. Besides them and the administrators—who are seen as originating another third of the new programs—the only important force for new majors seems to be the influence of state government on the state colleges. Several former teachers colleges have been undergoing forced growth because of the states' decision to transform them into multipurpose institutions, and their new programs are viewed as originating in the state capital.

The dynamics of these two different sources of change—internal stimulus versus external mandate—are considerably different. Here are some examples of new home-grown programs, stimulated by the faculty and administration:

>   *A department chairman at a new state university, speaking of a new major in Spanish:* The department and the school of arts had enough students and faculty to make it possible.
>   *The chairman of a state university department of geological sciences:* Geophysics is the coming thing. Since we're one of the leading schools of geology in the country we're trying to keep [the university] a major geology school, and therefore the academic planning committee of the department recommended it. There was no opposition: it's what was necessary to keep up with the other pace-setters.
>   *A professor of psychology at an Ivy League university, regarding a program in child psychology:* A new laboratory building with extra space for staff and students was constructed. The department had facilities to fill, and we debated adding more of the same program or opening a new area. The

psychology of childhood was a new field in the United States; we decided that we would get in early, and added it to the programs in experimental and physiological psychology.

The academic dean of an undergraduate college within an independent university: The ideas originate around here with senior professors. It's the senior men who make things happen. Take our linguistics major. A couple of people wanted to see it happen. They drew up the plan. They presented it to the Committee on Instruction. The Committee's the only obstacle to curricular development. The Committee decides everything. They're a tough one; and you have to fight your way through them. Junior men have a great deal of influence on their own courses; not otherwise.

The president of a Catholic university, regarding an undergraduate theology major: Theology has been a traditional requirement at [this university]. All Catholic students took a two-credit course in theology every semester. They were frankly awful courses. Some students would deny that they were Catholics in order to get out of them. Father ——— got a graduate program going in theology that was scholarly, and the new young professors that he brought in decided to try to strengthen the undergraduate courses by reducing the requirements and adding many electives. They did such a good job that students began to *want* to take the courses. And so they organized an undergraduate program as well.

An assistant professor at a religious teachers college: Physical education was just made a major in the school. The department felt it was necessary because of the lack of professionals in physical education in the Lutheran schools. No one person was responsible: it was the whole department.

The president of a state university, regarding a program in urban affairs: The essence of it was the development of a society and a world that was not reflected in our academic structure. The dean of our school of letters originated the idea, and he had a noon luncheon for the chairmen of six departments to discuss it. Then they took up the idea, and consultants were brought in. The chief obstacle was the unwillingness of departments to take the initiative in anything beyond their boundaries, so the leadership had to come from outside the departments.

Now for some comments about programs stimulated from outside the institutions:

Dynamics of Academic Reform

A professor at a New York state college: The major change came directly from Albany in changing from a teachers college to a liberal arts college. The private institutions were not accommodating the students who needed to get a liberal education, and so the legislature decided to expand the teacher's colleges to meet their needs.

A professor of modern languages at an urban state university, regarding a social service major: The president feels very strongly the need to respond to the needs of the city. And there was pressure from the legislature and the city government to do something about [the city] and its mess.

The chairman of sociology at the same institution: The curriculum in social service was urged by the welfare agencies in the city, and the new curriculum in corrections was urged by the parole board. People are needed in these fields, and they must be prepared on the undergraduate level as well as the graduate level so that they can go right out into their chosen field without having to go on for a future degree in graduate school. Dr. ———— in sociology came up with the final design after spending a year studying various agencies and schools around the nation to see what they were doing.

A department chairman at a state college: The new counseling and special education programs for the schools stemmed from the State Department of Education.

A president of a state teachers college, regarding a two-year nursing program: Our local hospital administrator hounded me more than anyone else. We're good friends, and so I know his interest. The doctors in the town have not been quite so vocal, although the chairman of our board is a physician. We've also been having trouble keeping nurses in our own infirmary on the campus, and so I knew of the difficulty. I asked the last session of the legislature that we be one of four institutions who would have authority to begin a two-year nursing program, and we got the right.

And the vice-president of a state university, regarding a similar nursing program: I am not sure whether this should be our responsibility, but the governor of the state made the decision and provided the funds, requesting that the university introduce an associate-degree program in nursing. I have gone along with the idea, although I really don't think that the university should be associated with it. Possibly other institutions in the community and the state—hospitals, perhaps—it

86

should be their responsibility. There is a great need to provide new programs like this for the community, both Negro and white, around the university and within the state. And so the governor is pushing for it and providing the funds, and consequently it was introduced here.

These examples of new programs illustrate a fact that became evident during the study—namely, that the sources of initiative differ somewhat for majors in different fields. In the examples reported to us, outside influence is more evident in the origins of majors in the social sciences and the vocations, where social agencies and business and industry seek staff members trained for these particular occupations. On the other hand, faculty and departmental initiative is highest in the humanities, where administrative and outside influence is less than in any of the other fields.

Changes in Requirements and in Curricular Organization. Students are occasionally seen as originating changes in degree requirements and in the organization of the curriculum. One of their particular targets has been ROTC. On at least four of the 110 campuses during the five years, changes appear to have been made in military training as a result of student influence: at three of them to abolish it or make it elective rather than compulsory, and at the fourth, to introduce it for the first time.

Students have been having an impact on other requirements as well. At a midwestern city university, their complaints helped eliminate a comprehensive examination in English that all graduating seniors had been required to pass. At two of the nine predominantly Negro colleges in our sample, professors report that student disturbances and sit-ins have led to significant changes in regulations. At a private university, declining enrollments in science have sparked the reorganization of the science curriculum; and at two Ivy League colleges, dissatisfied students have banded together to study their education and propose changes in it.

Administrators, however, are seen to be the primary originators for most of the alterations in requirements and curricular organization. Even to the faculty members, they appear to play this role more frequently than do professors themselves. In half of the cases reported to us, administrators are identified as originators of the plan, just as they are in the cases involving the introduction of a new academic calendar, such as a January "minimester" or the quarter system.

In the following illustrations, the role of the new administrator in facilitating some of these changes may be obvious. But note, too, the variety of factors involved in the decision—among them, student, faculty, and trustee concerns, the help of foundations, the threat of disaccreditation, and—to begin with—the transformation of the secondary schools.

The president of an independent college: Of all of our recent developments, the major revision has been our 1962–63 curriculum reorganization, and this stemmed from the secondary school revolution in mathematics and science. There was no ferment here when I came in 195_, but it emerged as the prior training of students became evident to the math and science departments. It was their professors, finding that their students were coming better prepared than they had planned, that forced the college into rearranging its curriculum. The scientists had to battle the humanitarians, who couldn't see that their students had changed at all. And, of course, they hadn't. To the humanitarians, they still couldn't read and write.

In the past, we had had year-long introductory courses in each department. But we had to split these up into semester courses and give alternatives for the second semester. Along with this, we made a mechanical change from five courses per semester to four; and as a result, we had to phase out the upper-level courses because of the new limit.

A new president of an art institute: I made a list of the things that I sensed needed to be done, and one of the first ones was the reorganization of the freshman program. The first year was conservative: it was just like it was when I went to school. The sophomore year was creative, but students were having to do in the sophomore year what they should have gotten in the first year. It was the smoothest change I ever encountered. The only problem was the old director of the freshman program. We smoothed the problem by putting him on leave for a year and then bringing him back in a different position. We appointed two brilliant new men to build up the freshman program, and it worked out excellently. And from this reorganization of the freshman year we have now restructured the full four-year program.

The president of a Catholic women's college, describing the origins of a system of four courses per term: The initiative came mostly from a few really alive people who've talked to me, and we've tried to get things going. We realized that too many courses were being offered for two credits, and so I invited a group of people to my office to discuss the problem. We decided on a four-course system, with each course meeting three days a week. We presented it to the faculty on a trial basis, and on this basis they were willing to go ahead.

The president of another Catholic women's college: I came in 195_ as a professor of chemistry. At that time, the department chairmen were considering changes in the college program. They proposed at one of their curriculum committee meetings that they ought to have a faculty committee free over the summer to think about reorganizing both the curriculum and calendar. I was elected to that committee and was made chairman of it. The faculty felt students were having to take too many courses each semester and that the curriculum was too structured so that interdisciplinary and interdepartmental programs could not be adequately offered. The committee sent out a questionnaire to students and faculty members, and from the answers they drew up a set of proposals. Over the last couple of years the proposals have been—well, in *many* cases have been—put into operation.

The new president of an independent college: My early conversations with the trustees led me to believe that they were not interested in change, and so I originally declined the offer of the presidency. Later they came back and inquired about my reasons, and when I explained my reservations, they assured me that my impressions were wrong: they were concerned about reorganizing the institution, too. And so I accepted, and indeed my first impressions have proved wrong. . . .

The graduation requirements needed to be reduced to 120 hours—for one reason in order to admit junior transfers from the community colleges. The speech requirement finally was cut back from nineteen hours to twelve hours. Although the idea had been around before I came, no one dared to talk about it because the chairman of the speech department was the most influential person with the former president. He had a friend in power. And so I probably triggered the idea with my coming. I personally thought that maybe the speech requirement could be squeezed back to nine hours, and the speech therapists even thought it could be squeezed back to six hours, but most everyone agreed that it should at least be only twelve hours, except for the speech department itself.

The president of an independent women's college: We were invited to send a team to the Danforth Foundation conference in Colorado, as many institutions are on a rotating basis. Three faculty members went and their enthusiasm led to a special committee of the faculty that we called the "Central Committee" that worked for two years between 1965 and 1967 and came up with a beautifully written report and called for a study of the curriculum. We completed this study just the past year, which will change our distribution requirements this next fall and allow increased flexibility.

The president of a Protestant college: My predecessor had been president for 42 years, and when I first arrived in the fall of 196_ we started on a major review of the curriculum. The college was under a cloud from the Middle States Association: it had two years to show cause why its accreditations should not be revoked. We had to demonstrate change in those two years, and with general support of the faculty, the dean and I and a faculty committee developed a core curriculum that put mathematics and foreign languages into all three tracks of the curriculum. It worked out well, and since then the changes have been refinements by and large. Here the departments have assumed the leadership again.

A New Unit of the Institution. Administrators were seen as the originators of new instructional units on campus in over 55 per cent of the cases. Thus they appear to play a role even more significant in originating an entirely new section or division of the institution than in curricular organization. One reason for this fact was alluded to by a chairman at a state university when he observed, "As long as finances aren't involved, the department has the most influence, but anything at all that involves finances, the administration steps in and they are the most influential." The creation of medical schools at two institutions was specifically attributed in both cases to the president, and here are four other instances of similar developments:

Agents of Change

A department chairman at a state university, describing the origins of an arts school and a symphony-in-residence: The chancellor does not concern himself with the existing curriculum. That is, he has never interposed himself against the proposals of the Academic Affairs Committee and the Senate. But he has been instrumental in creating totally new programs, such as the school of music, and in bringing the ——— symphony here for its summer seasons. Several years ago he asked the Senate if it would be willing to authorize a school of performing arts and permit the school to offer courses and credits on a somewhat different basis than the usual academic curriculum. And the Senate gave its approval, with some limitations. So ultimately we will have a school of performing arts because of his initiative. It's been mostly that that chancellor has been keeping his eyes open. At lunch a year ago in January or February, one of the trustees of the ——— symphony mentioned to him that the symphony was looking for a summer home so that it could extend its concert season, and the chancellor said to him, "Why don't you come to ———?" And by the next June the pavilion had been built and the conductor was raising his baton to lead the inaugural concert.

An administrator at a state university, describing a new professional school of community service and public affairs that will operate at the undergraduate level: It's really a school of applied behavioral sciences. Many students had to take an academic major even if they didn't want to go on to graduate school. Often a girl would say, "What can I do with a major in sociology?" We designed this curriculum to meet this need. It covers a broad area of community services from mental retardation to recreation work and public administration. . . .

The idea came from a widely-shared feeling among the faculty in the behavioral sciences and also in law, journalism, and other fields that somehow the university was not really fulfilling its obligations either to the undergraduates themselves or to society. [The president] took the initiative and appointed a fifteen-member committee with Dean ——— as chairman —an interdisciplinary committee that came up with the idea. It brought in consultants, and after the committee proposed the plan, [the president] went out and got a million dollars from the Wallace Foundation for the work of the new school.

91

A provost, describing a new center for the arts: It's harder for a large group to bring about change than for an individual like a dean. From my point of view as a physicist, it's an example of entropy. You can't make "first-order" changes—significant changes—at an institution by a vote of a hundred people. Our center would never have been built if we had had to have a vote of our constituency. A number of committees—half a dozen or more—were formed to discuss particular issues of the center, but the faculty was never called together to approve the idea. It stemmed from the president, who had a deep interest in developing this area of our program, and from the trustees' vote to commit eight million dollars to it. It has never been our tradition here to take major decisions such as this one or about new facilities to the faculty for vote.

Another provost at a private university: Something needed to be done about biology. The arts school was teaching zoology while the agriculture school had biology. The president, coming into office, realized that this was not adequate. The dissatisfaction came from him and not from the departments. It was one of his top priorities, and the provost and vice-president agreed. They got money for a consultant who came in and recommended a new division of biological sciences. And after making the report, the consultant was finally convinced to take the headship of the division.

The faculty is never averse to experiments; but here you had to break the authority structure of the schools, and so some delicate negotiations had to go on. Money was quite secondary here. The departments are always quite amenable to experimentation if money can be obtained to compensate them for the released time of professors.

Change of Institutional Status. In the most sweeping and potentially disruptive changes, where the boat is not merely rocked but rebuilt and redirected, our respondents identify outsiders, trustees, and administrators as almost completely responsible. State governments, in particular, have been reassigning functions among the state colleges; but other agencies as well are influencing other colleges into expanding to university status, merging with other institutions, turning public from being independent, or becoming independent from having been denominational.

Agents of Change

Among the 110 institutions, three mergers were occurring and a fourth college was beginning construction of a joint library with a neighboring college. At one Catholic women's college, the president agreed to a merger with the nearby men's college when the men's college decided to become coeducational and the possibility of this competition appeared too formidable to withstand. At an independent university and a technological institute, an administrator reported:

> The actual initiative came from the presidents of the two institutions, who saw that the two had complementary programs. They brought in outside consultants to study the possibility of merger, and the decision came about as the result of a recommendation by these consultants.

The severity of some reorganizations is illustrated by the president's comments at a new state university that grew out of an existing private college:

> This university was created by the legislature several years ago when it bought ———— College, a small downtown private college. Every institution has a trajectory of its own, and ————'s was different from what ours had to be. I regret that the changes have had to come from the top, but it has been a process of imposed social change. I've had to replace the total administrative staff—the vice president for business, the librarian, the director of public information, the bookstore manager. It's taken two years, but yesterday we finally appointed an academic vice-president. . . .
> The conventional departmental organization and monopolies were not satisfactory for a state university. For instance, political science was submerged under history, so I had to pull it out and make it a department of its own. We needed some program of general education, so I picked seven people who were not tied into the existing department chairmanships. I did not assign the task to any existing committee—it would have died. I bought them copies of books; I sent them on visits. There were mutterings and wailings, and we ran into the usual thickets, but we got the idea through the faculty when we said that it would only be an experimental program

93

with a review every month. . . . The department chairmen are continually proposing the conventional expansion of conventional programs. On the other hand, the administration is trying to develop new programs and new ideas.

In summary, then, academics—whether professors, department chairmen, or administrators—tend to see themselves as more important in the process of academic reform than their colleagues, but they tend to agree that their importance varies with the extent of the changes involved. Students and faculty are seen as playing their biggest role in initiating course and program changes; administrators are seen as the prime movers behind changes in requirements and the addition of new units to the institution; and outsiders are more influential as the source for major reorganization than anywhere else.[3]

Turning to the patterns of influence for and against academic change, our respondents tend to agree that administrators and faculty members are the most influential people at the institutions in terms of the academic program. Although they still assign greater influence to themselves and their particular group than to other groups, they agree far more closely on who is influential than on who initiates change. Even professors and department chairmen, as well as administrators, view administrators as more influential in affecting the academic program than any other group, as Table 5 shows. In terms of influence, administrators are followed by the faculty and then by department chairmen and departments, with students and trustees each deemed significant in less than 3 per cent of the total.

Some differences occur in the distribution of influence within different types of institutions. The faculty are mentioned *most* frequently as influential at the independent universities, where tradi-

---

[3] Among these influential outsiders, interestingly enough, the federal government is only infrequently named. Most commonly identified as influential in the changes are state agencies—not only at state institutions but occasionally at private colleges in connection with the requirements for state certification of teachers. In decreasing frequency, other external sources are local interest groups, such as hospitals and industry, foundations, accrediting agencies, alumni, and the federal government.

Table 5

Percent of Respondents Identifying Most Influental Groups

Group Identified as Most Influential

Respondents	Administrators (excluding the president alone)	Faculty	Department Chairmen and Departments	President alone	Committees	Students	Trustees	Total
Administrators	36.8	31.2	12.0	11.2	2.4	3.2	3.2	100.0
Department Chairmen	33.9	23.4	24.8	3.7	5.5	2.8	0.9	100.0
Professors	39.2	30.5	15.9	4.3	5.8	1.4	2.9	100.0
All Respondents	36.4	30.0	17.5	6.9	4.3	2.6	2.3	100.0

tionally the faculties have had much autonomy in curricular decisions. The faculty appears to be *least* influential at the religious colleges, where administrators for obvious reasons are frequently named. Department and division chairmen hold sway particularly at the state colleges. And influence seems most broadly shared or dispersed among all parties at the independent colleges, where administrators play some part and the faculty does not alone dominate as in the independent universities.[4]

Besides telling who seems to have the most influence over the academic program, our respondents also indicated whether they think of these influential people as a force for stability or for change in the program. As Table 6 shows, by and large they see administrators and the faculty at large more often as agents of change than they do department chairmen and departments or committees, which are viewed as particularly conservative. The influential presidents are seen as progressive far more often by administrators than by chairmen and professors. Similarly, the few trustees who were mentioned as influential are seen as progressive by the administrators while those mentioned by the chairmen and professors appear as conservatives. Only the few students who were mentioned as influential are viewed almost exclusively as oriented toward change.

We next asked the same question about the major influences on the academic program from outside the institution. While it could be argued that the major outside influence on the shape of the undergraduate program is from the graduate schools, only a few of the respondents think so. More of them see state governments and accrediting agencies as influential than any other outside source. Table 7 shows how frequently these groups were mentioned as well as the direction that our respondents see their influence taking on the curriculum. The influence of churches and graduate schools, although infrequently mentioned, is felt as particularly con-

---

[4] These impressions of the participants coincide with those of recent analysts of the higher education system, such as Talcott Parsons and Gerald Platt, who see the independent university as the prototype of academic values and the model of emulation by professors. ("The Academic Profession: A Pilot Study," duplicated, March 1968.)

Table 5

Percent of Influential Members Viewed as a Force for Change[a]

Influential Group

Respondents	Administrators (excluding the president alone)	Faculty	Department Chairmen and Departments	President alone	Committees	Students	Trustees	Average
Administrators	52.2	51.3	33.3	92.9	33.3	100.0	75.0	56.0
Department Chairmen	24.3	29.0	25.9	50.0	33.3	100.0	0.0	29.4
Professors	51.9	47.6	45.4	33.3	50.0	0.0	0.0	46.4
All Respondents	42.7	42.9	32.1	76.2	38.5	87.5	42.9	44.3

[a] This table indicates, for example, that among the administrators we interviewed who consider administrators as a group to be the most influential regarding the curriculum, 52.2 per cent of them see this group as a force for change. The remaining percentage, in this case the 47.8 per cent who do not consider the administrative group as a force for change, view it either as a force for stability in the academic program or as a fluctuating force.

Table 7

MOST INFLUENTIAL EXTERNAL GROUPS
AND DIRECTION OF INFLUENCE[a]

	Direction of Influence (Per Cent)			
Most Influential External Group (listed in terms of frequency)	For Stability	Varies	For Change	Total
State Government (29 cases)	55.2	10.3	34.5	100.0
Accrediting Agencies (27)	44.5	22.2	33.3	100.0
Other Colleges and Universities (19)	10.5	10.5	79.0	100.0
Employers (18)	33.3	16.7	50.0	100.0
Churches (16)	62.4	18.8	18.8	100.0
Local Interests (16)	18.8	25.0	56.2	100.0
Federal Government (14)	0.0	21.4	78.6	100.0
Professional or Scholarly Associations (14)	21.4	7.1	71.5	100.0
Alumni (13)	61.5	7.7	30.8	100.0
Foundations (7)	0.0	0.0	100.0	100.0
Graduate Schools (6)	60.0	20.0	20.0	100.0
Social Trends (4)	0.0	0.0	100.0	100.0
Donors (3)	0.0	0.0	100.0	100.0
Average (193 cases)	33.7	14.5	51.8	100.0

[a] This table indicates, as an illustration, that of the 29 respondents who mentioned state governments as the most influential outside force on the academic program, 55.2 per cent of them, or 16, consider state government as a force for stability, while 10.3 per cent see it as a variable force and 34.5 per cent view it as a force for change.

servative, while the effect of foundations, other colleges and universities, and the federal government is seen as a force for change. (Since few systematic differences of opinion among the three groups of respondents appeared in response to this question, Table 7 combines all their responses. The only major difference among the administrators and faculty members here involves the influence of alumni: Administrators see them primarily as a source of change while the chairmen and professors who mention them consider them to be conservative.)

One fact from these opinions about the influence of various groups gives a clue about the obstacles to academic change. The external groups that our respondents mentioned are on the average somewhat more often seen as supporting change than are the groups within the institution. In other words, despite the conservative influence of the churches, the graduate schools, and alumni, our respondents do not perceive the obstacles to academic change to be from external but from internal sources. Neither legislative vigilantes nor the John Birch Society nor any other outside group seem to our respondents to be the major obstacle to academic change at their institution. In fact, in answer to a specific question about the major obstacles, not one of the 185 people who mentioned any obstacle at all referred to religious or denominational pressures, and only three of them mentioned trustees as the impediment. Educators thus feel far more free from major constraints from outside sources in their efforts at academic reform than they do from internal obstacles.

Some respondents note the constraints of a *lack* of outside support: 16 per cent attribute the greatest problem to a lack of funds. "It's money," the academic vice-president of an independent university declared. "The other obstacles are so far down the list that they're insignificant. The first, second, third, fourth, fifth, sixth, seventh, eighth, and ninth problems are money." But over 80 per cent of the other respondents differed with him, and Table 8 shows the other major problems that they named.

Half of all of the respondents assigned blame either to the faculty or administration, with the faculty and departments mentioned most frequently of all. Among administrations, 46 per cent blame some inadequacy of the faculty—such as "entrenched departments," "faculty provincialism," "overspecialization," and "inadequate graduate training." More interestingly, over a third of the faculty concur. Here are some of their reasons:

99

Table 8

OBSTACLES TO ACADEMIC CHANGE

Obstacles to Change (Per Cent)

Respondents	Faculty or Departments	General Inertia or Conservatism	Lack of Funds or Resources	Administration	Lack of an Adequate Staff	Confusion over or Problem with Goals	Trustees	External Influence	Miscellaneous[a]	Total
Administrators	45.9	22.9	12.0	3.6	6.0	2.4	2.4	0.0	4.8	100.0
Department Chairmen	36.4	14.5	18.8	13.1	4.3	4.3	1.4	0.0	7.2	100.0
Professors	38.1	14.9	17.0	12.8	2.3	8.5	0.0	0.0	6.4	100.0
All Respondents	40.8	18.1	15.6	9.0	4.5	4.5	1.5	0.0	6.0	100.0

[a] Among the miscellaneous obstacles are these: too rapid growth of the institution and subsequent loss of communication; small size of the college; lack of mutual understanding among departments; the institution's system of committees; the need to convince department chairmen of the need for change; too little time and too many other commitments.

Agents of Change

The chairman of an education department at a Catholic women's college: We've had some beautiful obstacles—real beauts. Some of the old-time ladies on the faculty, in particular. We have a liberal and conservative bloc here. The nuns are in the liberal bloc. The laywomen are the convervatives: they have been here the longest and represent the traditionalists. Thankfully the most obstreperous one is retiring now. Selling about five or six of the older tenured ladies on the idea of our new program was our biggest problem, but now they claim that they invented it. Our president wins out either by getting outside funds or else by clouting them on the head.

A professor who has taught five years at a Protestant college: It's a small core of people who've been here since 1812. They believe that if you sit tight for twenty years it'll blow over.

The president of a municipal university: A group of older faculty. After World War II the university brought in a lot of professors. It paid low salaries then, and we would have questioned some of them if they were to be appointed now. But these professors are now all about five years from retirement, and some of them have become chairmen.

A vice-president of a Catholic university: Faculty resistance, by and large. Most faculty members are fairly obsolete if they've been out of study for five or six years. They're obsolete in general, and they may be obsolete even in their own field, particularly if it's something with very specific new knowledge, for instance, biology. They're afraid that with their background they'll have no place in any new curriculum.

The provost of an independent university: I think that you've got the built-in reaction of conservative factions in any faculty that consider *any* change in standards as a *lowering* of standards.

And the president of a small state college in New England seemed to have the most perplexing problem of all with the faculty: "Getting them to think of change is hard enough—but getting them to stop making changes once they've started is just as hard."

Thirteen per cent of the professors and the same percentage of department chairmen identify administrators as the major obstacle—as do one president and two other administrators themselves.

101

> *A chairman at a private university:* The usual obstacle used to be the president. It still would be if the board hadn't forced him out.
>
> *An associate professor at a Catholic university:* The faculty has been trying for years to put over many changes. The administration won't listen, even though the Church at Vatican II says it must listen. The faculty's letters to the administration have received no answers. A lack of communication is wished for on the part of certain administrators. There's a feeling around here that the faculty doesn't have the judgment to make changes. They're asked to do something and at the last minute an administration member steps in and puts in his own views and changes things.

Some respondents are more global in their view. Eighteen per cent of the responses do not blame any one group, but general inertia instead. "It's the natural conservatism of faculty, president, and board," said the president of an Ivy League university. And another president stated:

> Organizations just get lethargic as they grow older. They have policies for policies' sake. And soon the policies become rituals. And pretty soon it's almost like a religious order and the organization is ready for burial.

Occasionally the problem is philosophical in nature. A young professor of journalism at a Catholic women's college stated that one obstacle was this:

> A narrow definition of the liberal arts. There's a frowning on any type of *doing* anything rather than just *studying* it. We're fighting the idea, for example, that drama does not have to be produced on the stage—that students need to only *read* about it.

The administrators tend slightly more often than the faculty members to consider the impediments to change as institution-wide rather than the result of one or another specific obstacle. But the administrators and the faculty are alike in each tending to attribute less blame to themselves than the other does: the faculty is more culpable in the administrators' view than the faculty believes, while administrators, naturally, seem more of a nuisance to faculty than to themselves. Here again, as with their views of their own importance in bringing about reform, their attitudes tend toward what can perhaps best be termed as "polarized provincialism."

This provincialism, we begin to suspect, has serious consequences for the process of academic reform. Probably everyone connected with an institution of any kind likes to think of himself as the savior of the organization, the champion of its cause and the defender of its trust. No doubt this sense of responsibility and determination makes for vigorous debate and lively competition within the institution. But in academic life it may also account for some of the seemingly endemic antagonism that exists between administrators and faculty members over the curriculum. We have long wondered why, for example, when groups of presidents congregate, their oaths tend to become bluest when the conversation turns to the faculty. And conversely, when members of the AAUP and faculty associations meet, the gnashing of teeth seems loudest about administrative officers. Both groups seem to view the other with suspicion. On the one hand, some administrators aver that the faculty, if left to itself, will ruin the curriculum by a lack of vision— by laboring like myopic ants "with grains of dust, making Herculean conflicts with blades of grass" and killing off interest in subjects, no matter how palpitant with life, by asphyxiation.[5] And on the other hand, professors often believe that the faculty must alone be sovereign over educational policy if the curriculum is to remain undefiled from the "captains of erudition" in the offices of the "Keeper of the Tape and Sealing Wax."[6]

It now appears from our interviews that at least one part of the reason for this frequent enmity is that both administrators and faculty members tend to conceive of themselves as the primary

[5] Charles A. Bennett, "Is Teaching a Narcotic?" *The Bookman*, March 1929, p. 26, quoted by W. H. Cowley, "A Short History of American Higher Education" (unpublished draft), 1961.

[6] Thorstein Veblen, *The Higher Learning in America: A Memorandum on the Conduct of Universities by Businessmen.* New York: B. W. Huebsch, 1918, pp. 85, 105.

103

source of curricular improvement. Each sees itself as critical in the process, and as less reactionary and obstructionist than the other. Holding such disparate views of their own leadership and initiative, they understandably become competitive and defensive. The very position from which they view academic change is inescapably limited in perspective. They are aware of immediate problems, and actively engaged in overcoming them—whether the problem is an unsatisfactory text book in learning theory or the collaboration of an engineering school and a medical school in the development of artificial organs—but they are caught in the parochialism inherent in any one role. They sense that they themselves are willing, indeed eager, to make changes; therefore the obstacles must lie elsewhere.

Luckily, the reservoirs of personal good will and humility help overcome part of the tendency toward polarized provincialism. Perhaps the information from our study about this tendency can help reduce the enmity as well. But most important of all from our point of view, the fact of provinciality tends to cast doubt on the conviction of some faculty members and some administrators that the only answer to academic change lies on the one hand in greater faculty control or on the other in greater administrative inititaive.

CHAPTER V

Correlates of Dynamism

I consider that a great step is made in a reformation when it has been granted that the present
system is open to examination, and not stereo-
typed for all ages. Wherever that is done, light
will break in. All my labor about education 'hath
this extent—no more.' It begins to be admitted
that college systems may be examined. When this
is done there is hope of amendment.[1]

Francis Wayland

[1] Undated letter (about 1855 or 1856) to the Reverend Rufus An-
derson, quoted by Francis Wayland and H. L. Wayland, *A Memoir of the
Life and Labors of Francis Wayland, D.D., LL.D. . . . by His Sons*, Vol. 2.
New York: Sheldon and Company, 1868, p. 69.

The opinions about the sources of academic reform held by individuals in academic life are important in understanding the problem of curricular change; but since these impressions of the causes of change are to some extent inescapably limited because of their perspective, how can the sources of reform be identified objectively? Searching for evidence in historical documents leads to some clues. Observing in detail the genesis and development of new ideas at several colleges and universities provides further evidence. Beyond these techniques lies the comparative examination of the characteristics of a number of institutions, isolating the features that distinguish the most dynamic institutions from the most static ones and then studying these particular features to learn their effect.

We used all of these methods in the Study of Institutional Vitality in order to understand the origins of academic reform. We wanted to account for the changes that have been taking place in the educational program, and hence, as a major part of the project, we correlated all of the information that seemed important to us about the colleges and universities we were studying to the facts about academic change at these institutions.

Two guidelines seemed clear. First, we needed to complete a comparative study. That is, we could not examine merely the "best" cases, the colleges that showed the most reform. While it is always tempting to study only success—as one tends to do in remembering particular students who make good, or certain professors who seem to be effective teachers, or universities that are internationally famous—we knew that we could not claim to know the characteristics of dynamic academic institutions and the sources of their vitality unless we also looked at other institutions to make sure that these same characteristics were absent.

Second, we needed to study a multitude of characteristics to learn which were most important. Some studies properly deal with the relationships between two or three major variables, such as the influence of a professor's attitude toward television on his willingness to use closed-circuit TV, or the effect of financial resources and communication on the process of innovation, or the functions of differing administrative styles on productivity. If we had thought

106

that one or two major characteristics lay at the heart of academic reform, we might have chosen that path; but from all the evidence we had, the problem was more complex than this. From historical data it appeared that resources and the vulnerability of an institution to outside pressure were critical factors along with individual advocacy, the turnover of personnel, and institutional structure and traditions. From the study of organizational change at large, other characteristics also seemed important—not only cold hard cash, charisma, and competition, but cosmopolitanism, institutionalization, leadership, morale, pecking orders, and role specifications. And from the participants in academic change themselves, such as the men and women interviewed, it was evident that the attitudes and behavior of key members of the institution were closely involved. We knew that these and other factors form a web of interdependent relationships, but we wanted to gather as much information as possible about them in order to measure their relation to academic change and thus weigh their influence in stimulating change.

From all of the evidence, it seemed that the sources of academic change lie less in organizational renown or success than in organizational instability. That is, most of them appear to point to conditions of institutional vulnerability, flexibility, and openness as likely correlates of curricular change. As a result, we predicted that academic change would turn out to be primarily a by-product of organizational instability as measured by such factors as fluctuation in the resources available to the institution, shifts in the staff of the institution, and by an institutional structure that is particularly vulnerable to individual influence.

We should immediately make clear that we did not wish this condition to be true. Instead, we would hope that ideally changes in course content, in programs, and in requirements and regulations would occur continually even in the most secure and stable colleges and universities; and, of course, they obviously do occur in some of these institutions. But we suspected that a high level of academic change on these measures would more likely be related to instability, and in particular, to unstable resources, a shifting staff, and a vulnerable structure than to stability. If this hypothesis turned

107

out to be true, and everything else were equal, the most evidence of curricular change would be found at the weakest, most marginal, most down-and-out colleges, where perennial crisis stimulates the most frantic adaptability. Everett Hughes has referred to these institutions as "Available Jones" colleges. Like the fellow with that name in "Li'l Abner," they are ready to try anything in order to keep going. And at the opposite extreme, the most successful, prestigious, and wealthy universities would demonstrate the least amount of change. Proud of their traditions, uninterested in attracting new clientele, but interested in retaining their present status, they would adopt few academic innovations and then only after they had proved acceptable in less elite institutions. This, at least, was our suspicion.

To test this idea required data on a whole series of characteristics. Thus resources would tend to be unstable, for example, if endowment constituted a small proportion of the institution's income and student fees formed a major share; if the institution was not relatively prestigious or well-known, and if the most influential patrons of the institution (including students, if they were an important source of income) expected academic change at the institution. Instability among the staff would be evident if the rate of turnover in positions of power was high, if the faculty was recruited from a wide variety of sources rather than from one major source and particularly from inbreeding within the institution, and if the most influential members of the institution were a force for change in the academic program. The institution would be structurally more vulnerable to change if, among other factors, a small number of hurdles would be required to implement curricular proposals, if members participated broadly in decisions without the need for institutional consensus, and if their work was not highly specified— that is, if they had few restrictions placed on their own interpretation of their own duties. To obtain this and related information, we sought data on some ninety separate facts at each institution. The list of these variables appears in Appendix D; they include facts on enrollment, location, salary schedules, turnover of professors and department chairmen, amount of inbreeding, selectivity of the institution, sources of income, the proportion of faculty with tenure, requirements on taking attendance, and the participation of faculty, students, and trustees in curricular decisions. Some of this information could be gathered by means of the telephone interviews with administrators, department chairmen, and professors that were mentioned in the last chapter. The rest came from national surveys of higher education, directories of educational institutions, and college catalogs. Not all the information for each item was available on every institution, and some of the information was less reliable than we would have liked, as the examples in Appendix D illustrate. But we used the best data available to compare with the information we had already gathered on changes in the curriculum.

Turning to what we found when we correlated all of the facts and figures that we had gathered, at the outset we should state that we did not uncover the "causes" of reform—that is, we did not find universal principles that invariably account for change in one institution and its absence in another. We did, however, find some significant relationships that lead us to suspect that our hypothesis is at least in the right direction. That is, it seems evident from the data that academic change is a function, at least in part and among other things, of organizational instability.

To enlarge on this statement, as a beginning here are some relationships that we did *not* find: We did not find that academic reform, as we defined it and attempted to measure it, is occurring primarily in any one type or group of institutions. Neither the undergraduate colleges nor the universities, neither the public institutions nor the private, have a monopoly on it. Instead, there are virtually no statistically significant differences between the institutions grouped either by their level of program (college versus university) or by their type of control (public, independent, or religious).

This is not to say that great differences do not exist among individual institutions. Obviously they do. As we mentioned before, for example, the small sample of two-year colleges appears on the average to be far more static in course offerings than the senior institutions. But little in our data suggests that among senior colleges and universities, any one general type of institution is significantly more dynamic on our measures of academic change than any other type.[2] Thus our findings do not support the partisan champions or critics of any particular type of institution—be it the state university or the private liberal arts college—in regard to their dynamism and extent of reform. Other factors than their general type are far more influential.

Moreover, our measures of academic change appear to have little relation to most traditional measures of institutional reputation, such as the amount of income per student, the proportion of doctorates held by the faculty, the extent of endowment income, the rank of faculty salaries, or the academic origins of the faculty. These characteristics, sometimes mistakenly employed to measure academic "quality," do not appear to lead to a high level of reform. Nor do they lead, as our hypothesis proposed, to a significantly low level of reform. Wealth and prestige, it continues to seem, can contribute either to innovation or to stability, but by themselves they do not appear to stimulate one or the other.

In short, we sense no evidence from this study to support two common academic stereotypes: the provincial undergraduate college that is stagnant because of its genteel poverty, and the conservative and traditional university that is rigid because of its wealth. More is at work here, in other words, than simply wealth or prestige or institutional type. In fact, certain characteristics appear to be related to one measure of academic change but not to others; and so before trying to identify the features of the institutions that appear to be the sources of academic reform in general, we had best look at the correlates of each type of academic change that we measured. After individually examining the characteristics associated with course reform, replacement of programs, and

[2] The only two statistically significant differences that occurred out of a possible seventy-five among our six major types of institutions were these: First, the religious colleges, which had altered their graduation requirements as a group more than any of the other institutions, scored significantly higher (at the 5 per cent level) on this measure than did the religious universities. And second, the independent colleges, which as a group had shown the most reform in their course offerings, scored significantly higher on this measure than the independent universities, which by and large had altered their course offerings far less. But none of the remaining seventy-three possible differences was statistically significant.

changes of requirements and regulations, we summarize our findings about the sources of academic change at large.

Course Reform. Recall our general hypothesis: that academic change would be associated with instability of the organization, as measured by such factors as unstable resources, staffing, and structure. In terms of the reform of course content within the departments, we suspected that the major source of instability would be the turnover of the teaching staff. As professors leave and retire and new instructors and professors are hired, we guessed that the new men would alter the previous course offerings considerably— at first in their lectures and class sessions and reading assignments, and then in the catalog description of the courses, which we used as a measure of course reform. This measure is not entirely satisfactory, as it under-represents the amount of actual change in course content, according to the opinion of some of the professors that we interviewed who teach the courses, and particularly at those institutions that have not revised their bulletins or catalogs much in recent years. This difficulty, however, does not influence the fact that in the largest departments that we studied, the amount of change in course descriptions is significantly related to changes in the faculty. That is, in departments made up of ten or more professors in 1962, a high rate of faculty turnover between 1962 and 1967 was closely associated with a high rate of change in course descriptions and offerings. There is somewhat less but still a significant relation between faculty turnover and course reform in medium-sized departments with from five to nine professors; but overall, in the total number of departments that we studied, the relationship between faculty turnover and course reform is not statistically significant.[3] The reason for this difference in terms of de-

---

[3] In the sixty-three large departments, the correlation coefficient is .348, significant at the 1.0 per cent level. In the seventy-nine medium departments it is .246, significant at the 5 per cent level; but overall it falls to .166. Departments, incidentally, tend to be smaller than we had anticipated. In 1962 all 426 had a mean of 5.8 professors (not counting lecturers or instructors); a median of four; and a mode (that is, the largest number of cases, which in this study was seventy-seven departments) of two professors.

partment size may stem from the likelihood that professors in large departments have more option to introduce and discard courses of particular interest to them, while in the smallest departments with one or two men, the same basic courses with the same fundamental content may be deemed necessary regardless of who is employed to teach them.

More important than faculty turnover, it develops, is turnover in the department chairmanship. The replacement of one department chairman by his successor does significantly affect the rate of course reform within the departments as measured by course descriptions. The reasons why a change in chairmen plays a greater role in course change than turnover in faculty are probably twofold: the chairman at many institutions not only has power to assign courses to particular faculty members and to influence the momentum for changes in them, but he also may control the catalog copy about departmental listings.

In spite of this statistical relationship between the chairmanship and course change, not much of the variation among departments in their rate of reform can be attributed to this single factor —only 4 per cent of the variation at most.[4] Thus, change in the chairmanship—and turnover of faculty in the larger departments— is influential in the process, but far from crucial to it.

Another way of illustrating this finding is to compare the departments that appear to have changed their courses the most with those that seem to have changed them the least. By taking approximately a third of the 426 departments—those that fall outside one standard deviation from the mean score of 22.6 per cent for reform in their courses—we can compare seventy-three departments which have changed less than 1.0 per cent of their courses with seventy-three that have changed more than 40 per cent of them—including the four departments mentioned in Chapter Three that have altered their courses completely. Table 9 shows some of

---

[4] The correlation coefficient is .208, significant at the 5 per cent level. A multiple regression analysis of change in the chairmanship, turnover of professors, and net change in the size of the faculty indicates that all three have a total multiple correlation coefficient of .264, with the largest departments having an R of .349.

Table 9

CHARACTERISTICS OF DEPARTMENTS DIFFERING IN AMOUNT OF COURSE REFORM

	Departments			
Characteristic	Highest (Most Dynamic) Departments (73)	Medium Departments (280)	Lowest (Most Static) Departments (73)	All Departments (426)
Criterion Variables:				
Per Cent of Course Reform (Used to distinguish the three groups)	57.7	19.3	0.0	22.6
Change in Requirements for Majors (Five-point scale, *none* to *much*)	2.6	2.0	1.4	2.0
Predictor Variables:				
Per Cent of Departments with New Chairmen Between 1962 and 1967	73.6	59.7	38.8	58.3
Average Per Cent of Faculty Turnover Between 1962 and 1967	37.6	30.6	25.9	31.1
Number of Professors as of 1962	4.6	7.1	3.6	5.8
Per Cent of Change in Number of Professors Between 1962 and 1967	86.1	67.9	59.4	69.5
Number of Courses Listed as of 1962	20.8	26.1	15.8	22.5
Per Cent of Change in Number of Courses Listed Between 1962 and 1967	41.4	36.7	57.5	41.1
Per Cent of Inbreeding Among Professors as of 1962	18.7	20.3	22.6	20.6
Distribution Among Areas of the Curriculum (Per Cent):				
Humanities Departments	21.9	25.0	30.2	25.6
Social Science Departments	30.2	23.6	26.0	25.1
Natural Science Departments	26.0	26.8	17.8	25.1
Vocational Departments	21.9	24.6	26.0	24.2
Total	100.0	100.0	100.0	100.0

113

the differences between these two extreme groups as well as a comparison with the remaining majority of departments. The seventy-three most dynamic departments differ in these ways from those that have changed the least: First, a new chairman has replaced the old chairman in 74 per cent of them, compared to 39 per cent of the others, where some chairmen have been in office as long as twenty-four years. (In all departments combined, 58 per cent of the 1962 chairmen were no longer chairmen in 1967.) Second, turnover rates of faculty are higher: a median of 40 per cent and a mean of 38 per cent compared to 20 and 26 per cent for the others. Fifty-four of the dynamic departments have had at least some replacements among their professors, in comparison with only forty of the most static departments. But the two groups of departments differ only slightly in the extent of inbreeding among their professors and in their rates of course expansion and faculty expansion. Nor do they differ greatly in terms of field of knowledge. Because of the substantial changes occurring in religious and philosophical thought, we had expected to find a large number of humanities departments among the most dynamic group; but no such difference appeared, as Table 9 shows.

Next, we looked for differences between the most dynamic and most static departments in their operation and organization. We had interviewed twenty-two faculty members of the seventy-three most dynamic departments and twenty-four members of the most static ones, and we returned to these interviews to see whether any other factors seem to distinguish the two groups. We recognize that this evaluation is only impressionistic, but two general characteristics appear to differentiate them:

One is a difference in attitude toward students and outsiders. The twenty-two faculty members at the most dynamic institutions more frequently indicate a receptivity to their students' ideas and those of their constituents than do their opposites at the most static departments. They more often see students exerting influence on curricular decisions; students are more often able to choose their own courses; and the departments more frequently seem close to other clientele beyond students. As an illustration of this attitude, the chairman of a dynamic mathematics department volunteered the comment that "students form a proper part of the picture. Your consumer is the guide to acceptance in any economic unit." At one dynamic psychology department, student evaluations of each course go not only to the professor involved but to the total departmental faculty and the chairman. And in response to the question, "Among the faculty is there greater interest in offering *prescribed* programs of study or in allowing students latitude to *elect* most of their courses?" the members of the dynamic departments more often favor the elective system than do their opposites. At one of the static departments a professor explained his preference for prescription in these words: "If it's left to the student, he will not take a broad program; and this is the purpose of a liberal arts college." At the static departments, in other words, students are more likely to be told, not asked. Illustrating the difference in ties to the community, a professor of business at a dynamic state university commented, "The university has an obligation to the region, so indirectly the region influences the program." And at a dynamic Catholic college for women, the sisters sensed a need in the community for preschool education and were creating interdepartmental programs out of the psychology and education departments to meet this need.

A second difference seems to lie in attitudes of powerlessness and satisfaction. The respondents from the static departments more frequently indicated a feeling of powerlessness—a resentment of pressure and unilateral decisions from the administration—and greater satisfaction with what had gone on in the past. A psychology professor at a religious women's college reported, "The president didn't know that she didn't know anything about academic matters, and the president's secretary ranked higher than the faculty in influence." An instructor in music at a state university complained, "There are a few select faculty members who are on key committees year after year." The chairman of an economics department of a private university confided that the president "wanted to make the place like Hamilton College was in the 1920s." And a history professor at a state university commented:

The dean has so much power that things don't get proposed unless he favors them. Decisions tend to come down to the department from the policy committee, dominated by the dean. . . . The State Board of Education finally says what can't be done. Fear of their disapproval guides actions here.

Among the off-hand comments from the faculty interviews, here are some others from members of the most static departments:

Until we find a better way of doing things, most of us would prefer to be a little conservative and use the tested methods.

Sometimes you Americans experiment more than is necessary.

Our faculty is a force for stability, but you always have one or two around who want change for change's sake.

And at a southeastern university, a young professor thought that the faculty favored stability because, he claimed, "They've come here to die."

In contrast, among the dynamic departments occurred these comments:

Too many things continue just because they exist—not for real reasons. The institution has been too jealous of its past. It's tried to perpetuate its past too much.

The department chairman in special education at a state university reported, "I was hired to make changes." And the chairman of psychology at a Protestant college in the south stated:

Five years ago the department had just begun. Psychology wasn't an independent major. The academic dean presented the challenge to me: "Make the department known in the southeast. Come up with something inventive."

These are, however, only examples; and theories are not proven by case examples. The evidence to support our hypothesis about course reform is not clear-cut. Some obviously dynamic departments possess the stabilizing characteristics that we would think lead to rigidity, while some static departments are far from stable in their personnel and structure. But beyond these impressionistic conclusions, some additional evidence from the institutions at large exists which tends to support the idea that course reform is a function of institutional instability. From the changes in courses at the several departments that we studied in each institution, we calculated an average rate of course reform for the institution at large. Examining the differences among types of institutions, we found that the independent colleges as a group tend to score slightly higher on this measure of course reform than the other types, as was noted in Chapter Three. Then correlating this measure with the ninety separate variables that are listed in Appendix D, we found that nine variables from that list correlate significantly with course reform:[5]

Variable	Correlation
Much change in the number of courses offered at the institution	*.402*
More concern for recruiting the best students than the best faculty	*.310*
The most influential members of the institution are perceived as being a force for change in the academic program	.239
Department chairmen do not tend to serve until they retire	.235
Population of city in which the institution is located is large	.216
Taking of attendance by professors is not expected	.214
Student fees constitute a large proportion of current income	.211
Administrators are perceived to be influential in determining educational policy	.201
High per cent of change in department chairmen between 1962 and 1967	.200

These variables are in the anticipated direction, with indicators of

[5] The italicized figures for the first two variables indicate that the probability of a correlation this high or higher occurring by chance is less than 1.0 per cent. The probability of the remaining correlations occurring by chance is less than 5 per cent.

organizational instability positively associated with course change. First the institutions that demonstrate the most course reform tend to be changing the number of courses they offer the most. Second, the people that we interviewed at these institutions tend to sense a greater problem in recent years in attracting the best students to the institution than in attracting the best faculty. Third, they perceive of the most influential members of the institution as being interested in curricular change. Fourth, they tend to see administrators as influential in curricular decisions. Fifth, department chairmen at these institutions more often do not remain in office until they retire as professors. Sixth, the institutions tend to be located in urban areas, where social change and intellectual communication are rapid. Seventh, the restrictions on a professor's behavior (such as having to take attendance of students in class) tend to be fewer. Eighth, a high proportion of institutional income stems from student fees. And ninth, a high proportion of turnover has occurred among department chairmen in the past five years.

In short, although the trend is not strong, course reform tends to occur significantly more frequently at institutions marked by such characteristics of vulnerability for change as alterations in the size of the curriculum, a concern and need to recruit students, an urban rather than a pastoral environment, turnover of personnel in positions of power, and freedom from such restrictions as attendance taking. The most dynamic departments tend to be characterized particularly by turnover in their chairmen, and some scattered impressionistic evidence points to the possibility of a tendency toward widespread *participation*—participation of students, of constituents, of faculty and administration—while the more static departments tend toward *powerlessness*—toward being controlled and toward controlling their students.[6]

Changes in Majors. Chapter Three described the alterations that have been occurring in the programs that colleges and

---

[6] Were we to redo the study, we would include some direct measure on a departmental basis of student pressure for curricular change. We suspect from other findings that this might relate more closely to the amount of course change than most of these present measures do.

118

universities are offering as majors—the decline of the arcadian subjects, the continued splintering of the academic disciplines, the slow emergence of a few area-centered, problem-centered, period-centered, or issue-centered majors, and the occasional toleration of individualized student-planned programs. Chapter Four noted that the faculty members and administrators whom we interviewed reported that these changes were coming about primarily because of the faculty's interest in providing more educational opportunities for students. A number of replacements occurred, of course, because of declining student interest in the older programs. According to the interviews, "No business" was the reason for the demise of Greek at one state university. At another university, commercial education was dropped because of "no students." At a third, scientific German and Russian foundered on "a lack of students." And at a Catholic women's college, a professor reported, "Not enough students were majoring in sociology or anthropology, so the North Central Association advised us to drop them."

As could be expected, the greatest *expansion* in undergraduate programs is tending to occur at institutions with burgeoning enrollments, and in particular at the state colleges. And interestingly enough, the rate of dropping programs, such as Greek, physical education, or secretarial science, and replacing them with new ones, be they Russian, American studies, or wildlife management, is highest also in the expanding institutions. This latter measure—the rate of replacement of one major by another—is characteristic not only of expanding institutions but also of colleges rather than universities, of unrenowned institutions in comparison to well-known ones, and of institutions where the departments and the senior faculty had relatively less than usual influence over educational policy.[7]

In short, the institutions that were most frequently dropping old majors and adding new ones are those that are characterized particularly by instability in regard to students. They are more often

[7] As with the correlates of course reform, the italicized figures indicate that the probability of a correlation this high or higher occurring by chance is less than 1.0 per cent while that of the remaining correlations is less than 5 per cent.

119

Variable	Correlation
High per cent of change in total enrollment between 1961 and 1966	*.310*
Institution not selected frequently by high school students who scored high on the National Merit Scholarship examinations	*.301*
Undergraduate institution rather than university-level institution	*.290*
High per cent of expansion in total enrollment between 1961 and 1966	.264
Influence of the senior faculty on educational policy perceived as low	.205
Influence of the departments on educational policy perceived as low	.204
The institution is perceived as oriented toward change rather than toward the avoidance of change	.202
Change in the number of courses offered by the institution	.200
Relatively low academic status of institution using conventional measures	.194

than not undergraduate institutions that are expanding rapidly, and they are not particularly renowned in terms of attracting the most academically able undergraduates. Moreover, they tend not to be dominated in terms of influence by their departments and the tenured faculty, with the lack of influence of senior faculty being a function of institutional expansion—whereby the young Turks outnumber the oldsters.

Changes in Requirements and Regulations. The remaining three measures of academic change involve revisions in the published requirements for earning a degree, majoring in a particular subject, and student conduct in the classroom and on campus. Chapter Four noted that the men and women whom we interviewed tend to see these changes as stemming primarily from dissatisfaction with the requirements on the part of administrators and some students and faculty members. Here, for example, is an illustration of a change in the degree requirements of a small Catholic men's college and the view of the new chairman of the philosophy department about how the change came about:

> Formerly we required students to take four courses in philosophy and theology. Now we have reduced the requirement by one-half and we have changed from a neo-Thomistic approach to a more pluralistic one and permit students to choose among the courses. The reasons were, first, the changes in the membership of the philosophy department and then in the interests and capabilities of the students. Trailing these by quite a bit was the change in Roman Catholic attitudes generally, and fourth was pressure from other departments. We consulted with the chairman of philosophy in other Jesuit institutions, with the chairman of philosophy in other Catholic colleges, and third, with chairmen in non-church-related colleges.

This illustration is particularly appropriate here, for it turns out that the most changes in requirements have been occurring at the undergraduate religious colleges. But a variety of characteristics other than simply institutional type are even more closely related to these changes, and from the ninety listed in Appendix D, here are the ones that are significantly correlated with them:[8]

Variable	*Correlation*
Change in Degree Requirements	
Much change in the number of courses offered by the institution	*.331*
Much change in the composition of the governing board .	*.305*
More concern for recruiting the best students than the best faculty	*.261*
Much expansion of the number of major programs offered by the college	.229
Student fees constitute a large proportion of current income	.228
The most influential members of the institution are perceived as being a force for change in the academic program	.222

[8] Again, the italicized figures indicate a correlation coefficient significant at the 1.0 per cent level.

121

Variable	Correlation

A low proportion of faculty hold tenure .... .216

Much change in the number of major programs offered by the college .... .212

Institution not selected frequently by high school students who scored high on the National Merit Scholarship examinations .... .206

High per cent of change in department chairmen between 1962 and 1967 .... .205

Change in Majoring Requirements

The most influential members of the institution are perceived as being a force for change in the academic program .... *.367*

Much change in the composition of the governing board . *.332*

Much change in the number of courses offered by the institution .... *.305*

The trustees are perceived as being a force for change in the curriculum .... .277

A small proportion of institutional income comes from federal funds .... .242

Much change in the number of major programs offered by the college .... .220

Institution not selected frequently by high school students who scored high on the National Merit Scholarship examinations .... .202

Change in Student Regulations

Much change in score on academic progressiveness between 1961 and 1967 .... *.298*

Much expansion in the number of major programs offered by the college .... *.275*

Much change in the number of major programs offered by the college .... *.274*

The trustees are perceived as being a force for change in the curriculum .... .241

A low proportion of faculty hold tenure .... .237

The faculty tends to have come from undergraduate colleges of a different type than that of the institution itself .... .234

Total enrollment in 1961 was small .... .232

Total undergraduate and first professional enrollment in 1961 was small .... .210

122

Correlates of Dynamism

Some of these features—the expansion of the institution, its lack of renown, and a concern for change on the part of influential members of the institution—also correlate with measures of course reform and change in programs. In addition, however, several other characteristics are significant only here: among them, a good deal of turnover in the membership of the governing board and the perception that the governing board is oriented toward change rather than toward the status quo. Moreover, the institutions which have altered their regulations of student conduct the most tend to be among the smallest in our sample.

Looking at these correlates of published changes in requirements and at the fact that the changes have been occurring more commonly in the undergraduate colleges than in the universities, we are led to suspect that two trends may possibly be at work here. On the one hand, the small colleges—and particularly the religious colleges—for one reason or another may be trying to catch up with the practices regarding degrees, majors, and classroom conduct already adopted at other institutions. And on the other hand, the large institutions—and particularly the universities—may be suffering from some of the problems of size and bureaucracy that prohibit them from reacting to the possibility of change as readily as the small institutions.

The correlates of each of the five separate measures of academic change tend to lend support to the belief that academic reform is associated with factors of instability and flexibility. Thus they include such characteristics as change in the size of the institution and an interest in academic change rather than stability on the part of the most influential members of the institution. But of all these characteristics, which ones are most typical of the most dynamic institutions academically and least typical of the most static institutions? Which ones differentiate the radically changing colleges from the most unchanging ones?

To find out, we identified the institutions that had changed the most and the least on several measures of academic change, not merely on one of them; and then we compared the most dynamic institutions of all—nineteen of them—with the nineteen most static ones.[9] Comparing these two extreme groups on all of the factors that we believed might contribute to the differences between them, we discovered to begin with that on several characteristics their average scores are virtually identical. The most static institutions by and large are no more inbred in their faculties than are the dynamic ones. Their minimum salaries are almost identical. The proportion of their operating income from their major source of support is approximately the same. There is no greater communication between trustees and faculty at one than at another. And their trustees are perceived as equally uninfluential in educational policies. In other words, nothing in our data suggests that the major sources of difference between the academically most dynamic and the most static institutions lie in the background of their faculties, in the proportion of support that they receive from their major source of financing, or in pressure from their trustees. While these factors undoubtedly play some role at some institutions, they do not differentiate at all the static group from the dynamic one.

[9] To do so, we first identified the institutions that fell beyond one standard deviation of the mean score, or as close to the standard deviation as possible, on each of the five measures of change. Since we were interested in the institutions that had changed greatly on at least two of these measures and in those that had changed the least on several of them, we selected the nineteen institutions that scored among the highest on at least two measures and were not among the lowest on more than one measure (two of the nineteen had one low score each); and we contrasted them with the nineteen institutions that scored among the lowest on more than one measure and among none of the highest. We validated the resulting two groups of institutions on a measure of academic innovation completely independent from our measures of reform and found that the two groups are significantly different on it as well. The innovation measure came from a study by Professor Michael Brick at Teachers College, who recently completed a survey of innovations in undergraduate colleges throughout the nation that covered developments since 1961 in such areas as independent study for all students, freshman seminars, non-western studies, learning-living programs, and off-campus study. (See *Innovations in Liberal Arts Colleges.* New York: Teachers College Press, 1969.) Studying the information on eight of these innovations that he received from the institutions in our study, we found that, on the average, all of the institutions had each adopted one such innovation since 1961. The nineteen most dynamic institutions, however, had adopted on the average 1.5 of these innovations; while the most static ones had adopted only 0.3, or less than a half of one apiece.

Correlates of Dynamism

Next, on a number of factors that we thought might be important, the two groups do show some differences—but not enough that the differences are likely to be caused by anything other than chance. For example, the most dynamic institutions tend to exhibit higher rates of turnover in their faculty and administrative staffs— among presidents, department chairmen, and faculty members in selected departments—but the differences are too small to be statistically significant. Some of the most dynamic institutions have experienced little change in their administration or faculty, while some of the most static institutions have such high rates of turnover that they border on outright transiency.

Thus our suspicion that the turnover of personnel would account for the differences in the amount of academic reform at our institutions is not confirmed. Similarly the number of hurdles or decision points that are involved at the institution in the addition of a course to the curriculum does not appear to have a significant impact: the most static institutions have a slightly higher average number of hurdles than the most dynamic group—but again, this difference is most likely attributable to chance.

With this as background, what does distinguish the most dynamic from the most static group? First of all, while all types and levels of institution are represented in both the most dynamic and static groups, the colleges, and particularly the religious colleges, are well-represented in the dynamic group—while the universities are under-represented. Table 10 indicates that only two of the nineteen most dynamic institutions, or less than 11 per cent of them, are universities. Yet the universities comprise 37 per cent of the total sample and 47 per cent of the most static institutions. Moreover, the religious colleges seem unusually dynamic: ten of the nineteen, or 53 per cent of them, are religious colleges—five of them Catholic and five Protestant—compared to 27 per cent of all the institutions and only 16 per cent of the most static group. In contrast to the most dynamic institutions, among the nineteen most static institutions the independent universities are more over-represented than any other type: they account for 21 per cent of the static group, compared to only 13 per cent in the sample at large.

125

Table 10

DISTRIBUTION OF INSTITUTIONS ON ACADEMIC REFORM

	Groups of Institutions (Per Cent)			
Type of Institution	Highest Scoring Institutions (19)	Medium Institutions (72)	Lowest Scoring Institutions (19)	All Institutions (110)
All Four- and Five-Year Colleges	89.5	58.3	52.6	62.7
Public Colleges	26.3	19.4	26.3	21.8
Independent Colleges	10.5	15.3	10.5	13.6
Religious Colleges	52.6	23.6	15.8	27.3
All Doctoral-level Institutions	10.5	41.7	47.4	37.3
Public Universities	5.2	16.7	15.8	14.5
Independent Universities	5.2	12.5	21.0	12.7
Religious Universities	0.0	12.5	10.5	10.0
All 110 Institutions	100.0	100.0	100.0	100.0

Consequently we suspect that the concern expressed by some educators over the dominance of the undergraduate colleges by the graduate schools may at least in part be justified, for the universities appear to exhibit less flexibility in their undergraduate programs than do the separate undergraduate colleges. Certainly a university provides a stable home for undergraduate studies, but it imposes more restrictions on them than the separate college does. Part of these restrictions undoubtedly stem from the university's graduate orientation, but part may be caused by other factors, such as success, that—as the next paragraphs show—are also more common among the most static institutions.

Second, as Table 11 indicates, the most dynamic institutions

126

are significantly more dependent financially on attracting students than the most static group. They are not as prominent nationally nor as attractive to able prospective students, as the preferences of National Merit Scholarship finalists show. More of them obtain their major funds from student fees (48 per cent of their total current income came from students in 1962–63 in comparison to 28 per cent for the static group). They are not as wealthy in terms of total educational and general income per student. And they are more frequently oriented to seeking the best students rather than the best faculty. In sum, they are less renowned, more vulnerable, and of necessity more adaptive. And these characteristics have tended to distinguish undergraduate colleges more frequently in recent years than they have the universities.

Third, although the most dynamic institutions do not have a significantly higher turnover rate among their faculty members than the most static ones, the faculties of the most dynamic institutions are changing by a combination of expansion and turnover at a significantly faster rate than at the other institutions. And their personnel have different characteristics: On the average, less than a third of their faculty members have tenure (with some of the most dynamic institutions having no tenure at all), while half of the faculty at the more static group have tenure. The junior members of the faculty at dynamic institutions are seen as exerting far more influence on educational policy. Department chairmen far more commonly relinquish the chairmanship before they retire as professors. Their most influential members are thought of as being a force for change in the educational program rather than for stability. And even their trustees are seen as more interested in change than are those of the static group.

And fourth, they are more frequently located in metropolitan centers and are changing their number of course offerings significantly more than the most static institutions. And thus they are more vulnerable to the instability of a rapidly changing environment and the effects of a change in institutional scale than are the rural and more stable institutions.

In short, no one single characteristic alone clearly distin-

127

Table 11

CHARACTERISTICS OF INSTITUTIONS DIFFERING IN AMOUNT OF ACADEMIC REFORM

Characteristic	Groups of Institutions			
	Highest Scoring Institutions (19)	Medium Institutions (71)[a]	Lowest Scoring Institutions (19)	All Institutions (110)
Criterion Variables (used to distinguish the three groups):				
Change in Requirements for Majoring[b]	2.6	2.1	1.4	2.1
Per Cent of Course Reform[b]	39.5	22.4	10.0	23.2
Change in Degree Requirements[b]	2.6	2.0	1.2	2.0
Per Cent of Replacement of Major Programs	15.2	6.6	0.3	7.3
Change in Student Regulations[b]	2.5	1.6	1.4	1.7
Predictor Variables:				
Level of Program	Between bachelor's and master's degree	Master's degree	Between master's and doctorate	Master's degree
Frequency of Selection by Able Students (a score based on the proportion of National Merit Scholarship finalists seeking admission to the number of freshmen admitted. The national average score is 50 with more frequently-selected institutions scoring higher).	36.1	45.8	53.8	45.7

128

Predictor Variables (continued):

	Highest Scoring Institutions (19)	Medium Institutions (71)[a]	Lowest Scoring Institutions (19)	All Institutions (110)
Department Chairmen Serve Until They Retire as Professors	No	Some do	Usually do	No
Total Educational and General Income per Student, 1962 (Decile rank nationally)	4.3	6.2	6.6	5.9
Student Fees as a Per Cent of Income	47.7	32.6	28.5	35.4
Perceived Problem in Recruiting the Best Faculty versus the Best Students (Five-point scale, with 1 indicating a concern for recruiting faculty and 5 for students)	3.0 (Students)	2.1 (About equal)	1.8 (Faculty)	2.4 (About equal)
Change in Score on Academic Progressiveness Between 1962 and 1967	3.0	2.3	1.3	2.1
Perceived Orientation of the Most Influential Members of the Institution (Five-point scale, with 1 indicating an orientation toward the status quo and 5 toward change in the academic program)	3.8	3.5	2.7	3.4
Per Cent of Change in the Number of Courses Offered by the Institution Between 1962 and 1967	65.0	45.9	43.2	45.5
Perceived Influence of Junior Faculty (Seven-point scale: *none to much*)	4.8	4.7	4.1	4.6
Per Cent of Faculty Expansion and Turnover Between 1962 and 1967	134.2	116.9	102.8	117.5
Population of City or Town in Which College is Located, 1960	404,600	187,200	107,200	215,400
Proportion (Per Cent) of Faculty Holding Tenure	32.8	40.2	50.0	40.5
Perceived Orientation of Trustees (Six-point scale, with 1 indicating a force for stability and 6 a force for change in the curriculum)	2.8	2.1	1.5	2.2

Note: These are the characteristics, including all five measures of academic reform and the predictor variables listed in Appendix D, which most distinguish the highest-scoring institutions from the lowest-scoring institutions in terms of academic reform. The variables are listed in descending order of differentiation, as measured by a T-test of the means of the highest and lowest-scoring groups.

[a] One institution is not included in the medium group because of insufficient data.
[b] Based on a five-point scale, with 1 indicating no change and 5 indicating much.

guishes the institutions undergoing the most reform from those that are changing the least. Instead, a whole series of interrelated factors appear to be in part influential, operating systematically both to permit and to force reform. Some of these influences are environmental, such as an institution's location in an urban region or an undergraduate program's location in an institution dominated by graduate education. Some are structural, such as an institution's expansion and its proportion of tenured faculty. Still others are cultural or interpersonal, involving the very ethos and life style of the institution, such as an orientation of members in favor of change, a need to attract students and support, and influence among the junior faculty members.

All of these factors point toward conditions of organizational change and all of them influence and reinforce one another. The expansion of an institution can permit reform through diversity and new blood. Similarly, the institution that is on the borderline of renown or status may be more adaptive in attempting to improve its condition than is the prestigious college. But none of these factors can be termed the *cause* of academic reform in terms of its being unilaterally and invariably effective. Each of them instead appears to be to some extent a *source* of reform: a factor that along with others has some influence on the process of curricular change.

The effects of some of these factors can be seen more clearly by looking at the handful of institutions from all 110 in the sample that we found to be inexplicably dynamic or static. Four of the most dynamic institutions academically were relatively renowned; they had not by and large expanded greatly; and they did not show much change in their faculty and administrative staffs. Because of the relationship of these characteristics to academic change, as we have just reported, we would have expected these four institutions to show little change in their curricula—but they had changed a great deal. In contrast, four of the most static institutions were less renowned and had expanded considerably and replaced a larger than usual number of their staff. We would have thought that these institutions would demonstrate more reform in their programs than their opposites—but they do not. Why? To try to isolate the answer, we reviewed all the information we have on them, just as we did earlier with the departments that differed the most in reorganizing their courses. And as with the departments, the following five differences should be recognized as *impressions* from this evidence.

The first difference lies in environmental influences: the few inexplicably dynamic colleges appear to be more frequently swept along by social trends. For example, two of them are Catholic women's colleges, both of which have been feeling the effects of Vatican II and rethinking their entire role as educational institutions. Said the president of one of them:

> We kept raising the basic question for the college: "Does it have any reason for existence?" And we concluded that its reason for existence had to be that of a highly experimental institution—free to move and move quickly, whereas bureaucratic institutions—the universities—are powerful but slow.

The few inexplicably static institutions, on the other hand, seem caught in a constraining environment: One of them thus functions as a unit of a state-college system that until recently has been operated by the state department of education. And their members whom we interviewed more often see the major sources of influence on them—such as the church or the graduate schools—as a force for stability rather than for change.

Second, the role of students differs. At the four dynamic institutions, students are seen as having some influence on the curriculum—going so far as participating in equal numbers with the faculty on the College Council. At the four static institutions, however, students are seen as having little influence and little legitimate role in curricular decisions. "The students shouldn't have too much of a role because of our nature as a church-related institution," stated one professor. Moreover, at three of the four dynamic institutions, our respondents favored an elective curriculum for students; but at all four of the static colleges, they favored a prescribed curriculum. Said a department chairman at one of the latter colleges: "Most students we get are of average ability and they really need standardized programs and a great deal of direction. Innovation is not very useful in working with them." Interestingly enough, rebellion had already broken out at one of these static institutions: a three-day sit-in by students over a series of fifty demands has since led to the reform of many regulations.

Third, their faculties differ. Between 50 and 70 per cent of the faculty of the static institutions are on tenure, while no more than 50 per cent are tenured at the dynamic institutions, one of which does not grant tenure at all. The dynamic institutions place fewer restrictions on professors than do the static ones: they do not expect professors to take attendance in class, necessarily give examinations, or report their absence to their superior.

Fourth, the role of department heads differs. Department heads at the static institutions all serve unlimited terms—typically until they retire, and they tend numerically to dominate the curriculum committee of the institution. At the dynamic ones, in contrast, department chairmen tend to serve term appointments and hence leave the chairman's office before they retire, and while at one of them the curriculum committee consists entirely of chairmen, in the others chairmen comprise no more than half of the committee's membership.

And fifth, the direction of influence differs. At the static institutions, we sensed general satisfaction with the institution as it is, except for some vocal malcontents. The most influential members of the institution are seen as being interested primarily in stability rather than change. "Everything evolves from the president," stated a professor at one of them. "We have a dictatorship. We're supposed to have parliamentary procedures, but we don't have a parliament. . . ." At the dynamic institutions, in contrast, the presidents appear to play a less conservative role: several of them seem to have an ideal of higher education which is not yet fulfilled, as well as the ability to generate interest in the venture of fulfilling it. The president of one of them reported his own philosophy in these words:

> I carry a long needle, and that's my job—to needle people. The board was concerned about the direction of the college when I came fifteen years ago, and I came to either do some-

thing with it or close it up. We were a typical church-related college. I cooked up the idea of making a laboratory out of the institution. I have the opinion that most of our educational practices are outmoded and require modernization. I don't know what they should be, but we're searching for them.

In sum, the few otherwise inexplicably static institutions by and large are less open than their opposites to influence for change from either their students or their environment. They tend to be more oriented toward the status quo, more hierarchical and, in particular, more patriarchal. By patriarchy—the supremacy of a father within a family—we mean a system distinguished by two major characteristics: by the centralization of initiative, where power is concentrated in one person or one group of members; and by seniority, where promotion occurs primarily on the basis of age or length of service. The four inexplicably static institutions, which otherwise might have been expected to have undergone considerable reform, appear to illustrate these patriarchal characteristics by the low level of influence of their students, the unlimited tenure of their department chairmen, and the dominance of their curriculum committees by chairmen. Indeed, the nineteen most static institutions differ from the nineteen most dynamic on several variables related to patriarchy, including a low level of influence of their junior faculty; and among all the institutions in the sample, these variables also correlated negatively with measures of academic change.

Of the several structural or sociological characteristics of the colleges and universities that we studied, this feature of patriarchy seems to us to be unexpectedly inimical to academic reform as we measured it. The centralization of power in the most senior members apparently tends to influence the amount of change for the worse. It restricts the possibility of change by restricting the power of younger members. By itself, however, it may not always have this effect; and hence even more directly important for the amount of change appear to be two other factors: the *attitude* toward educational change of the people in positions of power at the institution, regardless of who they are, and the *pressure* toward change that is exerted on the institution from its major source of support and constituency or public. Recall that the most dynamic institutions tend to be particularly dependent on attracting students to finance their operations. They are most vulnerable to the interests of their clientele and most concerned about seeking the best prospective students. They are more frequently located in urban environments. And the most influential members of these institutions, as well as their trustees, tend to be perceived as encouraging change in their educational programs. Thus perceptions, attitudes, structure, administrative style, external pressure, and market conditions —all contribute to the process of academic reform or to the status quo. From the evidence of this study, they are far more closely related to reform than usual measures of academic status, such as the renown of the institution, the proportion of doctorates among the faculty, the extent of inbreeding within the faculty, or the level of the institution's degree program.

These characteristics that influence reform, moreover, tend to form a mutually-reinforcing constellation. A factor analysis of all of the variables that we examined in the study isolated several groups of characteristics that are related to one another. One group of them basically involves expansion—the expansion of enrollments, programs, and courses. But another factor appears to concern the flexibility of the institution apart from simple expansion, and these are the characteristics that contribute the most to this factor of institutional flexibility:

Variable	*Factor Loading*
Students perceived as influential in curricular decisions ..	.514
Small undergraduate and first professional enrollment, 1961	.455
High per cent of course reform	.452
The most influential outsiders are perceived as a force for change in the academic program	.438
Much change in degree requirements	.435
Small total enrollment, 1961	.431
High level of scholarship funds per total educational and general income	.419

Little expansion of the faculty between 1962 and 1967 .. .414

Undergraduate program rather than doctoral-level program .... .405

Chairmen are usually appointed from within the present faculty .... .395

Students perceived as influential in determining educational policy .... .372

Much change in the requirements for majoring in selected departments .... .370

Junior faculty perceived as influential in determining educational policy .... .370

Much change in the number as well as content of courses offered in selected departments .... .368

These characteristics—small size, the participation of students and junior faculty, an undergraduate emphasis, and an influence for change—depict institutions that are not typically bureaucratic, patriarchal, or immune from pressure: they are more typically "open" institutions.

The next and concluding chapter reiterates the limitations of the data in this study and discusses their significance. But to summarize briefly here the findings regarding the question of whether academic reform is related to measures of organizational instability or stability, we found less relationship than we had expected between our measures of academic change and our measures of institutional instability, and thus we can not claim to have found the causes of change. Every one of the significant relationships that we did find, however, is in the direction of a positive relation between change and instability. Thus academic change as we measured it is not found primarily at high prestige institutions, at universities, or on large campuses. Instead it tends to be associated with conditions of environmental, structural, and individual adaptivity—including, among others, expansion, urbanity, a need to recruit students, limited tenure in department chairmanships, and a positive orientation toward change—which interact together in influencing the rate of reform.

CHAPTER

Sources of Reform

*A*ll experience proves
that Universities, like
other corporations, can
only be reformed from
without.[1]

William Hamilton

[1] "On the State of the English Universities. With More Especial
Reference to Oxford," *Edinburgh Review, 53,* 106, June 1831, 427. Reproduced in *Discussions on Philosophy and Literature, Education and University Reform.* New York: Harper, 1853, p. 429.

$\mathscr{A}$t 10 o'clock on the morning of October 24, 1928, Edward S. Harkness, an alumnus of Yale and heir to the Standard Oil fortune of his father, arrived in the office of President A. Lawrence Lowell of Harvard and offered Lowell several million dollars to build a new housing system for Harvard's students. He had arranged the appointment with Lowell after waiting two years for his alma mater to accept the same offer, and after becoming discouraged by the inability of Yale to reach agreement on a plan. Lowell immediately accepted Harkness' generosity, and as a result, Harvard launched the first major attempt in American higher education to try to reintegrate student life with student learning.

The contrast between Harvard and Yale in this one situation is probably the most famous difference between two American universities in their response to an educational opportunity. The outcome had major consequences for relating the college curriculum to the extracurriculum, and it illustrates several important issues of college and university reform.

By the summer of 1928, Yale was still vacillating on the idea of building new facilities to house its undergraduate students. In 1926 Harkness had informed Yale's president, James Rowland Angell, that he would finance such a project; and in 1927 Angell had appointed a faculty planning committee for it. But the committee could not agree on a plan. One member favored an honors college; another wanted a unit for humanities and social science students; and others pushed for accommodations for freshmen. By the spring of 1928 the committee could only recommend further study of the idea of dividing Yale College into a series of small residential units; by the summer, Angell was unable to obtain a decision within the faculty or Yale's corporation for immediate subdivision; and Harkness' deadline of July 1 arrived and passed not only without any action but without even a note of regret from Angell.

In contrast, when Harkness then foresook Yale and journeyed to Harvard to meet President Lowell that fall, Lowell was ready for him. He had been concerned about the problem of undergraduate living even before assuming Harvard's presidency in 1909; he had heard of Yale's problems over its plans, and he was prepared to seek Harkness' aid not merely for one or two new dormitories, but, if Harkness was willing, for residential units to house all of Harvard's undergraduates. When Harkness proved interested, Lowell moved quickly. In November he got Harvard's Faculty of Arts and Sciences to accept the idea; in December the Harvard Corporation and Overseers approved it; by January 5, 1929, he could show Harkness preliminary architectural plans; by June construction began; and by the time the seven Harvard houses were completed, Harkness had contributed $13,365,000 to them. Meanwhile Yale, mortified at Harvard's acceptance, had overcome its problems. Its corporation had taken leadership away from Angell and the faculty committee and had reached agreement on a similar residential system. Finally, in January, 1930, Harkness relented and agreed to finance it, too.[2]

Why, in this significant case of educational innovation, was Harvard able to act while Yale seemed powerless to move? Lowell himself attributed the difference to Harvard's traditions—the most persistent of which, he claimed, was the tradition of change. From his perspective, Yale made fewer experiments—and fewer mistakes. But some analysts have attributed the difference to A. Lawrence Lowell himself: his dominating personality, his persevering strategy, his adroit manipulation of the situation. And others have pointed to the power that the Harvard presidency had accumulated under both Eliot and Lowell, in contrast to the lack of power of Angell's office at Yale, which had remained weak throughout President Porter's tottering reign, through Hadley's indecisive tenure, and into Angell's day. Angell, for example, unlike Lowell, could not nominate candidates for faculty appointment; he could not preside at faculty meetings nor designate a representative in his absence; he could not initiate legislation; he could not even choose the deans for Yale's colleges and schools—all of these being faculty prerogatives at Yale.

[2] Facts about this entire development can be found primarily in George Wilson Pierson's *Yale: The University College, 1921–1937* (New Haven: Yale University Press, 1955) and in Henry Aaron Yeomans, *Abbott Lawrence Lowell, 1856–1943* (Cambridge: Harvard University Press, 1948) and in the files of the Harvard and Yale University Archives.

These explanations are undoubtedly correct as far as they go, since leadership and the possibility of leadership were obviously involved, but from our perspective they appear insufficient. The differences between Harvard and Yale were more numerous and complex. For example, poor housing for students and the associated problems of poor food, inadequate recreation, and social isolation were perceived to be more serious in Cambridge than in New Haven. Second, Yale was rent by greater friction and controversy than Harvard: its faculty was still divided over the lingering problems between Sheffield Scientific School and Yale College, and the faculty bridled at the interference of the corporation and the alumni in setting educational policy while the corporation was annoyed at the intransigence of the faculty. Yale's faculty in the eyes of its historian, George W. Pierson, was a "states-rights republic, permeated by traditions of self-government," while Harvard's faculty to Samuel Eliot Morison seemed "a mere registering body."[3] Yale's organization thus permitted action primarily through negotiation and reaction among its units, while Harvard's allowed for action through the presidency. Moreover, Yale's orientation in general was educationally conservative. For the previous century, since its faculty's 1828 report, Yale had represented the fountainhead of tradition for American colleges. Thus change, to be easily accepted, needed to be seen as a return to values that had once been safe but now were threatened. In New Haven, therefore, the rhetoric about student housing tended to focus on making the old collegiate values more secure, while in Cambridge it centered on making the nation's oldest college constantly the youngest.

Thus we are doubtful about labeling only one element within the two institutions as the cause of their contrasting reactions to Harkness' offer. The whole web of institutional conditions —traditions, norms, beliefs, structure, roles, power—contributed to the difference in their receptivity to the opportunity. Their separate histories had produced in each a distinctive ethos that affected their receptivity to change, arrangements that influenced the considera-

[3] Both statements appear in Pierson's *Yale: The University College, 1921–1937,* p. 596.

tion of change, individuals and offices that decided the direction of change, procedures that determined its speed, and perceptions that shaped its extent.

These differences between Harvard and Yale in this situation point to the first conclusion that we would draw from the data in this book: different reactions to educational opportunity cannot be attributed to one difference alone among institutions, but rather result from a variety of differences in organization and operation. In one institution at one time any particular situation may serve to precipitate dramatic change—the death of a potential benefactor, the unauthorized occupation of campus buildings, the election of a new president. Yet nothing we have found in our study denies the evidence of multiple causation. Academic change, like other social phenomena, has innumerable roots, none of which by itself is alone important. This may be discouraging to anyone seeking the easiest means of effecting reform, but it deserves emphasis. We have unearthed no academic philosopher's stone: no one device, no one mechanism, no one technique that seems alone adequate to bring about academic change. Instead, a whole network of factors is involved in the process, each influencing the other; and it seems that a constellation of several factors tends to be present in different kinds of change. Colleges and universities, like other organizations, are systemic by nature. To alter their operations significantly requires effort on several fronts at several levels and by several means.

This evidence should not lead to the conclusion that certain factors are no more important in stimulating academic reform than others, for it seems clear that some are particularly significant. One basic factor is simply the possibility of benefit or reward. Program change within any organization or institution is unlikely unless the change appears to lead to greater reward than does the present program. There is little reason for a university to build a new comprehensive housing system for its students, as did Harvard and then Yale, or to revitalize its program of general education or introduce new subjects into the curriculum or admit new groups of students unless the change looks as if it will be an improvement—unless the institution or the students or at least some group will benefit from

140

it. Without potential reward, in brief, change is unlikely. The evidence from the statistical analysis of recent curricular changes supports this general conclusion, since the highest levels of academic change between 1962 and 1967 turned out to be occurring most frequently (1) at institutions which, among other factors, were the most dependent on student enrollment for financial support and thus where a curriculum that was interesting and attractive to students was more necessary than at institutions with other bases of support, (2) at institutions that were located in urban areas—where social change has necessitated institutional change, and (3) at undergraduate institutions that were independent of universities— where the reward for undergraduate curricular reform has been greater than in the undergraduate divisions of the universities, dominated as they are by the graduate departments.

A second factor is individual influence. It seems clear that to bring about change in colleges and universities, as in other organizations, advocacy is imperative to overcome innate institutional inertia. Call it inspiration, leadership, persuasion, or politicking; without it change is unlikely. The advocate not only welds a unity of interest out of the diverse interests of members; he can point to the possible rewards of change—convincing members and patrons of unmet challenges, new opportunities, and desirable responsibilities, be they student housing or free electives or spectroastronomy. All the evidence from history as well as from the observations of men and women engaged in academic life about the importance of individual initiative in stimulating change is borne out by the statistical evidence of this study: academic change tends to be highest at colleges and universities where the most influential members of the institution are seen as forces for change rather than for stability.

Third, the structure of the institution has an effect on the process of change through its openness to influence. Thus the very fact of expansion—be it an increase in enrollments, in faculty, or in programs—tends to lead not simply to new courses and majors but to the reform of old ones. Moreover, the amount of influence of students and junior faculty in comparison to senior faculty is also related to these changes. And the reform of courses tends to be related to turnover in the department chairmanship and to the professor's freedom from detailed specifications regarding his role as teacher. These features lead to influence from a variety of sources —from turnover, from the junior members, from newcomers to the institution—and while they thus appear to contribute to institutional instability, they permit institutional adapability.

Perhaps the most important conclusion of all, however, about the factors that are influential in academic reform concerns their origin. Are the sources of educational change primariily internal, from within colleges and universities themselves—such as the spontaneous innovations of creative professors and imaginative administrators? Or are they by and large external to the institutions —imposed, of necessity, on reluctant academics by outside forces and groups? This question not only stirs antagonistic arguments but raises major issues of university governance: issues of academic freedom, faculty prerogatives, professional autonomy, policy determination, and institutional accountability. It involves the problem of the best social policy regarding higher education and its control.

As the data from the interviews in Chapter Four revealed, people's attitudes on this question are influenced by their own position. Professors, daily involved in their own efforts at improvement, naturally tend to see themselves and their colleagues on the faculty as the initiators of change, just as administrators, actively working on some of the same problems, more often see themselves as the key source of impetus. If state legislators or the members of governing boards or student leaders were asked about the sources of change, their reactions would probably display the same tendency. Thus to consider this issue as objectively as possible, it is necessary to examine it beyond one's own parochial perspective. We have tried to do so, and we have reached the conclusion that the sources of academic reform—as well as the constraints on reform—are primarily external to the academic system. Here are the reasons for this conclusion: To be implemented, every academic improvement requires the initiative of an individual person, be he student, professor, or layman. But initiative is seldom completely spontaneous. It results as a reaction to changing conditions—changing knowledge, values, and events—and the most powerful and influential conditions tend to be those outside of academic life and academic institutions. They determine the boundaries of change and the options open to initiative.

In the most general theoretical terms, any open system, by virtue of its being open, is susceptible to massive alteration from its environment. For example, the dominant influences on the existence of any biological organism are environmental: if a load of bricks drops on someone, he's in trouble. Similarly, the major sources of change in the economic system lie outside the economic system itself in society at large. The major constraints on personality development appear to be cultural and social. And the most powerful influences on the educational system are those from outsiders. "No educational system, at any level, will ever transcend the general postulates of the community in which it works . . . ," Harold Laski wrote in *The American Democracy.* "For an educational system does not exist in a vacuum. It exists always within a social system which makes its own nature and purpose the framework within which the nature and purpose of its educational idea must function."[4] Just as a static society prohibits educational innovation, dynamic societies expect innovation and support those educational enterprises which provide it. All educational institutions require an economic and social base of support: without external support they cannot exist, and the direction of their support determines the direction that the educational system takes. Without Standard Oil and Edward S. Harkness, Harvard and Yale would not enjoy the residential housing they now have. Similarly, without the ferment within Roman Catholic thought over the past decade, many Catholic colleges would not be undergoing their current dramatic reformation.[5]

[4] Harold Laski, *The American Democracy: A Commentary and an Interpretation.* New York: Viking, 1948, p. 382.

[5] Here are three illustrations of this general social fact, one each from industry, the schools, and higher education: (1) The rapid shift from railway to airline travel in the United States since World War II came about not simply from the initiative of the airlines, but from the development of air technology and airfield construction during the war. (2) Most public high schools operate under the legal obligation of meeting state education requirements, which in some states specify the number of minutes a day to

Dynamics of Academic Reform

Besides this fundamental significance of external support for the existenece of the institution, it seems that without change in this external support, large-scale academic reform is unlikely. Small improvements and alterations will most likely occur from within the institution—so long as they maintain the existing tendencies or remain within the traditions of the institution. But the redirection or reorientation of any institution, must, of necessity, come from without. In other words, all things being equal, so long as support can be found for pursuing the existing program of a voluntary organization, the present program will continue to exist. It is unrealistic, in our judgment as a result of this study, to expect a change in direction from within the institution itself.

The evidence of history all points to the near inevitability of this institutional inertia. In the thirteenth century at the University of Paris, teaching from the physical and metaphysical works of Aristotle was forbidden, and algebra, geography, and the last books of Euclid's *Elements* could be taught by interested masters only by special permission. In the nineteenth century in England, Benjamin Jowett and the other young tutors at Oxford sought to break the impregnable control of the masters and called for the intervention of the Crown to liberalize the universities on the grounds that "we cannot reform ourselves."[6] Today, in Ohio, the staff members in business administration at a small liberal arts college are surreptitiously teaching computer programming under a seminar course number because the faculty of the college has refused to allow computer programming to be offered in the catalog for credit. As Jo-

---

be spent on particular subjects, and the informal necessity of meeting college entrance requirements. What happens in the school classrooms is largely determined outside the schools—and, to a great extent, by the textbook publishing industry. (3) Changes in knowledge and in the program of the schools and the graduate schools continually affect undergraduate curricula. When mathematical societies design a model undergraduate program for "pregraduate" mathematicians, when students are interested in enrolling in it, and when rewards seem clear for offering it, mathematics departments will tend to adopt it.

[6] Letter to Roundell Palmer, November 1847, reproduced in Geoffrey Faber, *Jowett: A Portrait with Background.* London: Faber and Faber, 1957, p. 197.

seph Ben-David and Abraham Zloczower have pointed out in their studies of higher education, the universities of the world have not been responsible for the development of science; instead the impetus of science has been responsible for the development of today's universities.[7]

Evidence about the importance of external sources of reform also comes from the administrators and faculty members who were interviewed as part of the Study of Institutional Vitality. While they primarily see themselves as the initiators of change, they see outsiders proportionally more often stimulating major organizational changes—such as institutional mergers or shifts in function from a teacher training to a multipurpose institution—than smaller changes. And overall they perceive the most influential external groups, such as government, business, and local interests, as slightly more frequently a force for academic change than they do the personnel of their own institutions, such as the faculty and administration.

The personnel of any organization, including the faculty members of a college, quite rightly believe in what they are doing. Most of them are committed to activities and functions that they will not by themselves abandon or neglect except by external intervention. Unless they are trapped in a situation of being forced to do what they dislike, such as teaching six sections of freshman composition, they are likely to continue doing the same thing—hopefully, of course, better and better—until they become convinced to do something else. Thus because of the nature of voluntary organizations, the advocate of change will most likely be an outsider.

Support for this view that extensive academic reform is unlikely without some external intervention comes also from the statistical analysis of curricular change at a sample of 110 colleges and universities that was reported in Chapter Five. The most dynamic institutions in this sample tended to be those that, among other things, were most dependent on attracting students—in particular, some of the private colleges that were not expanding greatly. Typi-

[7] "Universities and Academic Systems in Modern Societies," *European Journal of Sociology, 3,* 1, 1962, 45–84.

cally they were not as prestigious; they did not have the national renown of the more stable universities, and their students had a greater voice in the formation of institutional policy. Conversely, among the least dynamic institutions were the few public community colleges we surveyed as a supplement to our main analysis. Although they were expanding greatly, they demonstrated little change in their existing courses. Like the public schools, they seemed to be providing a service to a captive audience.

In short, we conclude that while the responsiveness of an institution to change can be significantly affected by internal factors, the institution will seldom alter its functions without external influence. Outsiders initiate; institutions react.

This evidence helps explain, we believe, the relatively small amount of change that has taken place in American higher education during the past decade. Some observers have expressed surprise over this lack of change;[8] but from our perspective as a result of this study, the low level of change seems understandable. "The spirit of monopolists is narrow, lazy, and oppressive," Edward Gibbon said regarding the monopoly of Cambridge and Oxford in eighteenth-century England;[9] and, for better or worse, American colleges and universities have collectively approached the status of a monopoly in American culture within the past decade. No other route except college is now available to a high school graduate who seeks success in much of American life. Apart from the skilled trades, only the fields of entertainment, art, and sports remain readily open to youngsters who are not academically certified, and even the field of professional sports now relies on intercollegiate athletes as its major recruiting group. Moreover, in recent years the Army lay in wait for young men who were not enrolled as students.

Thus American higher education has been in a seller's market for the past decade. Most colleges and universities have been

[8] For example, see Paul L. Dressel and Frances H. DeLisle, *Undergraduate Curriculum Trends*. Washington, D.C.: American Council on Education, 1969, pp. 74–75.

[9] Edward Gibbon, quoted by George Macaulay Trevelyan, *British History in the Nineteenth Century and After: 1782–1919*. London: Longmans, Green, 1937, p. 26.

offering a scarce and valuable commodity to an expanding market of students, and have been able for the first time in decades, if not in history, to say in effect: "Take what we offer you or go elsewhere. We have other customers besides you." And, as the members of the Cox Commission noted in their investigation of the Columbia University disturbances of 1968, even though the college curriculum has not often in fact been irrelevant, many colleges have not bothered to make clear to students its relevance.[10]

During this same time, the colleges and universities have considered themselves in a severe faculty shortage, with adequately experienced professors in short supply. More than at any time in the past, professors in most fields have been able to demand—and receive—lucrative salaries and perquisites. As a result, institutions have been competing more for faculty than for students; and most arrangements of the academic program, including office hours, teaching loads, and instructional methods, have been organized for the benefit of professors rather than students, while the curriculum —as the trends described in Chapter Three show—has followed the specialized academic interests of the faculty. Thus the natural tendency of any group over a long period of time—that of serving its own interest first rather than those of its clients or constituency— has been heightened by the power that academics have wielded over decisions in higher education during recent decades. Indeed, at no time in American higher education have students been as powerless vis-à-vis their institutions as they were from 1955 to 1965.

Historically, students have been, as Frederick Rudolph rightly says, "the most creative and imaginative force in the shaping of the American college and university."[11] In the past, they have

---

[10] Archibald Cox, et al., Crisis at Columbia: Report of the Fact-Finding Commission Appointed to Investigate the Disturbances at Columbia University in April and May 1968. New York: Vintage, 1968, p. 16.

[11] Frederick Rudolph, "Neglect of Students as a Historical Tradition," in Lawrence E. Dennis and Joseph F. Kauffman (ed.), The College and the Student. Washington, D.C.: American Council on Education, 1966, p. 47. For a historical review of student influence on American higher education, see Fred Farley Harcleroad, "Influence of Organized Student Opinion on American College Curricula: An Historical Survey," Ph.D. dissertation, Stanford University, 1948.

rebelled against outmoded curricula, taken the initiative for their own education through the extracurriculum, and pressed the colleges to add new knowledge to the classroom. Even within the past decade in Canada, students have succeeded in revolutionizing the French-Canadian universities, which until then had continued to prepare their graduates for the preindustrial society of the nineteenth century. But only sporadically in one or another American college have recent students been equally influential.

The reason seems to stem in large part from the fact that the role of the American college student since the middle 1950s has become encapsulated by being rendered passive. The power—real though invisible—that students shared in earlier decades with faculty members and administrators has declined. Earlier generations of students could often set the level of classroom production required of them by the simple device of restricting their output without threat of faculty retaliation. Professors might have wanted fifteen-page term papers, but were often gratified to get ten pages. Student representatives, such as the student body president or the president of the campus interfraternity council, could meet with college officials on somewhat equal terms to work out informal agreements on campus policy.

More recent students, however, despite appearances to the contrary, have been successively disenfranchised. With the recent surplus of applicants for admission, faculty members have been more free to raise the threat of academic failure and dismissal, and at the same time an increasing number of students have come to believe that college graduation is necessary for their personal success and have thus been reluctant to jeopardize their future by attacking the one means of this success. Thus with pressure from above to restrict the influence of students, coupled with their acquiescence in a largely impotent role, students—the largest and most immediate bloc of clients of colleges and universities—have in most institutions become encapsulated. They have proven insignificant, until the late 1960s, in effecting academic reform.

Many Americans mistakenly believe that students have recently had great power over curricular matters, and a majority of them apparently think that students already possess too much power. (In a Gallup poll of December, 1968, for example, more than half of the persons over thirty years old who were interviewed stated that they did not think college students should have a "greater say concerning the academic side of colleges.")[12] The fact is, however, that students have possessed little power at all during the past decade. They have not controlled the resources that would effect change, and they have not had the opportunity of a buyer's market to exercise their options.

In sum, we submit that the past decade has been a relatively unique period in American higher education regarding power over the curriculum: for the first time the colleges and universities had far more autonomy than ever before to set their own requirements without outside interference. And the evident dissatisfaction and rebellion of students, we suggest, is in good part directly the result.

Most groups of people and organizations seek to free themselves from as much external influence as possible in order to become autonomous and self-directing. For educational institutions, the major means to this end is to become financially independent by amassing unrestricted endowment. In this way, external pressure of any kind can be restricted. But this opportunity of complete autonomy within higher education does not seem to produce academic or curricular change, despite its potential benefit for intellectual freedom. Instead it seems to perpetuate conventionality. Just as departments within colleges, if left to their own initiative, may grow increasingly homogenized, replacing their members with sympathetic and intellectually inbred colleagues, favoring an insider out of friendship over an unknown outsider, and even maintaining mediocrity out of self-interest,[13] so institutions isolated from any exter-

[12] Gallup Poll, December 6–8, 1968, reported in the *New York Times,* January 8, 1969, p. 40.

[13] "A weak faculty cannot be expected to favor the appointment of stronger men," Peter Blau has noted, "and even a strong faculty is likely to favor men with orientations similar to their own, to the detriment of diversity of approaches." ("The University as a Distinctive Organization," in R. H. Ingham (ed.), *Institutional Backgrounds of Adult Education: Dynamics of Change in the Modern University.* Boston: Center for the Study of Liberal Education for Adults, 1966, page 112.) And I. Bernard Cohen, the historian

nal pressure are likely to continue on their chosen path—as Oxford and Cambridge demonstrated during the eighteenth and nineteenth centuries until the Royal Commission of 1850, as the German universities demonstrated when they controlled every avenue to advancement in German professional and public life, and as American colleges illustrate by naturally retaining their existing functions if they can continue to support them and if the functions retain academic respectability.

In sum, we believe that advocates for complete autonomy for colleges and universities in the area of academic policy put greater faith in the willingness of the vested interests of faculty members and administrators to serve the public interest without external stimulus and supervision than any of these examples would suggest is warranted. The champions of self-regulation, whether in the tobacco industry, automobile manufacturing, the securities market, the medical profession, or colleges and universities, hold that these organizations can be expected in their own self-interest to tend adequately toward the public interest. Other observers, however, have concluded that although institutional self-reform may be possible without external intervention, it is unlikely, and that while self-regulation is desirable, it seldom suffices for public protection. No priesthood, it has been said, ever institutes its own reforms; no military service can be expected to do so; no professional association is so altruistic that it will not at some point confuse public welfare and its own; and colleges and universities tend, as do all other public trusts, toward serving the interests of their personnel—their teachers and administrators—before those of their clientele.[14] To suggest that the public underwrite higher education but leave its goals and policies to the mercy of academics alone would be naive. A college where academic policy is entirely the prerogative of its personnel—the faculty and administration—influenced by no other

---

of science, senses that this is one reason why departments of history may be less suitable for the growth of history of science as a specialty than a separate department which is co-equal with both history and the sciences. ("Discussion," in A. C. Crombie (ed.), *Scientific Change*. New York: Basic Books, 1963, page 778.)

[14] The most recent statement of this position occurs in Irving Kris-

group, including the governing board, seems unlikely to lead curricular reform and likely to resist it. It is too isolated from the sources of reform to do more than merely follow prevailing academic mores.

But we do not want to be misunderstood. In being suspicious of academic autonomy and isolation as contributing to continuous academic reform, we are not thereby suggesting that reform will be more continuous if control were vested at the other extreme—in some outside organization. America has had enough experience with this system of control—in which a college operates as an appendage of a larger unit, whether of a religious group, a state department of education, or the local community—to know its effects. Under these conditions, curricular change can either be stopped altogether or drastically enforced.

The community college that is operated as a segment of a local school system, the two-year campus of a state university that is governed from the central campus, the denominational college

tol's proposal for "A Different Way to Restructure the University." "No social group really possesses the imaginative capacity to have a liberal and reformist perspective on itself; individual members of the group may and do —but the group as a whole cannot. Otherwise the history of human society would be what it is not: an amiable progression of thoughtful self-reformations by classes and institutions. So the beginning of wisdom, in thinking about our universities, is to assume that the professors are a class with a vested interest in, and an implicit ideological commitment to, the *status quo* broadly defined, and that reform will have to be imposed upon them as upon everyone else." (*The New York Times Magazine,* December 8, 1968, p. 50.) Nearly two hundred years ago Adam Smith wrote in the same vein in *The Wealth of Nations,* as Theodore Caplow and Reece McGee noted in *The Academic Marketplace* (New York: Basic Books, 1958, p. 5). Among other commentators have been Ralf Dahrendorf concerning the German universities ("Starr und Offenheit der deutschen Universität: die Chancen der Reform," *European Journal of Sociology, 3,* 2, 290), and Eric Ashby regarding the English universities (*Technology and the Academics: An Essay on Universities and the Scientific Revolution.* London: Macmillan, 1963). See also Clark Kerr's *The Uses of the University* (Cambridge: Harvard University Press, 1964, pp. 105–106), and Homer D. Babbidge, Jr., "The Outsiders: External Forces Affecting American Higher Education," in R. H. Ingham (ed.), *Institutional Backgrounds of Adult Education: Dynamics of Change in the Modern University* (Boston: Center for the Study of Liberal Education for Adults, 1966, pp. 81–89).

that is considered to be the educational arm of a church, the teachers college that is dominated by the surrounding school districts, the state university that has succumbed to the control of the state purchasing office, the state personnel department, and the state building construction agency—all of these institutions tend, as do appendages, to respond automatically to the dictates of these other organizations. Appendages do not act; they twitch. And changes within an appended institution will of necessity be dictated by other groups, sometimes imposed swiftly, other times delayed for decades. The institution is forced to provide only those services that the sponsor desires and is willing to underwrite. One local college that we know of cannot even alter the flower plantings on the campus without preparing itself for showers of protest from the townspeople.

In short, while on the one hand some colleges may be overly isolated from their environment, others are encapsulated and prevented from taking any independent action by the dominance of a sponsoring group. Neither of these relationships to the environment encourages continuous academic reform. And thus other relationships are needed.

From all of the evidence so far, what can we suggest these relationships should be? Before turning to them, the limits of our evidence need to be specified. Scholars and researchers, like mapmakers, are always tempted to go beyond the facts and extrapolate into the unknown. Cartographers in the past liked to sketch in their best guesses about the land, rather than to leave an area of the map blank; but because this led to what has been called "hypothetical geography," the best mapmakers of today indicate the difference between evidence and speculation to warn the reader of the unexplored. Similarly, scholars should not claim knowledge without justification. They should indicate the sources of their conclusions and identify which of them are based on reliable knowledge and which of them are best guesses—extrapolations or speculations from available evidence.

Using this rule, five features of this study require reemphasis before sketching out some extrapolations from it. First, this study concerns the sources of academic *reform* and not the sources of academic *quality*. The major problem facing American colleges and universities, in our opinion, is not the ignorance of educators about effective teaching and learning but their difficulties in instituting changes that will lead to better teaching and learning. We thus view adaptability as a means to greater effectiveness. The best curriculum, from our perspective, is above all an evolving curriculum —particularly if its evolution involves planning and its innovations involve evaluation. And yet curricular change is not by itself an indicator of educational quality or effectiveness. In this study, we have made no independent measures of effectiveness at the institutions we analyzed; we have not compared our measures of reform to any measures of educational quality; we do not suggest that a dynamic institution in terms of our measures of academic change is necessarily a more effective institution educationally than a static one; and any implication that reform and quality are synonymous would be unjustified.

Second, the measures of reform in this study—the reorganization of courses, replacement of programs, and changes in requirements and regulations—are deliberately not evaluative. For example, they do not judge the social, economic, or human gain and loss when secretarial study or Greek is eliminated from the program of a state university and agricultural climatology or African studies is introduced. Each of these changes counts equally. The reason lies in the fact that for this study we have tried to learn the sources of academic reform, whether or not we ourselves applauded or abhorred the particular change itself. The dynamics of change remain the same regardless of our opinions of the desirability of the change, and understanding the process does not imply endorsing or equating all of the changes studied.

Third, the measures of academic change used in the study tend to under-report the amount of change actually going on when compared to the judgments of the professors involved. We used the institutions' own descriptive information about their programs as the basis of our statistical measures; and some institutions keep their information more current and valid than others. Our evidence about academic change, therefore, is subject to the vagaries of academic catalogs—publications which tend to be revised more frequently at some institutions than others and which tend everywhere to change more slowly than the institutions they supposedly describe.

Fourth, much of the information about the correlates of academic change—the data about personnel, enrollments, finances, policies, and procedures—comes from a variety of sources over which we have no quality control. For example, our interviews at each institution involved at most three people; they took place at the end of the period under study rather than at the beginning; and the differences of perception among the respondents from the same institution about certain institutional practices may have taught us as much about collective ignorance and about different frames of reference as about the practices themselves. Thus we cannot guarantee the reliability of all the data that we used, and, as with most studies, some of it is less reliable than we would have liked.

Finally, correlation is not necessarily causation. The relationships that we have found between academic reform and some characteristics of academic institutions may involve an element of causation, but it would be unjustifiable to conclude that these characteristics are the causes of academic reform. In a statistical study like this, at least a few statistically significant correlations are bound to result simply from chance. And none of the relationships that we found are so invariable that they can be termed causal: they provide clues about the sources of reform but they fail to point to any single factor as itself the source.

Taking these limitations of the study into account, what can we extrapolate about the sources of academic reform from the data that we have gathered? Ten characteristics seem to us to bear particular attention as likely contributors to continuous academic change, and they are listed below, beginning with the most obvious and moving to the most speculative.

A market is essential. Above all, a market for new ideas— a demand for improvement—is necessary. Just as the health of every academic discipline hinges on the support that it can acquire, so every dynamic college needs a congenial environment to support it. If it lacks this support—if it lacks reward or benefit for dynamism—it will fail.

A locally-based institution can deviate little from local norms; and if local norms are educationally conservative, the dynamic college must either move away or seek support from elsewhere to remain. A classroom discussion of Marx or Mao will cause phones to ring just as they do when gin punch appears at a faculty social in a dry community. This is the reason why the few famous avant-garde colleges in American higher education have been able to survive in a locally indifferent or hostile environment. Like Antioch in Ohio or Reed in Portland, they have obtained the support of a national constituency to overcome local suspicion. The failures, like Black Mountain in North Carolina, have lacked this support. (The same law holds true, of course, for a conservative college. A parochial institution faces difficulties when its local community becomes increasingly cosmopolitan.)

Historically, the evidence seems clear: resources and rewards must be available for academic reform. The greatest state-supported universities in the United States have arisen in the most progressive states—in the South before the 1840s and in the Midwest and along the Pacific coast thereafter. And some of them have been eclipsed as a result of shifts in the political climate, as Georgia and Virginia illustrated in the nineteenth century and Ohio State has demonstrated more recently. The statistical data we reported earlier tend to support this historical evidence. As mentioned before, the most academically adaptive institutions of those we studied tend to be located in urban environments—where social change has been not merely rapid but tumultuous. They tend to be most dependent on students for support. They are neither as wealthy nor as prestigious as the more static institutions. And they are not only dependent on students for support, but receptive to their opinions.

Thus we suggest that academic reform results above all from market pressures from outside the institution. We do not imply that all these pressures will be for change; sources of support—be they alumni, state legislatures, churches, philanthropic foundations, federal agencies, or students and their parents—differ in their support

155

of change. Even students can sometimes be a conservative educational force, and thus colleges that depend on attracting students to keep in business are tempted merely to copy their more successful competitors. While this is not necessarily bad, it is not ordinarily creative.

Since an institution that is almost completely dependent on finding students or satisfying the legislature or mollifying wealthy donors tends to be bound to their demands, either for tradition or for change, the best assurance of continuous reform, as well as the best protection against any one powerful external influence, is through *diversified* sources of support. Innovations in higher education seem most often introduced and most quickly adopted by institutions that are supported not by a local and a limited group but by a diversified national constituency. Not only have these institutions more freedom from any one controlling group, but they are subject to a greater variety of influences and advocates.

Hence in order to judge the potential of an institution for continuous reform, we would first ask these questions about it: What is its environment? What are its sources of support? What is its constituency? And what are their attitudes toward academic change?

New models are needed for emulation. Academic reform consists far more in the diffusion of educational ideas from one institution to another than in the creation of new ideas. The spread of freshman seminars, marine biology, credit by examinations, the philosophy of science, and other curricular changes is largely a phenomenon of academic fashion. (Nothing of course is wrong with fashion, as long as the innovation is adopted thoughtfully and adapted to local conditions.)

Thus for academic reform to occur, new models of institutions must continue to be created as examples, pace-setters, and competitors. Sometimes the new models can be created as units of existing institutions—such as the separate experimental colleges under Warren Bryan Martin at the University of the Pacific or under Joseph Tussman at Berkeley. Sometimes existing practices need only be copied by institutions of another tradition. For example, the president of a Jesuit college explained his rationale for introducing new majors in art and music on these grounds:

> In Jesuit education, among our twenty-eight colleges there's been far too much professional orientation and an orientation to philosophy and theology alone. We've ignored the whole aesthetic side of life, and that's what I'm trying to change here. . . .

But to go beyond existing academic convention, initiative cannot be expected to stem from the conventionally successful institution. For this reason, it is perhaps not surprising that the most academically dynamic institutions in our sample tend to be undergraduate colleges that are not affiliated with universities, rather than the undergraduate units of universities—conventionally organized, as they are, along scholarly lines.

If conventional institutions are reluctant to undertake new academic services, completely new institutions may be required as competition. To employ all the technological aids now available for education, to organize a curriculum on individualized lines and on other bases than the disciplines, or to award diplomas and degrees on the basis of achievement and competence alone rather than time-serving and chair-sitting—these may be radical enough departures to require new institutions for their inauguration. Educators have long fought the possibility of a national university, but federally-initiated institutions may be necessary to serve such functions as these if other means fail.

Thus we are led to ask: What competition exists for the institution or for the institutions as a system? What monopoly of educational services do they control? And what does the institution emulate?

Ideas need circulation. Educational reform has traditionally depended on the circulation of individuals from job to job—on a perpetual game of musical chairs, whereby instructors carry innovations with them from graduate school to their teaching and from one institution to another. But other mechanisms can be used for the circulation of ideas as well as people throughout the system of higher education.

157

These mechanisms for the circulation of ideas include professional meetings and journals, educational associations and newsletters, faculty retreats and workshops, interinstitutional seminars and tours. They increase the rate of change, since they allow individuals to learn new skills and attitudes on their job rather than merely carrying the same skills from one job to another. Yet most of the present channels of communication in academic life are based on the disciplines rather than on interdisciplinary concerns; and they do not permeate the total system of higher education to reach colleges where faculty members and administrators are isolated from ideas of value to them. For example, note the benefits of travel for two institutions that we studied:

> *The president of a Protestant college:* In 1966 I attended a Conference of Christian Colleges and heard about the "four-one-four" idea [a month's inter-session between two four-month semesters]. I brought it back from the conference, and we brought in a man from Luther College to our pre-session faculty conference that fall to describe it. The faculty was ready for it. By January, 1967, when the faculty approved it, we had great enthusiasm, and by May we had 74 projects submitted for trial. It has stirred our faculty up.
>
> *The vice-president for academic affairs of a Catholic men's college:* The students had been complaining that we had too many required courses, so we undertook a major curriculum revision starting five years ago and lasting until last year. The English department had always been fiddling with their opening course, but this was the first time we had ever looked at the total curriculum. In the summer of 1965, we had a workshop of the Jesuit Education Association in San Francisco, and it was invaluable for me to learn at that meeting what other institutions were doing—what they found successful and what they had found were problems. I stole the "forty course" idea from Holy Cross then. I decided that we needed to cut back our program to 120 hours, or forty courses of three credits each. I jumped in, and the faculty concurred in the decision.

In contrast, the president of a state college reported to us that the primary obstacle to introducing a new major in biology at the insituon was the belief on the part of "the old established folks" in botany and zoology that no one else taught botany and zoology together as biology.

One of the major benefits of the Higher Education Act of 1965 in its program to strengthen the nation's "developing" colleges has been its help in bringing some of these colleges within this circle of communication. Other projects, including *Change Magazine,* the Danforth Foundation workshops for liberal arts colleges, and the programs of the Union for Research and Experimentation in Higher Education, aim at increasing this communication. David Riesman has advocated sabbaticals for college teachers every three years to help keep them intellectually alive. All of these techniques can help in the circulation of ideas and the introduction of change. Thus we ask: How extensive is communication across institutional boundaries and beyond disciplinary limits? And what resources are available for observations of other institutions and for in-service education?

A number of "marginal" members are helpful. Because of the importance of external pressure and interinstitutional communication in the process of academic reform, continuous reform appears to depend on the influence of marginal or borderline members of the institution—*in* it but not *of* it—who can affect its operations by mediating between the institution and its environment.

By a marginal member of an institution we mean anyone associated with it whose livelihood is not dependent on it. If a person is financially or psychologically dependent on his membership in the institution, he is not marginal to it, but is instead an insider. Typical marginal members of colleges and universities are trustees, alumni, visiting lecturers, patrons, and consultants, as well as occasional administrators, professors, and students.[15]

---

[15] Among writers on this concept in higher education are Paul F. Lazarsfeld, "Innovation in Higher Education," *Expanding Horizons of Knowledge About Man: A Symposium* (New York: Yeshiva University, 1966, pp. 12–21). Lewis Mayhew talks of the "sociological stranger" and describes W. W. Charters' work at Stephens on pp. 40–41 of "Innovation in Collegiate Instruction: Strategies for Change" (*Southern Regional Education Board Research Monograph* No. 13, no date).

Thus, in a psychological sense, the marginal member is at the boundary of the organization. He is relatively invulnerable. Others know that they cannot control him, since his job is less important than his independence or principles. And in an organizational sense, a marginal member can act as an intermediary between the members of the organization and nonmembers. He is in an exposed position but at the same time is maneuverable in mediating pressures.

Note the position of the president in this regard. "When the president dare not resign, his powers are waning and soon he will be impotent," Henry Wriston observed after having served in the presidencies of both Lawrence and Brown. "He must be ready to give up his office if confidence is lacking."[16] Wriston himself immediately quit as president of Lawrence when the trustees decided to look into his expulsion of two students who had been caught cheating. Within two hours, an emissary of the board asked him to return.

Similarly, the financially independent professor can play a creative role in an institution because of his marginal position. If he is either independently wealthy or professionally in demand elsewhere, he is able to play a more forceful role in advocacy than a dependent member of the faculty since he can use the threat of resignation as leverage, if he chooses, for bringing about change. Likewise, the student who is neither dependent on scholarships or loans from the college nor inhibited by the belief that graduation is essential for his personal success can be more free to advocate institutional change than the student who is indebted to the institution or who feels dependent on it. And from our statistical study, it appears that the highest ranking institutions in terms of academic reform tend to have trustees—marginal members *par excellence*— who are perceived as interested in change rather than in the status quo.

We suspect that colleges and universities can be distinguished by the proportion of their members who are in this sense

[16] Henry M. Wriston, *Academic Procession*. New York: Columbia University Press, 1959, p. 67.

160

marginal to them—freedmen or *liberi* in contrast to members who feel captive or bound to them by demands other than loyalty. And we suggest that without the influence of such marginal members, most academic institutions will have difficulty in maintaining continuous reform.

Hence we would ask: Does the institution encourage independence or dependence on the part of its members? Is it open to examination? Does it solicit advice? And does it consider that marginal members such as trustees have a legitimate role in influencing educational policies of the institution?

For major reorganization, new members seem necessary. Colleges and universities undertake new functions by adding new members. In the nineteenth century they switched from the recitation system of instruction to the lecture system by hiring new generations of German-trained instructors. In the twentieth century, they have tried to repersonalize institutional life by adding staffs of student personnel workers. Thus the rate of academic change tends to vary with the rate of expansion and turnover in personnel. Encouragingly, turnover alone does not appear from the statistical evidence of this study to be as fundamental a mechanism for small-scale educational reform as we had pessimistically suspected it might be, but we sense that it remains the major mechanism for instituting and implementing major academic realignments in an institution.

These realignments may not necessarily be the deliberate consequences of new blood: they may result simply from the fact that reorganization disrupts traditional relationships. "When you get a new president, all the frustrations come to the surface," a professor at one college remarked. "All the discarded or buried ideas are dusted off and reexamined." For example, the arrival of a new president at an independent university led to changes in its admissions policy, according to the dean of its college of business:

> The initiative for recent changes has come from the new president, although none is really a black-and-white thing. There has been a feeling among the faculty that changes were needed, and the new president took over and listened to the

wishes of the faculty and helped put through the changes.
. . . They all initiated the development, but it wouldn't have
taken place if the old administration had still been here.

And a new president herself reported:

Our student education committee has been active since 1962.
They came to my office soon after I arrived and said to me,
"Theology is awful. We're only getting questions and answers
in it." I had to get rid of the extant theology department and
bring in all new people.

Moreover, the newcomer is likely to bring new perceptions
with him. In some cases the results will be small-scale—such as the
discovery by one new administrator of classroom space in basement
rooms that had been piled high with broken furniture, or the reali-
zation that irreplaceable institutional files are stored on the second
floor of a wooden house. In other cases, however, they may include
new visions of the role of the college in society. The new president
of a religious college told us during an interview :

I came into a college that was impaled on the dilemma of being a Bible college or a liberal arts college. . . . Until five
years or so ago there was a cleavage in the faculty's opinion
about which direction it should take. When I arrived it was
moving toward liberal arts status, and I immediately tried to
capture the enthusiasm in this direction. . . . I fanned some
embers during the process, but it was encouraging to see how
quickly the flames of enthusiasm leaped up.

And the president of a women's college said:

I've had to be careful never to make a first suggestion, but
I've been able to encourage the sparks in the faculty with the
power of the purse. I've been able to initiate some changes: A
recognition of non-western studies—African and Asian. A major internal press toward race relations—several years ago we
began reverse discrimination—unpublicized admission of Negro students—and we started some interdepartmental work on
race questions. We've brought respectability to creative work.

This community was bookish to the extent that the creative arts were passive; but now students are sculpting, not simply reading the history of sculpture.

Some colleges make sure, of course, that the newcomers bring as few disruptive ideas as possible with them. Andrew Greeley found in his study of Catholic colleges that some provinces and orders deliberately seek presidents who will not exert any leadership at the institution in order to avoid the possibility of independence.[17] At a Protestant college the president reported to us, "We probably could employ a Catholic now—but not a Jew. Or a Unitarian."

Even though our statistical analysis of academic change dealt mostly with small alterations in the curriculum rather than major institutional realignments, newcomers did prove important in these changes. The most dynamic institutions tend to be those where the faculty is both expanding and changing the most, where the junior faculty appear to have more influence in affecting educational policy than at other institutions, and where the proportion of tenured faculty is lowest. In addition, the most dynamic departments as measured by reforms in course offerings during the past five years tend more frequently to have witnessed a change in their chairmen during this same period.

So we ask: Who are sought as new members of the institution, and particularly for executive positions? And what limits are drawn regarding their qualifications? Must they be academically orthodox and impeccably conventional?

As may be evident already, these first five characteristics all have in common an element of openness to the environment: openness to outside influence, openness of competition, and to a variety of ideas, individuals, and new members. That these characteristics of openness carry with them the dangers of instability cannot be denied. But we suggest that without some instability—be it conflicts over financial support, debates over institutional goals, or the unknowns in recruiting outsiders—most colleges and universities will

[17] Andrew M. Greeley, *The Changing Catholic College*. Chicago: Aldine, 1967.

163

lack the needed external stimuli to change. The same generalization applies to the features of the colleges' internal organization and operation. As the remaining five characteristics illustrate, we sense that the most constantly responsive institutions seem structurally the most open. In one word, they can be termed latitudinarian.

The right people must be retained. As pointed out in the first chapter, the process of recruiting faculty and staff seems more important to academic reform than to change of program in other organizations. All efforts at reform through in-service training and communication must depend on the quality of person attracted to the institution and retained there. Robert Maynard Hutchins has said that ". . . vitality is given to an institution by the people who are there. If they are vital, they will attract other people who are also vital."[18] Like attracts like, and excitement attracts excitement. But whether vital people and advocates of new ideas stay on at the institution or leave hinges on the conditions that they find there—restrictions or opportunity; frustration or freedom.

Some institutions systematically impose limitations on the newcomer: not allowing new instructors, for instance, to vote with the rest of the faculty. (Of the 110 institutions in our sample, at least fifteen of them have such policies, according to the people we interviewed.) Some institutions unintentionally find themselves overstaffed at the senior levels and unable to offer a chance of advancement to younger staff, leading to transiency within the lower faculty ranks. "I tried to encourage some professors to leave by not increasing their salaries," stated the former president of one such institution. "I even reduced salaries in a couple of cases. But they still wouldn't go." Finally, some institutions exhibit a suspicious orientation toward the consideration of change. Robert Merton has observed these differences between creative and lethal organizational atmospheres:

Some are evocative, providing a system of direct and unplanned rewards for significant ideas, facilitating their effec-

[18] Robert M. Hutchins, "Trees Grew in Brooklyn: Robert M. Hutchins Interviewed by Frank K. Kelly," *The Center Magazine, 1,* 7, November 1968, 21. Santa Barbara: Center for the Study of Democratic Institutions.

tive transmission, and so generating further ideas. Other organizations provide a lethal environment for new ideas, which
are regarded as disruptive.[19]

Chief among these differences is the perceived attitude of influential
people at the institution. Recall that at the most dynamic institutions in our sample, the most influential members are seen by other
members as interested in change in the educational program rather
than in the status quo. Newcomers soon learn whether or not they
can try teaching a new course, or alter their course offerings as their
interests change, or obtain support to try a new technique. Observe
the ease with which courses can be changed at one small private
college, according to a division chairman:

> One of my men comes to me and says, "I'm sick of this
> course: it isn't drawing well." So I say, "O.K." It's a family
> situation and that settles it right there. Sometimes in our pol-
> icy committee, I'll mention it. "We're planning to drop Dav-
> enport's course in English literature. Does anyone have any
> objections?" And I'd probably ask him what he wanted to do
> instead, and if it sounded as if the new course wouldn't draw
> well, I'd probably call the department together to discuss it.
> But so far I've never done that.

At an unusually dynamic state college, the graduate dean said, "We
can approve a graduate-level course any Tuesday afternoon in the
Graduate Studies Committee. We don't need a year's wait, as they
do in some other systems."

Thus we would ask: What image does the institution present to its members: exciting, active, engaged? Or static, passive,
isolated? What is considered sacred: authority, standard operating
procedures, a tradition of tradition—or independence and a tradition of change? What seems to be rewarded? Participation, initiative, advocacy, and debate—or role adherence, specialization, and
conformity? And what is its climate—trusting or secretive, expres-
sive or constrained, appreciative or impersonal?

[19] Robert K. Merton, "The Environment of the Innovating Organization: Some Conjectures and Proposals," in Gary Steiner (ed.), *The Creative Organization*. Chicago: University of Chicago Press, 1965, p. 51.

Initiative is decentralized. We suspect that the major restriction to continuous reform on many campuses is the debilitating effects of a sense of powerlessness, whereby initiative seems impossible. Some institutions circumscribe the amount of discretion they permit any member to exercise: they create detailed job descriptions, publish innumerable regulations, frown on questions, and suppress advocacy. For instance, the governor's office that must approve all out-of-state travel, the chancellor who requires that his office approve all photographs taken on campus for off-campus use, the president who refuses to allow the dean of students to attend meetings of other deans of students, the dean who deletes a line-item budget request from a department chairman without consultation, the department that assigns existing course outlines and textbooks to a new professor for his courses, the academic senate whose members are appointed by the administration rather than selected by the faculty—all illustrate the overcentralization of initiative. Witness, too, the near paranoiac demand of a state commissioner of education for triplicate copies of recommendations for new faculty members:

> Each nomination will need to be accompanied by a letter of recommendation from the past employer of the candidate and the personal evaluation of the candidate by the President, Dean, and the Chairman of the Department of Instruction, or any other official staff member who participated in the interview of the candidate. The individual statements of evaluations should include such observations as educational philosophy and attitudes toward instructional practices, improvements needed in college instruction, attitudes toward the basic issues in public education, teacher education, and higher education.

This form of institutional autocracy appears to stem from particular historical roots. In the teachers colleges it results from the traditions of the normal schools and the public schools for strong executive authority as opposed to teacher and student docility. In technical institutions, it obviously stems from industrial influence. And in denominational colleges, its origins lie in the tradition of the all-powerful pastorate, where the cleric has ruled the congregation as preacher, administrator, and even director of the Ladies Aid. Indeed, most highly centralized or hierarchical colleges tend themselves to be dominated by other hierarchical organizations—the state department of education, the local industry, the church—and used for their ends.

At some institutions, centralization of initiative continues to be supported on the ground that it alone protects against the incompetence of an untrustworthy staff. Petty cash, it is assumed, leads to petty thievery. But we suspect that centralization contributes to the very conditions it supposedly guards against—since it discourages or repels faculty members who are able to be selective about their job and retains those who cannot afford to be. Thus centralized, line-item position and equipment budgets imposed on some state colleges prohibit them from moving quickly to meet new social needs and hiring the best faculty. In the long wait between recommending professors for appointment and their classification and approval by state agencies, the best professors can be bought up by other institutions.

Elsewhere, power may unintentionally become the prerogative of an oligarchy. Observe an anthropologist's frustration at a western state university:

> The people who have been here a long time have no energy and are not willing to do anything. Committees are chosen from people who are well-known at the university, and these are always the older faculty members. So there's no opportunity for change here.

In this connection, another university found that only 5 per cent of its committee appointments were being filled by assistant professors and only 15 per cent by associate professors—the remaining 80 per cent being occupied by full professors and administrators. Committees, moreover, can wield inordinate influence. In a recent study of curriculum committees at seven liberal arts colleges, William O'Connell found that none of them had any provision for reporting to the faculty the negative decisions that they make on curricular proposals: they merely report their positive recommendations and bottle up the rest, thus serving as an obstacle to the consideration of suggestions.[20] In 1965 Joseph Tussman won the opportunity to try his Experimental College after the Berkeley revolt only by outflanking the College of Letters and Science Committee on Courses and the Berkeley Division Committee on Courses when the Committee on Rules and Jurisdiction voted that the program did not need their authorization.

In contrast to these centralized conditions, the most dynamic institutions appear by and large to offer faculty members and students greater latitude of behavior. They select faculty whom they consider competent and students whom they deem able, and then they trust them. Here are three statements illustrating this decentralized approach:

> *The provost of a midwestern state university:* Ninety-nine per cent of a faculty will do twice as much as they think they can, as long as you don't get in their way. The trick is not to worry about mistakes, but to encourage them instead when they need a pat on the back—and encourage them even when they don't.
>
> *The dean of a Catholic men's college:* People look to the dean of the faculty to do everything. My basic decision has been to get the decisions made by the department heads themselves. That's what I've been trying to do as dean. We are now getting people up and saying "Can I try this?" and I've been saying to them, "Great! Write it up afterwards so we can know how it works out." I feel that's helping the situation.
>
> *A vice-president for academic affairs at a predominantly Negro college:* This office has been trying to move the decisions nearer to the point of implementation. The deans of the schools are getting to be a little bit more autonomous, and we are trying to push decisions back to the divisions, by establishing broad policies for all to follow.

Thus the most dynamic institutions in terms of the amount of reform of their courses tend to allow professors greater leeway in tak-

[20] William R. O'Connell, Jr., "The Curriculum Committee in the Liberal Arts College," Ed.D. dissertation, Teachers College, Columbia University, 1969.

ing attendance of students, and we have the impression that they more often allow students to elect much of their program of study while the most static institutions seem more often to expect students to take a prescribed program.

We should not imply that centralization of control cannot lead to great academic change, for this is not the case; the changes that can be wrought in higher education by a powerful administrator can be as great as in any other organization. But the process of academic change in the centralized institution hinges on the predilection of its central figure. Depending on his attitude, the entire institution can constantly be propelled rapidly in new directions or, conversely, can languish until rebellion or replacement occur. As with any autocracy, dramatic and coordinated change is possible, since decisions and their implementation can be swift—as President Lowell's response to the offer of Edward S. Harkness to build the Harvard houses illustrates. Yet centralization places so much influence in one person or clique that when the center goes dead, the institution of necessity follows. It appears to have the same effect as a flywheel in physics: when the powerful person has momentum, he keeps the rest of the mechanism moving; but when he stops, tremendous energy is required to overcome his inertia.

Thus we are led to inquire: How much discretion do people have in performing their tasks? How precise are their job descriptions? And how frequently are decisions made—in budgets, appointments, curricula, and other areas—without consulting the individuals involved?

Patriarchy is avoided. From our perspective, the worst type of centralization in terms of its effect on curricular change is what we have termed patriarchy. In a patriarchal institution, power is not merely concentrated in one person or group, but it is assigned on the basis of seniority and is thus held interminably or indefinitely by senior members. Decisions are made at the top of the hierarchy, often unilaterally by the president or senior professors; power and perquisites are won by age or length of service rather than other means—be it by competence or nepotism; and governance tends to devolve upon a geriatric oligarchy. For example, department chair-

169

manships are typically held by the oldest members of the departments, chairmen tend to serve as chairmen until they retire, few retirement limits are enforced on administrators, and trustees serve unlimited terms of office. Indeed, the one fact about the structure of a college that seems to us to indicate best the general orientation of the institution toward curricular reform is the tenure of department heads and department chairmen. Do they hold office until they retire as professors, as department heads traditionally have done? Or do they serve a limited term of office, as increasing numbers of department chairmen do? We do not claim that the difference between these two styles of departmental management will of itself cause a difference in the amount of curricular reform at the institution, despite the evidence of the significant role played by the department chairman in course changes within his department. The difference is, however, symptomatic of the institution's whole orientation toward seniority at large.

Seniority as the criterion for power in academic institutions was well-adapted to an earlier culture and to the role of higher education in a stable society. In fact, the centralization of initiative in the most senior members has been typical of most organizations in most societies throughout history. It continues to exist throughout much of American higher education—particularly, we believe, in rural, preindustrialized regions and at institutions that are most dependent on the support of ecclesiastical, industrial, or government agencies that also operate patriarchally. Patriarchy complemented the conservative orientation of the old-time American literary college toward the past, with its functions of conserving revealed religion, classical literature, and the record of history rather than creating new knowledge and new culture. Even today patriarchy may be functional for the most impoverished institutions, where continual crisis engenders centralized authority and where low salaries create a need for some reward to the most faithful. But patriarchy now seems unlikely to assist many impecunious colleges in overcoming their impoverishment, since funds for higher education are being provided less on the sentiment of the past, as they once were, than on the evidence of present effectiveness and in areas of teaching and research that are unsuited to the patriarchal tradition—in particular, the sciences and technologies.

Thus we suggest that patriarchy is an inadequate form of government in a rapidly changing society, as knowledge and competence become less directly related to an individual's length of service. Here, other criteria of merit besides longevity need to be considered. As the provost of a state university said to us about the problem, "There's nothing magic about being old."

Consider the issue of seniority in three different cases—first among department chairmen, then among presidents, and finally among trustees. The chairman of a department can influence its rate of course reform through his power in recruitment, promotion, course assignments, scheduling, committee appointments, and policy and priority decisions for the long-term direction of the department. At most institutions, he thus plays a more significant role in day-to-day and year-to-year academic decisions than do central administrators. Our evidence that course reform in the departments is correlated more closely with change in the chairmanship than with change among the faculty members themselves leads us to be increasingly concerned about the length of tenure of department heads and chairmen. "Most of them have served until they were very tired, or we were tired of them," commented one president. "Ten years, fifteen years—far too long."

As part of the trend away from patriarchy in society at large, more and more colleges are coming to adopt a policy of either reviewing chairmen periodically or specifying a term of office for them and expecting the chairmanship to be rotated among the faculty. For instance, at one state university, according to its chancellor, "Each year the dean takes a secret ballot in the departments as to whether they want a new chairman or want to continue with the same one. It's actually a one-year term, and very few men stay on until retirement." At a private university the president reported, "Within the last three years we have begun to elect chairmen for three-year terms, with the option of reelection for one more term. So I told one chairman that since he had served for six years already, he must be rotated out. His department wanted him out, but he claimed that they didn't. So I had each one of them come into my office and I asked them their opinion, and I got him out."

From our perspective, strict rotation either every year or every two or three years has a number of disadvantages: it reduces the influence of the incumbent too greatly and makes turnover too mechanical. But periodic review and a tradition of limited tenure for chairmen seem essential. Without such a tradition, the removal of an inadequate chairman prior to retirement is so difficult that it tends to be avoided by retaining him until he departs.

Similarly, we suspect that presidents have tended to serve in office for too long rather too short a time.[21] We have no data from our study to substantiate or deny the belief that innovation tends to decline at an institution the longer the president remains in office. We have seen enough evidence, however, of long-term executives coming to conceive of the institution as their personal creation that we sense long tenure may tend to decrease the possibility of alternative sources of initiative besides the "great man" or "founding father" himself. The clearest example of this danger occurred at one of the colleges we visited for a case study. There the president had tried to make the faculty obey the same regulations about smoking and dancing that were imposed on the students. Historically, the most famous example of patriarchy in the history of American higher education was Eliphalet Nott, who, as president of Union College for sixty-two years from 1804 to his death in 1866, holds the record for the lengthiest presidency. He led Union to national prominence by the 1850s, but—as Dixon Ryan Fox says in his history of Union—even at age eighty-eight, when an acting president was appointed to relieve him, "the old chief, with his brilliant record of more than half a century behind him, could not now content himself with being merely a ceremonial figure in his continuing office, and reached into administration with a frequent

---

[21] The average tenure of president in the relatively placid years before Berkeley was between ten and eleven years, according to a survey conducted by William K. Selden and reported in his "How Long Is a College President?" *Liberal Education, 46,* 1, March 1960, 5–15.

and capricious hand."[22] Union has never yet fully recovered.

Some inadequate presidents do not voluntarily relinquish the office because of the limited number of equal positions of high status to which they can move. "What more than one institution needs is a first-class funeral," an official of one accrediting agency told us, but death and retirement are inadequate mechanisms for turnover in the academic presidency. And the same problem of entrenchment can occur in any office, whether business manager, registrar, departmental secretary, or faculty parliamentarian, where "top-sergeant resistance," as Everett Hughes labels it, comes to control institutional practice even if these offices supposedly do not determine institutional policy.

The same infirmities can afflict the patriarchal governing board. Traditionally, two of every three private colleges have been governed by boards containing at least some self-perpetuating members with no limitation on their length of service.[23] The danger of impaired health and perspective among some of their older members contributes to their ineffectiveness. One former president confided over a drink, "The worst problem is that they fall asleep at board meetings. When a vote is taken they wake up and vote with the majority. Yet they're the ones who should act independently if anyone does."

Several devices can help reduce this problem. One device, of course, is term appointments, with the requirement that a member step down after one or two terms for at least a year. Another is a specified retirement age for trustees, such as seventy or seventy-two. While some boards would have difficulty adopting either of these limitations on length or age of service, some colleges have in part succeeded by creating the status of honorary or emeriti trustees for exceptional members who can continue beyond their term or retirement to serve on the board without vote.

In short, since the control of academic change naturally

[22] *Union College: An Unfinished History.* Schenectady: Graduate Council, Union College, 1945, p. 22.

[23] The figure comes from data gathered on 1,490 boards by August W. Eberle and students in the Department of Higher Education, Indiana University, in January, 1967. Duplicated report, January 27, 1969.

tends to flow toward the long-term members of all institutions, we are particularly suspicious of seniority as the basis of power. The continually-dynamic institution seems to benefit from the circulation of power among young and old. We therefore raise these questions: What policy does the institution have for regularly reviewing the appointment of department chairmen and administrators, and of assuring their selection on other bases than only seniority? Does the president attempt to consolidate his control over the institution during his tenure, or does he increasingly delegate a proportion of direct decisions to his associates? And does the institution have a retirement policy for trustees and expect board members to step off the board after specified terms of office?

Collegial consensus is also avoided. At the opposite extreme from this patriarchal style of operation, American society and American colleges are moving toward a new orientation, which has been termed collegial in nature.[24] Collegiality here indicates a community of equals. Instead of the father figure, it is typified by a peer relation—in university life, by the brotherhood of the professoriate. Collegiality can be viewed as the opposite of patriarchy because of these three main characteristics: (1) Initiative is dispersed throughout the organization rather than being concentrated in any one portion. Most members participate equally in decisions and policy formation. This fact is true of most professional organizations like universities, medical clinics, research institutes, and scholarly associations—although collegiality seldom extends to the members of the organizations that are considered to be clients—for example, to undergraduates in college or to patients in hospitals. (2) High status is achieved through renown rather than ascribed through seniority. While status distinctions are deemphasized, leadership is won by the professionally respected members. Thus de-

---

[24] Nicholas J. Demerath and his associates develop the concept of faculty collegiality on pages 215–238 of their *Power, Presidents, and Professors* (New York: Basic Books, 1967). Talcott Parsons and Gerald M. Platt discuss it in their "Considerations on the American Academic System," *Minerva, 6,* 4, Summer 1968, 497–523, especially p. 509; and in their preliminary report on their study of the American professor, "The American Academic Profession: A Pilot Study," duplicated, March, 1968.

partment chairmen at a collegial institution tend to be elected, and the winner of an election is likely to be the most widely-published member of the department. And (3) Positions of high status rotate among the members of the organization on a periodic basis, rather than being held interminably. Elections for department chairmen occur, for instance, on a set schedule.

By and large, collegiality is the model of most professional groups, including the academic disciplines. Policy decisions are made by consensus among the members, and they alone judge themselves competent to make decisions. Collegiality thus can offer an ideal blend of individualism within a loose confederation of equals. In colleges and universities, it seems to arise in part as a reaction against centralization. Having eliminated the father-figure of the presidential autocrat, faculties in their euphoria establish the democracy of equals—as Charles Beard, Alvin Johnson, and James Harvey Robinson did in 1919 when they banded together to form the prototype of the American collegial university—the New School for Social Research.

The collegial university has become the ideal model of an academic institution for many professors, and in the future more and more institutions will probably move toward this style of operation. Collegiality is well-suited for those colleges and universities that operate as holding companies for their faculty members— those institutions that exist for the purpose of providing professors with space, equipment, and apprentices, and where the combined interests of the faculty constitute the purposes of the whole.

But at some institutions, the *collegium* as a group dominates. Rather than permitting the individualism and independent initiative that collegiality implies, some faculties permit no initiative without the approval of the faculty at large. For example, the faculty that must vote as a body on every curricular change proposed at the institution, the department that will not delegate decisions to its representatives, the faculty that is reluctant to permit temporary experiments or rump-group independence, the faculty that votes against allowing students to select their own courses because it suspects that faculty advisers will steer their advisees toward their own discipline; in short, any majority that cannot trust a minority of its own members—all overcentralize power in the collectivity as a body.

Christopher Jencks has attributed the rigidity of the university curriculum in large part to this collegium orientation—to "the extraordinary difficulty of getting permission from one's colleagues to try anything new and exciting." He wrote in 1965:

> On virtually every major university campus in America there are professors who want to develop an interdisciplinary science program for non-scientists, start a small residential college where undergraduates will have a common curriculum and a chance to get to know a small group of faculty, or whatever. These ideas rarely get off the ground. Often they are vetoed by the rest of the faculty, or by one or another faculty committee.[25]

To protect against the tyranny of the collegium, Jencks advocates funding of professors' teaching experiments in the same way that professors' research projects have been financed: independently obtained from outside sources without collective control and direction by the faculty at large. Presently, however, the most successful tactic for innovation at collegial institutions remains that of obtaining permission to try the new idea only as an option or only for an experimental period. Thus at Wesleyan in 1926 Henry Wriston was able to get the faculty to agree to the idea of comprehensive examinations by specifying that only departments that wanted to give them to their students would do so, and Harvard succeeded in introducing its general education program in 1945 and its freshman seminar program in 1958 by authorizing them only for three-year trials. One of the most dynamic colleges in the sample of institutions for this study has been able to avoid a collegium orientation partly because of the deliberate philosophy of its president regarding her role. "I have conceived of the presidency," she says, "as an office for finding very creative people, giving them freedom, and protecting them from one another."

[25] Christopher Jencks, "A New Breed of BA's: Some Alternatives to Boredom and Unrest," *The New Republic,* October 23, 1965, p. 18.

Sources of Reform

Beyond this domination of the minority by the majority, the collegium orientation appears to present a second difficulty to academic reform. Thinking of themselves as independent professionals at heart, the faculty members of the collegial institution tend to reject all outside influence—including the intrusion of administrative initiative—in order to maintain their autonomy. They not only assume responsibility for deciding on means to the institution's ends, but they believe that nobody else legitimately can decide what these ends should be. Students are naive; laymen are ignorant; therefore the institution must be the private preserve of its professional personnel.

Under these conditions, academic reform in the collegial institution hinges almost entirely on the quality of the new professors that the faculty allows or attracts into the institution. When these professors are achievement-minded, nothing but a lack of consensus can prevent any reform they initiate; but when the majority of the faculty becomes tradition-oriented or declines in quality, no safeguards exist against academic atrophy. Thus we would ask: Must the faculty at large approve every curricular change proposed at the institution? And must any change be adopted for the total institution and be considered irrevocable, or does the faculty permit an "open-field" approach to change, with separate experiments throughout the institution?

The institution is avuncular. By now it is probably evident that these two styles of academic organization—the patriarchal and the collegium-oriented institution—seem to us to be inadequate models for continuous academic reform. The patriarchal institution tends toward massive but periodic changes and to vulnerability from the predilections of its patriarch and from outside organizations. The collegium-oriented institution tends toward the dominance of the majority over any advocates of innovation and toward isolation from all outsiders.

We pointed out earlier that the chances for academic reform seem to us from all the available evidence to be best at institutions that are open to influence from many sources in their environment and that are latitudinarian in their organization for responding to

177

these influences. Is there any one theme that distinguishes these institutions from those that operate on a patriarchal or a collegium orientation? Although the facts are scattered, we believe there is. Part of this theme is openness. The open institution, like the open society, is marked by characteristics that permit ameliorative change rather than require violent revolution: equality, toleration, advocacy, dissent. Related to this characteristic is professionalism. A professional organization is characterized by high levels of autonomy, self-government, and individualism among its members. They associate as colleagues, respecting each other's expertise and trusting each other's skills.

But we would suggest that the most common element in this theme can best be conceived as avuncularity. The term *avuncular* comes from the Latin word *avunculus,* referring to an uncle. The avuncular institution is characterized primarily by uncle-like relationships, in that the role of the uncle in many societies, including America, is that of a relative who provides experience but not discipline and who is available for aid without being omnipresent. While paternal and peer relationships may of course be present, these relationships of expertise and aid distinguish the avuncular institution from the patriarchal and the collegium-oriented institution.[26]

Three general characteristics identify the avuncular institution: (1) Initiative is neither permanently centralized nor dispersed. All members of the institution as well as outsiders are considered to be advocates, and while power is generally diffused, it is occasionaly centralized. Everyone connected with the institution—students, faculty, alumni, trustees, patrons—participate to some

[26] Our thinking on this concept was sparked by the ideas of Richard C. Hodgson, Abraham Zeleznick, and Daniel J. Lewison in their book, *The Executive Role Constellation* (Boston: Harvard Graduate School of Business Administration, 1965). On pages 496–497 they discuss three general executive role types: controlling and assertive, loving and supportive, and friendly and equalitarian. In passing it should be noted that one of the most famous anthropological studies of an uncle relationship—Malinowski's analysis of the role of the mother's brother in Trobriand Island culture—describes a relationship that is in effect paternal rather than avuncular.

extent and at one time or another in determining policy. For example, the trustees serve as active overseers, and although they commonly encourage initiative by faculty and administration, they are prepared to assume it themselves. (2) High status is assigned on the basis of expertise. Responsibilities are delegated to individuals because of their special competencies. Department chairmen are chosen, for example, on the basis of the particular demands of the chairman's role as an executive position, while the professor of horticulture is consulted for advice about campus landscaping and experienced students are expected to assist the neophytes. (3) Positions of status shift according to different tasks rather than in strict rotation. Positions are assigned neither on an interminable basis nor for stated periods. For example, rather than relying on standing committees, the institution organizes ad hoc committees frequently for specific purposes, and they disband when their task is done.

Consider some other illustrations. The governing board that is acquainted with many members of the institution and that holds periodic open meetings, the president who consults with the people involved by telephoning them or walking down the hall to their office before making a decision, the opportunity for students to elect their courses of study with the counsel of their faculty advisers, the tradition of a clear route of appeal for any institutional decision against a member, the custom of employing consultants and visiting professors, of inviting in guest lecturers and visiting committees, of post-audit rather than pre-audit, and of encouraging faculty members to hold joint appointments and to teach in areas of knowledge where they have competence in addition to their own department—all these exemplify an institution that emphasizes avuncular relationships of expertise and assistance.

Perhaps the most characteristic fiscal device of the avuncular institution is the discretionary fund. "Without it, I wouldn't get anything done," says the dean of an Ivy League college. And the provost of another one says:

A discretionary fund is essential—and it should not be trivial. I probably have $50,000 . . . so that we can try a program to see whether or not it works. To be a dean without a discretionary fund would be intolerable. It's better to tighten up your budget and to trust your deans with some leeway in funds than not to have a discretionary fund. Much of some colleges' problem, I sense, is that they have weak deans and weak department chairmen who cannot back people and support them when they have good ideas. I could go back to teaching physics if I wanted: I would not want to stay in this office if I did not have considerable funds for discretionary use.

In the avuncular institution these discretionary funds are not limited to central administrators to use. They are budgeted at every level—institutional, divisional, departmental—in order to permit widespread initiative. One innovative midwestern state university tries to maintain discretionary funds of at least $500,000 in order to set aside an amount equal to a percentage of the annual budget of each area of the university for use by that particular area.

The best illustration of an avuncular orientation, however, is the manner in which department chairmen are selected. Rather than being appointed unilaterally by the president for an indefinite term, as in the patriarchal institution, or elected for a set term by the department faculty, as in the collegium model, the chairman in an avuncular institution is appointed by the administrator after consultation with the department, and his appointment is periodically reviewed on the basis of contacts with the members of the department.

Although the American Association of University Professors naturally favors the election of chairmen, we suspect that election, as opposed to appointment, will serve to reinforce institutional stability rather than encourage change. An elected executive is more dependent than an appointed one on maintaining the existing social structure of the department—thus giving greater opportunity for mediocrity to perpetuate itself.

In brief, at the avuncular institution, expertise tempers the authority of patriarchy and the equality of the collegium. Members of the institution with special skills serve as advisers and consultants —a psychological statistician, for instance, on questions of institutional research regarding students; a professor of business administration on the introduction of program budgeting. Most important of all, however, this model of an institution assures a legitimate role for its marginal members—those persons at the boundary of the institution who can influence its policies: the consultant, the observer, the trustee. It permits these near-outsiders to participate in the formation of policy, and it allows expertise by these advisers and specialists from outside the institution to counter inbred parochialism. Hence avuncularity stimulates initiative better within the institution than does patriarchy, which tends toward authoritarian directives; and it encourages continual communication between the institution and its environment better than does collegiality, which tends toward isolationism.

Avuncularity, moreover, seems particularly well-suited as an operational model for educational institutions, since their fundamental purposes are basically avuncular in nature: they are concerned with learning and research by means of apprenticeship. The educator, of course, is implicitly an avuncular figure—a guide, a mature and knowledgeable helper, a resource and an aid—rather than a disciplinarian. And student personnel staff members explicitly play an avuncular role—assisting students with problems beyond the competence or the interest of most professors. Neither the patriarchal model nor the collegium model is adequate to encompass the special role of the student. He is neither a child, confined to the college, nor a completely equal citizen of the institutional republic. Through the college, he can explore the world and test new roles for himself, some of which will be exemplified by other students and by the faculty. Thus college is not a home for him—but it is home base.

In sum, we suspect that a distinctive structural characteristic of the continuously reforming and self-renewing institution is its avuncular style of operation. This conclusion, it should be emphasized, is an extrapolation from data: it attempts to account for a variety of evidence without itself directly stemming from this evidence. For example, a factor analysis of the statistical variables used in this study reveals no strong factor that might be labeled as avuncularity; but the influence of several related variables in affecting change—among them, external pressure, individual advocacy, widespread initiative, and an absence of patriarchy—point to avuncularity as a general institutional characteristic of potential importance. Within a college or university, an avuncular orientation places restraints on autocratic or oligarchic power because of its emphasis on advisement rather than authority; yet it permits coordinated action when action is necessary. And externally, it succeeds in mediating environmental pressures through the creative role of marginal members. Since colleges and universities depend for their existence on the support of their outside constituencies, these pressures from the environment cannot be neglected. They must be encouraged, but at the same time they cannot be allowed to overwhelm the institution. They must be filtered by individuals on the margin of the institution—a role that only the avuncular institution adequately provides.

Consider the implications of an avuncular orientation for three particular institutional roles: the executive, the consultant, and the trustee.

While the role of the faculty in curriculum reform is so widely accepted that it does not require endorsement here, the value of the administrator in this process requires recognition. As the respondents to the interviews in this study indicated, administrators remain the most influential individuals on most campuses in determining educational policy, and as the statistical data show, their attitude toward educational change relates significantly to the amount of change that occurs in the curriculum.

Even the American Association of University Professors (AAUP) has agreed that the academic executive must play a role in academic reform. Together with other educational associations, the AAUP has stated:

> As the chief planning officer of an institution, the president has a special obligation to innovate and initiate. The degree to which a president can envision new horizons for his institution, and can persuade others to see them and to work toward them, will often constitute the chief measure of his adminis-

tration. The president must at times, with or without support, infuse new life into a department; relatedly, he may at times be required, working within the concept of tenure, to solve problems of obsolescence. The president will necessarily utilize the judgments of the faculty, but in the interest of academic standards he may also seek outside evaluations by scholars of acknowledged competence.[27]

The problems that confronted Yale as late as the presidency of James Rowland Angell illustrate the significance of this presidential function, for until Yale's by-laws and statutes were revised during his tenure, Angell, like his predecessors, was unable to exert the leverage that was needed to open Yale to new ideas. The president who is denied this leverage by a defensive faculty, the administrator who must spend his time trying to extinguish one academic brush fire after another, who lacks assistance to permit him to undertake long-range planning as a major task, who hesitates to intervene to stop the downward spiral of a department or a whole section of the institution—these men cannot fulfill this executive responsibility.

But with the growth of faculty expertise and influence, the administrator must increasingly play an avuncular rather than a paternal role. In contrast to an emphasis on control in the patriarchal institution and on laissez-faire in the collegium model, the executive in the avuncular institution emphasizes his responsibility for stimulation, facilitation, and coordination. Perhaps it can best be labeled as a "watering can" responsibility. By it, the administrator encourages initiative and the advocacy of new ideas. John Corson suggested the watering can analogy from observing Victor Butterfield's role as president of Wesleyan. "Butterfield walks around the campus with a watering can," he said, "and wherever he finds an idea beginning to sprout he gives it a drink."

Consultants are professional uncle-figures. Most institutions

[27] American Association of University Professors, American Council on Education, and Association of Governing Boards of Universities and Colleges, "Statement on Government of Colleges and Universities," duplicated, 1966, p. 6, reprinted in Louis Joughin (ed.), *Academic Freedom and Tenure*. Milwaukee: University of Wisconsin Press, 1967, p. 97.

call in advisers for remedial aid only during crisis but not for long-term assistance at other times. We sense, however, that the most innovative institutions in American higher education continually rely on expert advice from outsiders. The president of one of the most dynamic colleges in our sample said:

> We've used a number of consultants, but not in the traditional ways. We've tried to get people with ideas about education to stop by and talk with us. We ask them, "What do you think of this? Or this?" We've got contacts around the country, and we bring them in to speak. . . . Too many consultants have the answers already. We don't want to imitate others by using their answers. We're interested in questions. . . . Meetings, conferences, visitors—they all help.

And here is a sample of the role an outside expert can play, from the president of a high-powered technological college:

> We found that taking a look at how our product has made out has been most informative—both by asking our graduates and by talking with their graduate-school advisors, since almost all of our graduates go on for advanced work. We called Paul Heist in to help on this project. Attrition was high— about 50 per cent of our students were not completing their program, and so we tried to improve that. . . . The reason attrition was high was that many students were transferring to other institutions. We found out that they were not doing as well on the Graduate Record Examinations as they would like in order to get into top graduate schools. So we all talked about it in the faculty; we got Paul Heist aboard in the faculty seminars on it; and we got the trustees interested in the problem.

As a result, the college has cut its attrition rate down to about 30 per cent.

Other institutions have benefited from the continuing assistance of a long-time consultant. At Rochester Institute of Technology and Stephens College, W. W. Charters served as a peripatetic educational adviser, and Ralph Tyler has continued this relationship with RIT. At Michigan State, Floyd Reeves played an influential role following the Second World War in helping plan its Basic

College, its Continuing Education Center, and other new programs. And Antioch for decades has invited educators to visit Yellow Springs and has sent its faculty members out to observe new practices elsewhere. These practices not only bring educational ideas and news to a campus; they also let the campus see itself through other eyes—through the eyes of a friendly but somewhat detached observer: the avuncular adviser.

Turning finally to the trustees, many academics historically have scoffed at the beneficial influence that laymen on the governing board can have as marginal members of a college. Admittedly trustee influence is not always creative, as the frustration of one administrator illustrates:

> Trustees should play a very, very, very minor role. They're uninformed. If they had an obsolete president or faculty member on the board, or even a vice-president, they might know what to do, but hell, they don't know anything about the curriculum. They're concerned with what downtown will say. You can't take a savings and loan man, a surgeon, and somebody else, and expect them to consider the institution. When it was a choice between maintaining intercollegiate football or supporting new programs in psychology, urban affairs, and Upward Bound programs, they killed these three proposals to make sure that football was retained. They were worried about what downtown would say about it.

And trustees have sometimes failed to remember their limited role in dealing with curricular issues by getting entangled in decisions on specific courses and requirements. They may not know the dictum that A. Lawrence Lowell gave the Harvard Board of Overseers about their proper role when they once attempted to overstep it. "Laymen should not attempt to direct experts about the method of attaining results," Lowell instructed them, "but only indicate the results to be obtained."[28]

Part of the problem of trusteeship stems from the fact that the role of the trustee is perhaps the most ambiguous in academic life, calling as it does for overseeing without administering and pas-

[28] *Report of the President of Harvard College, 1919–1920.* Cambridge: Harvard University, 1921, p. 25. In that one sentence Lowell sum-

sivity without abdication. Yet we suggest that effective trusteeship by laymen can help stimulate continuous academic reform better than any other device. On the one hand, it can avoid the danger of direct outside pressure from other organizations. Acting as a semipermeable membrane between the institution and its environment, the governing board can filter and temper environmental influence. In this way, a lay governing board protects against direct action from outside—whether from a legislature or a government agency or other sources. (Lacking such a filtering device, the German universities fell to Hitler on March 1, 1933, when he took over the German civil service, including its ministry of education.)

On the other hand, lay trusteeship avoids the danger of isolation from society by allowing continuous mediation between the institution and society. In this way, it contrasts with the collegial system of academic government that Oxford and Cambridge long exemplified, where, as Lord Bryce said, "the juniors drank and hunted and the seniors drank and slept,"[29] and where reforms have been achieved through periodic upheavals by parliamentary intervention and Royal Commissions.

Even by playing only its passive role of overseer, the governing board affects the rate of academic change. Among the institutions we studied, the administrators and faculty members that we interviewed at the most dynamic institutions sensed that their trustees are more of an influence for change than did the members of the most static institutions. At these static institutions, trustees were perceived as especially conservative. Moreover, at several institutions visited for this study, trustees had been responsible for stimu-

---

marized the basic relationship that should exist between any layman and any professional. He continued by giving an illustration of this relationship: "Many years ago the Board of Overseers, after careful examination, came to the conclusion that the writing of English by Harvard undergraduates was sadly defective. In this they were acting wholly within their proper province, and the result was a very notable improvement in the teaching of English composition. But if they had attempted to direct how the subject should be taught they would have been hopelessly beyond their province. They would not have known, as the instructing staff did, how it should be done, and they would have exasperated and disheartened the teachers."

[29] James Bryce, "The Future of the English Universities," p. 401.

lating major innovations in the curriculum—including experimental cluster colleges, off-campus study, and totally new divisions—because of their interest in educational development.

We submit that the governing board, more than any other unit of the institution, must be held responsible for assuring the continuity of academic reform. By its selection of the president, its setting of a level of aspiration for the institution, its efforts at financial support, its supervision of the budget, and its role as the continuous overseer of the institution, the board can assure a climate for educational change more powerfully than any other group of its members. For it to leave to the faculty and administration the initiation of all educational policies without retaining any initiative to establish the educational priorities and services of the institution is to allow inadequate recourse against academic entrenchment.

To play their governing role successfully, boards of trustees must above all be knowledgeable. They must be active; they must meet frequently; they must obtain information from sources other than simply the president. While they must respect the specialized competence of faculty members and administrators, they must not be cowed by it into leaving to them the formation of general institutional policies. In short, while they will ordinarily play a largely passive role of observation and supervision of the educational program, they cannot assume that the program will progress without their attention. The possibility of their taking the leadership in academic reform should serve as a goad to the faculty and administration. They must play the role of "Being a Cloud no Bigger than a Man's Hand," as Wilmarth S. Lewis, a Fellow of Yale, labels it.[30] "There it is," Lewis says, "the Cloud, always in the sky"— and always on the mental horizon of administrators and faculty members.

To end, we should repeat what we mentioned before. Our evidence is not clear-cut, and some conclusions that we have drawn from this evidence extend beyond our data. They are extrapola-

[30] Wilmarth S. Lewis, "The Trustees of the Privately Endowed University" (The 1952 Phi Beta Kappa Oration at Harvard), *American Scholar*, 22, 1, 1952–53, 19–20.

tions from all of our evidence and experience to date, and thus they are tentative, subject to criticism and verification. But on the basis of this evidence, our final questions about an institution in assessing its potential for continuous academic reform are these: What type of role most commonly characterizes the institution? Is it supportive, consultative, advisory—in brief, avuncular? And do its administrators, consultants, and trustees, as well as its faculty at large, commonly play this role?

In sum, this book has reported the results of a study of the sources of institutional vitality—the factors in institutional life that stimulate and sustain enterprising educational development. To obtain information about these factors, the staff of the Institute of Higher Education sought to learn how changes come about in the educational program: how colleges and universities alter their services, revamp their requirements, and reorganize their courses. In doing so, the staff examined the historical evidence about academic change, conducted a number of case studies at selected colleges and universities, and then systematically compared developments during the half-decade from 1962 to 1967 at more than a hundred institutions.

As a result of this study, it is clear that academic reform is not the province of only a few unique institutions. It occurs in some form and to some degree at every institution—at one with more difficulty, at another more continuously—but it occurs everywhere. Thus although great differences are apparent between individual institutions in terms of the measures of curricular change used in this study, none of the institutions was completely dormant on all of these measures. Moreover, while the separate undergraduate colleges have recently been undergoing more curricular change than the undergraduate divisions of universities, the average differences among the several types and levels of institution were statistically significant only rarely.

Second, the most frequent means of academic reform in recent years, as in the past, has been the piecemeal adding and dropping of programs, courses, and requirements—the small-scale process of gradual academic accretion and attrition—rather than radical transformation. Thus, for example, only four of the over four hun-

188

dred departments examined during the study completely reorganized their undergraduate program during the five-year period under review, in comparison to over three hundred that made at least some modifications but not total revisions. And of all the recent changes in the academic programs of the institutions, only five of the 224 that were reported to us by administrators and faculty members involved total restructuring of the curriculum.

Third, no one factor—no one specific characteristic—appears to be either a sufficient or an invariably necessary element in accounting for the differences that do exist among institutions in their amount of reform. Neither presidential leadership nor faculty collegiality nor low role specification nor high faculty turnover by themselves appear to contribute unilaterally to the process. Instead, a whole network of factors—attitudes, procedures, mechanisms, pressures—appear to be involved.

Fourth, although administrators and faculty members at institutions of higher education tend to think that the most important factor of all in the process of reform is the personal orientation of the members of the institution, environmental factors appear to play an equal, if not greater, role. Thus the rewards and resources that exist within American society for educational change—the market for higher education, the pressure for innovation, the competition among institutions—have a pervasive effect on academic reform. Indeed, the seller's market in higher education in recent years helps explain why relatively little change has occurred in the undergraduate curriculum in the past half-decade and why the trends within the curriculum have been primarily toward greater specialization in the academic disciplines.

Finally, while external resources and rewards are significant in affecting the process of reform, institutional differences in orientation and structure also affect the process. Among these differences are the attitude of the most influential members of the institution, the distribution of influence among members, and the simple expansion of the institution itself.

Some colleges and universities more than others, of course, are deliberately not adaptive. Their most influential patrons and members do not encourage innovation. They not only lack rewards for change, they have no wish for them. They do not want to accept new responsibilities or to set aside the old. They may see their function as that of preserving past glories and proud traditions, of standing as a bastion against the forces of decline, and of resisting the untried and the unfamiliar. For such institutions that seek to avoid the possibility of change, the evidence in this book may be of some help. It points toward some possible sources of flexibility to guard against and some likely sources of rigidity, such as patriarchy, to adopt in order to maintain the status quo. Inevitably, change will become necessary nonetheless—since, as American society changes, educational institutions that lose significance also lose support. But needed change can at least be delayed and postponed as long as possible through the use of proper techniques.

And for other colleges and universities—and for those faculty members, students, administrators, and trustees who want to help make their institutions more significant and more adaptive— the same evidence may be helpful in permitting more continuous reform. The most dynamic colleges and universities in this study tend to be marked not only by a need to reform but by the opportunity to reform. That is, beyond their obvious need for change—a perceived problem, an unmet demand, a potential reward—they possess the ability to change: the arrangements, the procedures, and traditions that make them responsive to this need.

Most American colleges and universities are attempting to increase their significance for their students and their services for society. Many of them are doing so despite the obstacles of their structure and traditions. Some of them are seriously restricted from doing so primarily because of these self-imposed impediments. But these obstacles can be reduced; and if an institution is to be dynamic, they should be. As the recent Commission of Inquiry at Oxford stated all too well, about the organization not only of Oxford but of every institution, "It is a bizarre achievement to show great skill in avoiding obstacles of one's own creation."[31]

[31] University of Oxford, *Report of Commission of Inquiry, I: Report, Recommendations, and Statutory Appendix.* Oxford: Clarendon Press, 1966, p. 31.

Appendix A

Literature on Change

The turmoil of contemporary society is stimulating increased analysis of social and institutional change. Surveys are being undertaken, conferences are being held, research institutes created, and consulting firms organized to understand and plan the process of organizational change. The literature on the topic is burgeoning; and this appendix reviews some items beyond those cited in footnotes that are of particular interest, first from the study of higher education itself and then from the field of organizational analysis at large.

The best collection in recent years of observations about the problem of academic reform are contained in a small volume, *Institutional Backgrounds of Adult Education: Dynamics of Change in the Modern University* (R. J. Ingham, editor. Boston: Center for the Study of Liberal Education for Adults at Boston University, 1966). Homer D. Babbidge, Peter M. Blau, Burton R. Clark, John Corson, Edmund Volkart, and other perceptive observers contributed articles to the volume from a symposium held at Syracuse University.

Most institutional histories of particular colleges and universities are not especially helpful in trying to assess the origins of change in higher education. They are reportorial rather than analytical, and tend to review the formal actions of administrators, faculty, and board, rather than the informal influence and negotiation involved in institutional alteration. Among the scholars of higher education at large, W. H. Cowley of Stanford has more than anyone else attempted to view change in higher education analytically and in cultural context. As part of his taxonomic study of American higher education, he has traced the growth of American academic institutions and their relations to "power saltations" as illustrated by industrial and technological revolutions; but much of his work unfortunately remains unpublished, including his "Overview of American Higher Education" and "A Short History of American Higher Education," both duplicated in 1961.

For the Planning Project for Advanced Training in Social Research at Columbia in the early 1950s, Bernhard J. Stern brought together materials describing the process of change in European and American higher education which were duplicated as "Historical Materials on Innovations in Higher Education" in May, 1953, but which also have not been published. From the Cowley and Stern materials, Ralph W. Gerard speculated on trends within higher education in "Problems in the Institutionalization of Higher Education: An Analysis Based on Historical Materials," *Behavioral Science,* Volume 2, Number 2 (April, 1957), pp. 134–146.

Three other scholars have written incisively on the process of academic change in recent years. The first is Joseph Ben-David of Hebrew University. See, for example, his article with Abraham Zloczower, "Universities and Academic Systems in Modern Societies," *European Journal of Sociology,* Volume 3, Number 1 (1962), pp. 45–84. Second, David Riesman's ideas about the straggling "snakelike" academic procession remain valuable. See Chapter One of his *Constraint and Variety in American Education* (Lincoln: University of Nebraska Press, 1956, or Doubleday Anchor Paperback A135, 1958). Third, for a study that Peter Blau and Terry Clark are beginning on the development of higher education, Clark has analyzed the reasons behind the "Institutionalization of Innovations in Higher Education," *Administrative Science Quarterly,* Volume 13, Number 1 (June, 1968), pp. 1–25.

Turning from the analysis of higher education at large to more limited studies of a few selected institutions, Andrew M. Greeley recently sought the causes of academic improvement at a group of Catholic colleges (*The Changing Catholic College,* Chicago: Aldine Publishing Company, 1967). He defined academic improvement in terms of the proportion of a college's seniors planning to go on to graduate or professional school, and found that the Catholic colleges in his sample that had made the greatest improvement recently were marked in particular by independent and intelligent administrative leadership. Similarly, Richard H. Davis found that the leadership style of the college president and the norms he encouraged among the faculty were more highly related to innovation at two colleges—one of the least innovative and one of the most innovative of those belonging to the North Central Association —than were differences between the faculties either in terms of their knowledge of current educational experimentation or in terms of psychological conservatism ("Personal and Organizational Variables Related to the Adoption of Educational Innovations in Liberal Arts Colleges," Ph.D. dissertation, University of Chicago, 1965).

In a case history of the introduction of television into the teaching process, Richard I. Evans studied the psychological variables involved in changed attitudes toward instructional television. At the institution where he conducted the experiment, the innovators were found to be from among the more "pragmatic" rather than "academic" areas of the university and were more financially secure (Richard I. Evans in collaboratiton with Peter K. Leppman, *Resistance to Innovation in Higher Education: A Social Psychological Experiment Focused on Television and the Establishment.* San Francisco: Jossey-Bass, 1968).

In a report published in 1961, Earl J. McGrath described the methods employed by fourteen independent liberal arts colleges in altering their curricula and, in particular, eliminating courses no longer needed or appropriate. He proposed that faculties have the responsibility "to undertake critical and continuing reviews of institutional offerings and to maintain an educational program consistent with the purposes of a liberal arts college," but he found that they had not done so in the colleges studied. He concluded that most presidents had no systematic plan for periodically reviewing the curriculum, deans were more concerned than presidents in having a broad and deep curriculum in comparison with other colleges, and the department chairmen were the most conservative force of all regarding the curriculum (*Memo to a College Faculty Member.* New York: Institute of Higher Education, Teachers College, 1961).

A number of proposals have been made within higher education to overcome some of these difficulties. One of the most noteworthy was made in 1959 when Beardsley Ruml and Donald Morrison suggested that the traditional decision-making structure of the faculty was incapable of accomplishing curricular reform adequate for the cause of liberal education. They proposed to substitute a "new and suitable instrument" created by the governing board in the form of either a reoriented presidency, a rededicated and strengthened Committee of the Faculty of the Curriculum, or a new "Council for Educational Policy and Program," to include members of the faculty, the administration and the trustees (*Memo to a College Trustee,* Prepared for the Fund for the Advancement of Education, McGraw-Hill Book Company, 1959). In 1960 Philip H. Coombs proposed the creation in colleges and universities, school systems, and state education departments of a position that he titled the Vice-President in Charge of Heresy in order to insure "that competent attention is given to the promotion of significant research and development, to keeping informed, and to the prompt application of important new ideas and techniques." This vice-president, as Coombs saw him, would be responsible for stimulating heresy instead of repressing it. ("The Technical Frontiers of Education," the twenty-seventh annual Sir John Adams lecture at the University of California, Los Angeles, March 15, 1960, p. 14.)

The best collection of material on change within the educational system at large and the lower schools in particular appears in *Innovation in Education,* Matthew B. Miles, editor (New York: Bureau of Publications, Teachers College, 1964). The articles in that volume identify some of the characteristics that contribute to resistance to change within school systems: they are composed of small and vertically fragmented units; they have heavy investments in materials supplied by textbook manufacturers; and they seldom attract or reward innovators—instead they tend to reward conformity and docility on the part of both students and teachers. Thus Henry M. Brickell observes that "teachers are not change-agents for innovations of major scope. When free to guide their own activities, teachers seldom suggest distinctively new types of working patterns for themselves." ("State Organization for Educational Change: A Case Study and a Proposal," in *Innovation in Education,* p. 503.) At the same time the ideology of the schools supports resistance to "outside interference," since teachers believe that they are professionals and as such reject initiative from non-teachers. "The teacher's role," Matthew Miles has noted, "is actually that

195

of a bureaucratic functionary who has little power to *initiate* system-wide change, but—because of the ideology concerning professionalism alluded to above—tends to resist innovative demands, like most professionals in bureaucratic organizations." ("Innovation in Education: Some Generalizations," in *Innovation in Education,* p. 634.)

The work of Paul Mort and his associates on adaptability of school systems indicates that differences in adaptiveness stem from differences among communities. He writes, "Explanation of the differences in educational adaptability of communities can be found in no small degree in the character of the population, particularly in the level of the public's understanding of what schools can do, and citizens' feeling of need for education for their children. This appears to set the posture of the community toward financial support, and toward what teachers are permitted to do—and tends to shape the staff by influencing personnel selected and kept in the community." ("Studies in Educational Innovation from the Institute of Administrative Research: An Overview," in *Innovation in Education,* p. 326). Within school systems, most analysts view the superintendent as the key figure in the process of change. "More than any other person at the local level, the superintendent has the authority to make decisions with regard to the organization and allocation of resources and personnel," Roland Pellegrin writes in explanation ("An Analysis of Sources and Processes of Innovation in Education," Eugene, Oregon: Center for the Advanced Study of Educational Administration, 1966). See in addition, Gordon N. Mackenzie, "Curricular Change: Participants, Power, and Processes," in *Innovation in Education.*

Among writers on organizational change at large, John W. Gardner has dealt directly with the problem of institutional reform. "How can we design a system that will continuously reform (i.e., renew) itself, beginning with presently specifiable ills and moving on to ills that we cannot now foresee?" he asked in *Self-Renewal: The Individual and the Innovative Society* (New York: Harper and Row, 1965, p. 5). He observes from other studies that apathy and lowered motivation are personal characteristics detrimental to self-renewal, while openness, courage to fail, motivation, independence, and flexibility are among the necessary characteristics. These qualities can be either hampered or stimulated by organizational factors, such as recruitment and rotation of personnel, communication, and pluralism.

In *The Active Society: A Theory of Societal and Political Processes* (New York: Free Press, 1968), Amitai Etzioni questions whether a continually self-renewing institution or society is possible. He suggests that "while maintenance processes are continually operative, processes of change are more sporadic and probably vary more in their intensity" (p. 389). Since change requires mobilization—a shift of energy and interests from individual and local concerns to organizational or societal concerns, he suspects that a constantly mobilized society is utopian although some of its features may possibly be institutionalized. Other recent books bearing on the problem of organizational change include *The Creative Organization,* by Gary A. Steiner (Chicago: The University of Chicago Press, 1965), which summarizes a seminar on this topic held at the Graduate School of Business of the University of Chicago in 1962; *The Handbook of Organizations,* James G. March, editor (Chicago: Rand McNally and Company, 1965), which contains William H. Starbuck's article on "Organizational Growth and Development"; and *The Social Psychology of Organizations* by Daniel Katz and Robert L. Kahn (New York: John Wiley, 1966).

The problem of adaptability within organizations has been discussed by Peter M. Blau in his *The Dynamics of Bureaucracy: A Study of Interpersonal Relations in Two Government Agencies* (Chicago: The University of Chicago Press, 1955) and by Donald A. Schon in *Technology and Change: The New Heraclitus* (New York: Delacorte Press, 1967). Schon's book analyzes the factors which distinguish three "mature" American industries—textiles, machine tools, and construction—from several growing industries including chemicals and aerospace.

The difficulty in introducing changes within hierarchical organizations is illustrated by William A. Sims' development of continuous-aim firing in the United States Navy, described by Elting E.

Morison, "A Case Study in Innovation," in Warren G. Bennis, Kenneth D. Benne, and Robert Chinn, editors, *The Planning of Change: Readings in the Applied Behavioral Sciences* (New York: Holt, Rinehart and Winston, 1964, pp. 592–605).

The importance of adequate resources in permitting change has recently been illustrated in a study of the local health offices of ninety-three American communities by Lawrence B. Mohr (*Determinants of Innovation in Organizations*. Ann Arbor: University of Michigan Institute of Public Administration, Michigan Governmental Studies, in press)'. Mohr found that increased resources had a pronounced positive effect on the number of innovative programs adopted by the departments. He suggests that innovation may be determined "as a multiplicative function of the motivation to innovate and the balance between the obstacles and resources bearing upon innovation. . . . If there is no motivation to innovate, there would probably be no innovation at all, no matter how abundant the resources; if there are no resources with which to overcome existing obstacles, even the strongest motivation would be unlikely to produce a great deal of innovation."

The significance of the attitudes of the most powerful members of an organization in influencing change has been demonstrated repeatedly. For some recent examples, see the case study of an innovative mental hospital in Ezra Stotland and Arthur L. Kobler, *Life and Death of a Mental Hospital* (Seattle: University of Washington Press, 1965)', a survey of the introduction of scientific knowledge into British industry, conducted by C. F. Carter and B. R. Williams, *Industry and Technical Progress: Factors Governing the Speed of Application of Science* (London: Oxford University Press, 1957)', and Robert Guest's study of an American automobile plant, *Organization Change: The Effect of Successful Leadership* (Homewood, Illinois: The Dorsey Press, Inc., and Richard D. Irwin, Inc., 1962)'.

Finally, the most comprehensive review of research on innovation at large is that by Everett M. Rogers in *Diffusion of Innovation* (New York: Free Press, 1962)'. From his review of this research, Rogers has abstracted five policies that he believes should lead, everything else being equal, to a self-renewing university. They are: testing the effectiveness of innovations, creating a mechanism to facilitate change, improving communication on innovation, selecting faculty oriented to innovation, and using informal channels of communication to diffuse information. ("The Communication of Innovations in a Complex Institution," *Educational Record,* Volume 49, Number 1 [Winter, 1968], pp. 67–77.)

Reports, ideas, and opinions about organizational change appear in a variety of publications, as the citations above illustrate. One particular publication, however, is devoted exclusively to the topic of change in higher education and is an excellent source of information: *Change Magazine,* edited by Peter Schrag and published at 59 East 54th Street, New York 10022. In addition to it, the journals of the several educational associations and the new newspaper, *The Chronicle of Higher Education,* report studies and developments in educational reform and innovation; and the scholarly journals in the academic disciplines contain an occasional item of importance.

APPENDIX B

Sampling and Analysis

The statistical information in Chapters Three, Four, and Five was obtained from 110 senior colleges and universities that were selected randomly on a stratified basis from the 1,164 accredited four-year colleges and universities in the forty-eight contiguous United States that were offering more than simply a purely occupational or professional program in 1966.

The 1966–67 *Education Directory,* Part Three, "Higher Education" of the United States Office of Education served as the source from which the sample was selected. From the 2,252 institutions that were listed in that edition, the staff of the Institute of Higher Education eliminated 320 that offered only a specifically vocational curriculum (those identified in the *Directory* as in categories *a, g,* or *i*) and those at level "V," which offered work at other than the associate, bachelor's, master's, or doctoral degree level, such as the Institute for Advanced Study in Princeton and the United States Department of Agriculture Graduate School in Washington, D.C.—neither of which offers degrees. For tactical reasons, we also eliminated the fifteen institutions in Alaska, Hawaii, and other noncontiguous areas of the United States. We also excluded from the population the 358 institutions which were not accredited by a nationally recognized accrediting agency, and from our detailed analysis we eliminated the 389 two-year institutions.

Had we picked a completely random sample from among the remaining 1,164 institutions in the population, we would most likely have had only a few universities to study, since only 10 per cent of all American institutions of higher education offer the doctor's degree. (These universities, however, due to their large size, enroll a much larger proportion of students than ten per cent.) We deliberately oversampled from them on a random basis as well as from colleges and universities that are independent of either state or religious control in order to assure an adequate sample of them for comparisons both in terms of the institutions' level of offering and type of control. The following table compares the resulting sample with the total population from which it was drawn:

201

Appendix B

LEVEL AND CONTROL OF INSTITUTIONS IN TOTAL POPULATION AND IN SAMPLE

Group	Type of Control (Per Cent)			
	Public Control	Inde-pendent Control	Religious Control	Total
Population (1,164):				
Four- and Five-Year Colleges	22.2	17.7	43.9	83.8
Doctoral-Level Institutions	8.8	4.7	2.7	16.2
Total Population	31.0	22.4	46.6	100.0
Sample (110):				
Four- and Five-Year Colleges	21.8	13.6	27.3	62.7
Doctoral-Level Institutions	14.5	12.7	10.0	37.3
Total Sample	36.4	26.4	37.3	100.0

To judge the representativeness of this sample, we compared the institutions in each of these six types within the sample with all of the institutions of this type, using several measures which seemed particularly relevant to this study and data from the ninth edition of *American Universities and Colleges* (Washington, D.C.: American Council on Education, 1964) which had been placed on computer tape for the College Data Bank of the Columbia University Bureau of Applied Social Research. The similarities and differences between the average scores of the sample and the population are shown on page 203. As a result, we concluded that our sample was sufficiently representative of the population to allow us to generalize from it.

Two biases of the sample did occur, however. More of the institutions that we selected are located in the eastern United States than is true of colleges and universities generally. Thirty-three per cent of the sample institutions are located in the northeastern states in comparison to 26 per cent nationally, while only 8 per cent of the sample are found in the mountain and Pacific states of the West, compared to 13 per cent of the institutions at large. Although this accidental under-representation of western institutions helped in reducing to some extent the telephone bills for the long-distance inter-

MEAN SCORES OF SAMPLE INSTITUTIONS AND POPULATION
ON SELECTED VARIABLES

Level and Type of Institution

Variable	Public Colleges	Independent Colleges	Religious Colleges	Public Universities	Independent Universities	Religious Universities	Total Institutions
Student Fees as a Per Cent of Total Educational and General Income, 1962							
Population:	17.3	51.9	44.3	15.3	34.4	42.4	37.5
Sample:	18.0	48.4	49.5	14.1	31.3	42.3	35.4
Per Cent of Students who Were Graduate Students, 1962							
Population:	11.7	10.7	14.2	16.7	30.8	24.7	15.3
Sample:	15.4	8.3	10.4	13.5	25.0	27.6	11.4
Per Cent of Undergraduates from Out of State, 1962							
Population:	9.2	48.8	33.9	16.8	48.6	38.9	30.0
Sample:	8.9	37.0	34.2	18.8	49.0	37.3	27.9
Ratio of Book Value Endowment to Total Current Income, 1962							
Population:	16.6	204.9	106.3	34.2	199.7	120.0	113.7
Sample:	27.7	140.9	73.4	12.4	191.0	144.9	100.8

views, if any systematic differences exist between eastern and western institutons in terms of academic reform, our results are slightly biased in the eastern direction. The second and hopefully inconsequential bias is an overabundance of institutions whose names begin with *W*. Eleven per cent of the colleges and universities in our sample happened to be so named, in comparison with 6 per cent in the nation at large.

To determine how much change had occurred in the curriculum of each of these 110 institutions between 1962 and 1967, we attempted to measure the amount of reform that had taken place in courses, the amount of replacement of major programs, and the amount of change that had been made in requirements and regulations. Here is what we looked for in each case:

Course Reform: To obtain a measure of course reform, we randomly selected four departments at each institution—one in the humanities, one in the behavioral sciences, one in the natural sciences, and one in the vocational fields such as education, business, or nursing—and determined a rate of course change for each of them. (A few institutions lack a department in a vocational field or in one of the science areas, and so we obtained 426 departments in all rather than 440 as originally planned.)

We tried to measure these changes, although with only partial adequacy, by comparing the description of each undergraduate course offered by the departments in 1962–63 and in 1967–68. That is, we attempted to determine how many courses had remained substantially unchanged during this five-year period and how many of them had been added, dropped, or substantively altered. To do so required considerable interpretation and judgment. The number of courses that were offered in the two years was not hard to count, but the changes in their content were more difficult to assess. Here, for example, is the description of a course that seems to us to be so different in content that we consider it a completely new course:

> 1962 PHILOSOPHY 201 *Introduction to Logic* 4 credits. Rules of valid deduction from premises and of methods of formulating valid generalizations from experience with emphasis on the methods of science.

1967 PHILOSOPHY 201 *Logic of Language* 4 credits.
A consideration of words, their combinations, functions, and malfunctions. Designed to have a practical
effect in improving communication of meanings.

But here are two descriptions of a course that we suspect was substantially the same in 1967 as in 1962, despite its different number
and slightly different wording:

1962 GEOGRAPHY 351 *Cartography* 5 credits. An introduction to map making. The course includes practical experience in map and chart construction as well
as study of the principles of grid representation, scale,
symbols, lettering, design, and reproduction.

1967 GEOGRAPHY 251 *Cartography* 4 credits. Practical
experience in map and chart construction; the principles of grid representation, scale, symbols, lettering, design, and reproduction.

To arrive at the rate of course reform for each department,
we measured the proportion of courses that had been dropped or
altered substantially in any department whose overall number of
courses increased between 1962 and 1967, and the number that had
been added or altered in any department whose number of courses
declined over those five years. In other words, the rate of course
reform is the proportion of courses that were dropped or changed
at departments that expanded their course offerings and the number that were added or changed at departments that cut back on
their number of courses. Course reform is thus not a measure of expansion or contraction in course offerings, but a measure of turnover in the content of the courses offered.

If anything, this measure tends to minimize the amount of
change in course content that actually occurs. As academicians
know from personal experience, catalog copy is not always a reliable reflection of reality. The difficulty lies not only in the subter-
fuge of some institutions that list unoffered courses, but in such
variables as the intransigence of some registrars and the poverty of
some printing and typesetting budgets (both of which tend to retain outdated copy) or the exuberance of a public-relations-minded

editor (which would indicate more change in the curriculum than really occurred.) That these factors affect the measure to some extent is evident from the fact that those institutions which scored high on reform of courses also appear by and large to have reorganized and rewritten their catalogs more often than the other institutions.

The reason we believe this particular measure tends to minimize the extent of change rather than exaggerate it is that we compared our conclusions from an analysis of catalog copy in fifty-two courses with the opinions of the instructors of these courses themselves. We asked them when the last major change had been made in the course from their point of view, and learned that our conclusions tended to indicate less change—not more—than they felt had occurred. Only in one course (an introductory sociology course at a state college) did we judge from the description that substantial change had occurred when the professor thought it had not, but in twelve of the fifty-two courses, the professors perceived more alteration than we. One of them, for instance, was using more textbooks than he had three years ago. Another, in a physical education course, was concentrating more on tennis than he had previously. And several of them reported that they had made small changes every year in the course. Despite these inadequacies of the measure, however, it does not appear to be an invalid indicator of course change: In three-fourths of the cases the professors and we agreed.

Replacement of Majors: We used the institutions' own criteria for what constitutes an undergraduate major program, and we measured the replacement of these programs in the same way that we calculated course reform. For example, if the college dropped two majors, such as secretarial science and rural sociology, but expanded its total number of programs, its replacement rate was the proportion that these two majors formed of all its programs in 1962. On the other hand, if a college cut back several majors, but opened only one new one—say, in communications—its rate of replacement is the proportion that this one new major is of the original programs.

Change in Requirements and Regulations: To obtain information on the other three measures of academic change, we compared the graduation requirements, the requirements for majoring in the departments, and the regulations regarding student life as stated by the institution, and scored each institution on a five-point scale ranging from *no change,* through *small, moderate,* and *major,* to *complete change.* As with the other measures, the scores assigned to these measures by the members of the institute staff were independently checked by another staff member. The scores tended to cluster at the lower end of the five-point scale; in the judgment of the staff, only the requirements for majoring changed enough on the average among the institutions during the five-year period to warrant a score of *1* or *small change.* The average scores for changes in graduation requirements and in student regulations lie between *0* and *1*—between *no change* at all and *small change.*

These five measures of academic change bear some relation to each other, as measured by a Pierson product-moment correlation. That is, an institution which scores high on one is likely to score somewhat high on another, as the following table indicates (the italicized figures indicate p < .01) :

CORRELATIONS AMONG FIVE MEASURES OF ACADEMIC CHANGE

	2. *Replacement of Major Programs*	3. *Change in Degree Requirements*
1. Reform of Course Offerings	*.348*	*.326*
2. Replacement of Major Programs		.180
3. Change in Degree Requirements		
4. Change in Majoring Requirements		

	4. *Change in Majoring Requirements*	5. *Change in Student Regulations*
1. Reform of Course Offerings	*.434*	.241
2. Replacement of Major Programs	.247	.200
3. Change in Degree Requirements	*.355*	*.342*
4. Change in Majoring Requirements		.180

Appendix B

The closest relationship of all among the five measures occurs between the average amount of course reform that has been made in four departments at an institution and the amount of change in the requirements for majoring in these departments. This is not surprising, since if departments change a number of their course offerings, they are probably likely to alter the requirements for majoring in the department, too.

But while the 110 colleges and universities tended to score either high on several of these measures or low on several—and thus some of them appeared to be in general more dynamic than others —it seems that academic change as we measured it is not a unitary phenomenon. Some colleges that had made dramatic reforms in areas such as their degree requirements did not alter other elements of their program greatly, even though the tendency was in the direction of doing so.

APPENDIX C

Telephone Interviews

To visit all 110 institutions that were studied for this project would have been prohibitively costly, yet facts and opinions were needed about the institutions from their members. The growing aversion of many people to the task of completing questionnaires led us to reject the possibility of a mail survey; and as a result, telephone interviewing proved an excellent compromise. Less expensive than face-to-face interviews and more flexible and revealing than questionnaires, phone interviews provided a balance between the personal contact of direct communication and the anonymity of distance. Since, to our knowledge, telephone interviewing had not previously been employed in this type of academic study, the procedures were somewhat novel and deserve description.[1] (For background on the use of telephone interviews in survey research generally, Chapter Five of Seymour Sudman's *Reducing the Cost of Surveys* [Chicago: Aldine Publishing Company, 1967] provides useful information).

At each institution we sought to interview an administrator (either the president in the case of the smaller institutions or the provost or vice-president for academic affairs in the case of the large universities), a department chairman from one of the four departments we had studied, and a professor of any rank from one of the other three departments. If we had started the study now, we would have included students; but in 1967 we could detect little overt student influence on most academic changes. Students were then still being advised of changes more than being consulted about them.

The three individuals at each institution received letters briefly describing the study and asking them to participate in it. They were asked to return a preaddressed postcard indicating the date and time they wished to be interviewed and the telephone number where they could be reached. Included with the letter was a list of the questions to be asked during the interviews. (A copy of the letter and sample of the list of questions follows.) No follow-up

---

[1] This description was prepared by Arthur Shriberg, who along with Robert Friis of the Institute staff organized the telephone interviewing for the Study of Institutional Vitality.

Telephone Interviews

letters were sent, although a few calls were made to assure adequate responses.

Teachers College • *Columbia University, New York, N.Y. 10027*

INSTITUTE OF HIGHER EDUCATION
STUDY OF INSTITUTIONAL VITALITY

Earl J. McGrath,
Director

JB Lon Hefferlin,
Associate Director

April 23, 1968

(Inside Address)

With the support of the Kettering Foundation, the Institute of Higher Education is studying the factors that contribute to the dynamism of institutions of higher education—to improvements in their curricula, to innovations in solving institutional problems, to the vitality of their operations. In this study we would like your observations and opinions.

Would you be willing to be interviewed over the telephone some day within the next month by one of our staff members? On the enclosed sheet I have listed the areas of information we would like to obtain from you. Your ideas, together with those from a number of presidents and other department chairmen and faculty, will help us learn more about two things: (1) the most important factors that contribute to institutional experimentation and innovation within American higher education, and (2) techniques that are effective in stimulating institutional self-renewal among colleges and universities.

Your ideas would be helpful to us in this study, and they will be used only for the study. They will be compiled, along with others, for our report to the Kettering Foundation and the academic community, but under no condition will they be identified as yours to anyone outside the Institute of Higher Education.

The telephone interview would take no more than twenty minutes of your time. You can indicate on the attached postcard the date and time you would like to be called, and unless you receive word from us you can expect to be called

211

then. (If you prefer to be interviewed at home in the evening, simply indicate that fact on the card.)

Since I believe this study will eventually benefit a number of colleges and universities, I hope you will be willing to be interviewed for it.

Sincerely,

JB Hefferlin, *Associate Director*
Study of Institutional Vitality

jbh/aa
encs.

The following list of questions was sent to each department chairman. A comparable list, containing several additional items and deleting several of these, was sent to the administrators and the professors.

STUDY OF INSTITUTIONAL VITALITY
INSTITUTE OF HIGHER EDUCATION

TEACHERS COLLEGE, COLUMBIA UNIVERSITY

Information Requested in Telephone Interview

(This list will be useful to have at hand during the interview.)

YOUR POSITION

Are you a graduate of your present institution?
How long have you taught at your institution?
What was your position before coming to the institution?
How long have you served as department chairman or department head?
Approximately how long did your predecessor serve as chairman?
At your institution, do department chairmen serve a set number of years or indefinitely?
How are department chairmen selected?
About how frequently at your institution are new department chairmen brought in from outside rather than being selected from inside the faculty?
    a. never
    b. less than a fourth of the time

c. about half the time
d. more than three-fourths of the time
e. always

OBSERVATIONS ABOUT THE ACADEMIC PROGRAM

1. We are particularly interested in the ways that *changes* come about in the educational programs of American colleges and universities. Where has the initiative come from for recent changes in the program of your institution?

2. Could you illustrate this with a particular example?
   2.1 What were the major reasons for this change?
   2.2 With what person or group did the idea originate?
   2.3 Who has taken the leadership or given it the most support?
   2.4 Who from outside the institution has been influential in the development?
   2.5 Was this change part of a larger reorganization or simply part of a continuous process of change?
   2.6 What have been the chief obstacles?
   2.7 Are these typically the major obstacles to academic change at your institution?

3. Where has the initiative come from for some other development at your institution?

FACTS ABOUT DECISION MAKING

4. If your department decided to offer several new courses and require students majoring in the department to take them, what steps would be involved in deciding whether or not to implement this idea? That is, what individuals or groups or committees would have to give their approval?
   4.1 Would the total faculty of the College vote on it?
   4.2 Would your governing board take any action on it?
   4.3 Of these individuals and groups, who would have the most influence, by and large?
   4.4 Of them, who would be involved only nominally or pro-forma?
   4.5 In the decision, what would your own role as department chairman typically be?
   4.6 What role would the dean and president ordinarily play?
   4.7 Has any such proposal been considered but tabled or rejected in the past several years?

5. If several professors proposed that a *new undergraduate major* should be offered at your institution, would the same steps be followed in deciding this issue?

6. From which of the following groups has the impetus for new undergraduate majors come in recent years at your institution?

213

Appendix C

a. the governing board	j. faculty-wide committees
b. president	k. the student body
c. dean/provost	l. alumni
d. other administrator	m. individual benefactors
e. department chairmen	n. the local community
f. senior faculty members	o. the constituency
g. junior faculty members	p. government agencies
h. the faculty in general	q. foundations
i. department committees	r. other ....

ATTITUDES TOWARD THE CURRICULUM

7. From your perspective, is too much attention being placed on "innovation" and experimentation in higher education to the neglect of established standards and programs?

8. Concerning the commitment of professors to their discipline on the one hand and to their institution on the other, would you say that most of the faculty at your institution consider themselves first of all as members of their *discipline* or as members of the *institution?*
   8.1 Do you generally approve of or encourage this attitude?

9. Among the faculty, is there greater interest in offering *prescribed programs* of study or in *allowing students latitude* to elect most of their courses?
   9.1 What is your own personal attitude on this issue?

10. Among the faculty, is there greater interest in doing a better job with the *present* program or in creating *new* programs and moving into new areas of activity?
    10.1 What is your own personal attitude on this issue?

11. How much support for your work and interests do you feel that you and your colleagues receive at your institution?

    1. none   2. little   3. some   4. much
    5. a great deal

12. Do you believe that students should have a role in curricular policy decisions?
    12.1 By and large, would your fellow department chairmen tend to agree with you on this issue?
    12.2 What influence, if any, do students *now* have on curricular decisions at your institution?

    1. none   2. little   3. some   4. much   5. most
    6. all or almost all

13. Do you believe that trustees should have a role in curricular policy decisions?
    13.1 And by and large, would your fellow department chairman tend to agree with you on *this* issue?
    13.2 What influence, if any, do trustees *now* have on curricular decisions?

1. none   2. little   3. some   4. much   5. most
6. all or almost all

13.3   Are they generally an influence for stability or for change?
14. Does your institution have a Curriculum Committee or an Educational Policies Committee that deals with academic policy?
    14.1   If so, approximately what proportion of its members are department chairmen?
    14.2   In your opinion, does it serve a very important role in curricular changes?
    14.3   And is it generally an influence for stability or change?

PERSONNEL SELECTION AND BUDGET PREPARATION

15. Who takes *primary* responsibility at your institution for recruiting new faculty members?

16. Who also *assists* in faculty recruitment?

17. Is it usually possible to bring a prospective faculty member to the campus, or are a good many new faculty members hired without a visit?

18. Who makes the decision about appointing a new faculty member?

19. In the past several years, have you sensed that your institution has had a bigger problem in recruiting the best *faculty members* or in recruiting the best *students?*

20. What is your institution's policy regarding the number of years that faculty members serve before being granted tenure?

21. What practice does your institution follow regarding faculty sabbaticals?

22. How are travel funds awarded to faculty members to attend professional meetings?

23. Do you prepare a departmental budget?

24. If so, to whom do you submit the budget for review and decision?

25. Can you transfer funds from one category of the budget to another during the year to finance a new course or a new teaching technique?

TEACHING EXPECTATIONS

26. If a professor at your institution cannot meet his class as scheduled, is he usually expected to notify the department chairman or someone else of this fact?

27. Are faculty members expected to take attendance of students?

28. And are faculty members generally expected to give mid-term and final examinations in their courses?

29. How much of a voice do the faculty members in most departments have in the decision on who is appointed to the department or who receives a promotion?

1. none   2. little   3. some   4. much   5. most
6. all or almost all

215

Appendix C

30. Some colleges limit new faculty members or untenured faculty members from serving on faculty committees or participating in policy decisions. Are new or untenured faculty members at your institution limited in these ways, or do they participate just like senior faculty members?

31. At your institution, do professors such as you have any regular contact with members of the governing board, such as at annual dinners or on joint committees, or are the only contacts with the governing board through the president?

32. Does it seem to you that most of the faculty members at your institution plan to make it their career home, or do most expect that eventually they might move on to another institution?

INFLUENCE AT YOUR INSTITUTION

33. Among outsiders to your institution, who tends to exert the most influence on your academic program?
    33.1   Are they generally a force for stability or for change?

34. Among insiders, who are the most influential people in terms of the academic program?
    34.1   And are they generally a force for stability or for change?

35. How much influence does each of these persons or groups have in determining educational policy?

	Great deal	Some	Very little	None
a. the governing board	4	3	2	1
b. administrators	4	3	2	1
c. department chairmen	4	3	2	1
d. other senior faculty members	4	3	2	1
e. junior faculty members	4	3	2	1
f. faculty coalitions and blocs	4	3	2	1
g. the faculty in general	4	3	2	1
h. particular faculty committees	4	3	2	1
i. departments	4	3	2	1
j. the student body	4	3	2	1
k. alumni	4	3	2	1
l. the local community	4	3	2	1
m. the institution's constituency	4	3	2	1
n. funding agencies	4	3	2	1
o. you, personally	4	3	2	1

36. Which of these attitudes best describes the most influential people at your institution concerning educational policy?
    a. "change for change's sake"
    b. willing to lead and support experimental educational ventures
    c. not hostile to innovation, but unwilling to get involved personally
    d. "nothing new must be tried for the first time"
    e. "if it is not *necessary* to change, it is necessary *not* to change"

37. Finally, if there is some particular person at your institution who seems to you to be especially interested in the educational program and its improvement, could we have his name? (We would enjoy calling him eventually for his observations.)

Thank you!

Note: The individuals mentioned in response to the final question, number 37, have not been contacted for the purposes of this report.

Responses: Perhaps not surprisingly, the administrators were more willing to be interviewed than the faculty members: 83 per cent of them participated, in contrast to only 67 per cent of the department chairmen and 63 per cent of the professors. Although we did not explore the reasons for this difference in response rates, several factors may have played a part: the interviews were conducted in late April and May of 1968, when faculty members were increasinigly busy with end-of-year course work. And some professors may have been more concerned than presidents and provosts about the anonymity of their responses, less sure about the utility of such a study, or possibly less concerned about the institution-wide problems of academic reform.

The tolerance of faculty members for participating in such a survey seems to have influenced the responses, as evidenced from the fact that 75 per cent of the social scientists participated in comparison with 55 per cent of the faculty members in the natural sciences, while members of humanities and vocational fields fell between these two extremes. One other factor probably played some role: the national publicity in April and May of 1968 about the disturbances at Columbia University—our own institution. The president of a college in the Mississippi valley thought us presumptuous to be inquiring about academic reform at his institution when we had problems of our own at home. "My only comment, therefore," he informed us, "is 'Physician, heal thyself.' "

In terms of institutional representation, both administrators and faculty members at the universities generally responded more frequently than those in the colleges, as the following table illustrates.

217

Appendix C

RATE OF PARTICIPATION IN TELEPHONE INTERVIEWS BY POSITION
OF RESPONDENTS AND BY TYPE OF INSTITUTION

	Position of Respondent		
	Adminis- trators (*110* *possible*)	Department Chairmen and Professors (*220* *possible*)	Total (*330* *possible*)
Type of Institution			
All Four- and Five-Year Colleges (69)	78.3	60.9	66.7
Public Colleges (24)	70.8	60.4	63.8
Independent Colleges (15)	86.6	56.6	66.6
Religious Colleges (30)	80.0	63.3	68.8
All Doctoral-Level Institutions (41)	90.2	72.0	78.0
Public Universities (16)	81.2	71.8	75.0
Independent Universities (14)	100.0	71.4	80.9
Religious Universities (11)	90.0	72.7	78.8
Average (110)	82.7	65.0	70.9

Thus in terms of likely biases in the responses, our respondents are weighted in favor of administrators and of the universities. They are particularly under-representative of chairmen and professors in the natural sciences. And from the evidence of typical survey experience, it seems likely that our respondents are probably somewhat more interested in the issues of academic change about which we asked them than were the administrators and faculty members who did not wish to participate.

Interviewing: Graduate students at Teachers College served as interviewers on the staff of the Institute of Higher Education. Each of the interviewers conducted a minimum of three practice interviews before interviewing the respondents. Using a pre-coded

218

copy of the interview schedule, the interviewer placed the call at the designated time, answered any questions the respondent might have concerning the study, and then proceeded with the structured interview, jotting down answers to open-ended questions and occasionally having to press for a codable response to a forced-choice question. After the interview, the staff member immediately tape-recorded as accurately as possible any particularly pertinent comments, completed the coding of the interview schedule, and then sent a note of thanks to the respondent.

Time estimates for the interviews proved conservative: although practice interviews lasted fifteen to twenty minutes, actual interviews averaged a half-hour and some extended up to an hour. As a result, the staff concluded that in future telephone surveys the interviews might better be scheduled during the evening when the respondents were at home. Not only would the long-distance rates be lower, but fewer interruptions might occur than took place in the faculty members' often crowded offices. In addition, the respondents whom we interviewed at home—approximately 10 per cent of the total—seemed to be somewhat more relaxed and involved in responding.

One other change might well have been made in procedure. The staff decided not to tape the interviews directly since we feared that the "beep" required by law and the awareness of being recorded would inhibit responses. In retrospect we believe that little would have been lost by requesting permission to record the conversation, since most of the respondents were uninhibited in their opinions, and much would have been gained in preserving a complete record of the conversation.

Perceived Originators of Change: Chapter Four reports the responses to some of the questions asked during the interviews. Each of the respondents was asked to describe a recent change in the program of his institution and then was asked, "With what group or person did the idea originate?" The following table lists the responses to this question for five different types of change and for each of the three groups of respondents—administrators, department chairmen, and professors.

GROUPS PERCEIVED AS ORIGINATING VARIOUS CURRICULAR CHANGES

	Originator							Total Responses	
Respondent	Adminis-trators	Depart-ment Chairmen	Pro-fessors	Commit-tees	Students	Trustees	Out-siders	Number	Per Cent
1. Change in a Course or the Addition of a Course									
Administrators	2	2	0	1	1	0	0	6	9.0
Department Chairmen	5	11	14	6	1	1	2	40	59.7
Professors	2	4	9	1	3	0	2	21	31.3
Total Respondents	9	17	23	8	5	1	4	67	100.0
Per Cent of Responses	13.4	25.5	34.4	11.9	7.4	1.5	5.9	100.0	
2. Addition of a Major Program of Study									
Administrators	47	22	37	1	7	2	10	126	75.9
Department Chairmen	8	6	7	2	0	0	1	24	14.5
Professors	2	5	9	0	0	0	0	16	9.6
Total Respondents	57	33	53	3	7	2	11	166	100.0
Per Cent of Responses	34.4	19.9	31.9	1.8	4.2	1.2	6.6	100.0	

3. Change in Graduation Requirements or Curricular Organization

								Total Respondents	Per Cent of Responses
Administrators	11	0	4	0	2	0	0	17	44.7
Department Chairmen	3	2	2	1	1	0	1	10	26.3
Professors	5	0	2	2	1	0	1	11	29.0
Total Respondents	19	2	8	3	4	0	2	38	100.0
Per Cent of Responses	50.0	5.3	21.0	7.9	10.5	0.0	5.3	100.0	

4. Addition of a New Unit to the Institution

								Total Respondents	Per Cent of Responses
Administrators	9	1	3	1	0	0	2	16	53.3
Department Chairmen	5	2	1	0	1	0	0	9	30.0
Professors	3	0	2	0	0	0	0	5	16.7
Total Respondents	17	3	6	1	1	0	2	30	100.0
Per Cent of Responses	56.7	10.0	20.0	3.3	3.3	0.0	6.7	100.0	

5. Change in the Institution's Status

								Total Respondents	Per Cent of Responses
Administrators	4	1	0	0	0	1	3	9	50.0
Department Chairmen	2	0	0	0	0	2	1	5	27.8
Professors	2	0	0	0	0	2	0	4	22.2
Total Respondents	8	1	0	0	0	5	4	18	100.0
Per Cent of Responses	44.4	5.6	0.0	0.0	0.0	27.8	22.2	100.0	

APPENDIX D

Variables Employed in Analysis

For the correlation analysis described in Chapter Five, information on the predictor variables was collected from several sources. Financial data came from *American Universities and Colleges* of the American Council on Education, salary information from the annual surveys of the American Association of University Professors, enrollment statistics from those of the United States Office of Education, facts on federal funding from publications of the National Science Foundation, information on institutional selectivity and status from the accumulated computer tapes of the College Data Bank of Columbia's Bureau of Applied Social Research, and facts and opinions about institutional procedures from individuals at the institutions themselves by means of telephone interviews with administrators, department chairmen, and professors. In the following list of predictor variables, the variables that are identified as "perceived" were obtained from these interviews.

PREDICTOR VARIABLES USED IN TESTING HYPOTHESIS REGARDING ACADEMIC CHANGE

Environmental Variables	*Number of Institutions*	*Mean*
Clientele		
Level of Program (Bachelor's, Master's, or Doctoral Degree)	110	*Master's*
Total Enrollment, Autumn, 1961	108	4,091
Total Undergraduate and First Professional Enrollment, Autumn, 1961	108	3,313
Full-time Undergraduate Enrollment as Per Cent of Total Full-time Enrollment, Autumn, 1961	108	96.0
Per Cent of Students who are Graduate Students, 1962	67	11.4
Per Cent of Undergraduates from Out of State, 1962	77	27.9
Selectivity of the Institution (1 to 5: unselective to most selective)	105	1.9

Appendix D

PREDICTOR VARIABLES USED IN TESTING HYPOTHESIS REGARDING ACADEMIC CHANGE

Environmental Variables	Number of Institu- tions	Mean
Frequency of Selection by Able Students (Score based on the National Merit Scholarship finalists seeking enrollment to the number of freshmen admitted—a normalized score with the average college nationally scoring 50, and more frequently chosen colleges scoring higher)	105	45.7

Financial Condition

Per Cent of Income Stemming from Major Source of Income	97	51.4
Per Cent of Income Stemming from Federal Funds, 1962–1963	72	15.0
Student Fees as a Per Cent of Total Current Income, 1962	101	35.4
Ratio of Book Value Endowment to Total Current Income, 1962	81	100.8
Cost of Tuition, Board and Room, 1962 ..	86	$1,217
Total Educational and General Income per Student, 1962 (decile rank)	85	5.9
Scholarship Funds as Per Cent of Total Educational and General Income	101	4.3
Per Cent of Undergraduates on Scholarship, 1962	69	27.2
AAUP Rating of Average Salary Scale, 1962-63	65	C–
AAUP Rating of Minimum Salary Scale, 1962–63	63	C–

Location

Population of City or Town in which College is Located, 1960	94	215,400
Distance from Nearest City over 50,000 ...	100	38 miles

Faculty Background

Per Cent of Inbred or Home-Grown Professors, 1962	92	22.8

Variables Employed in Analysis

Environmental Variables	Number of Institutions	Mean
Proportion of Faculty Trained at Local Graduate Schools (Per Cent)	109	50.9
National Prominence of Graduate Schools from which Professors Graduated (six-point scale, 0 to 5: not prominent to most prominent)	109	2.7
Similarity Between the Institution and Type of Institution from which Professors Graduated (ten-point scale, 0 to 9: alike to dissimilar in type)	110	4.8
Per Cent of Visiting Professors at the Institution, 1962–63	101	1.5
Frequency of Appointing Department Chairmen Directly from Outside (Per Cent)..	96	34.9
Proportion of Doctorates per Faculty (decile rank nationally)	91	5.7

Comparative Standing

Academic Status of Institution as determined by its Decile Rank Nationally on Size of Library, Library Books per Student, Educational and General Income per Student, Faculty-Student Ratio, and Doctorates per Faculty (possible scores range from zero to 50)	105	29.6
Academic Progressiveness, 1961: Score on number of educational innovations adopted by the institution, zero (none) to 16 (all)	104	2.1
Change in Score on Academic Progressiveness Between 1961 and 1967	104	2.1

Environmental Pressure

Perceived Orientation of Trustees. Six-point scale: 1 (oriented to the status quo) to 6 (oriented toward change in the curriculum)	101	2.2
Perceived Orientation of the Most Influential Outsiders at the Institution. Five-		

225

Appendix D

PREDICTOR VARIABLES USED IN TESTING HYPOTHESIS
REGARDING ACADEMIC CHANGE

Environmental Variables	*Number of Institutions*	*Mean*
point scale, 1 (oriented to the status quo) to 5 (oriented to change in the academic program)	103	3.5
Perceived Amount of Influence of Various External Groups in Determining Educational Policy. Seven-point scale, with 1 indicating no influence and 7 indicating a great deal of influence.		
Governing Board	103	3.5
Alumni	103	2.3
Local Community	103	2.1
The Institution's Constituency	103	3.2
Funding Agencies	103	3.3
Perceived Problem in Recruiting the Best Faculty versus the Best Students. Five-point scale, with 1 representing a concern for recruiting faculty and 5 representing a concern for recruiting students	98	2.4

Organizational Variables

Changes in Size

	Number of Institutions	*Mean*
Per Cent of Change in the Number of Major Programs Offered by the Institution Between 1962 and 1967 for Undergraduates	110	21.4
Per Cent of Change in the Number of Courses Offered by Selected Departments Between 1962 and 1967 primarily for Undergraduates	110	45.5
Per Cent of Expansion in the Number of Major Programs Offered by the Institution for Undergraduates Between 1962 and 1967	110	18.6
Per Cent of Expansion in the Number of Courses Offered by Selected Departments primarily for Undergraduates Between 1962 and 1967	110	26.6

226

Variables Employed in Analysis

Environmental Variables	Number of Institutions	Mean
Per Cent of Expansion in the Number of Professors in Selected Departments Between 1962 and 1967	110	46.2
Per Cent of Expansion in Total Enrollment Between 1961 and 1966	108	48.3
Per Cent of Expansion in Total Undergraduate Enrollment, 1961 to 1967	108	50.5
Per Cent of Expansion in Total Full-time Undergraduate Enrollment Between 1961 and 1967	108	56.2
Per Cent of Expansion in Total Full-time Enrollment, 1961 to 1967	108	68.4

Turnover of Personnel

Per Cent of Change in Presidents Between 1962 and 1967	110	39.1
Length of Tenure of Current President, as of 1968	110	4½ years
Per Cent of Change of Chairmen in Selected Departments, 1962 to 1967	95	56.4
Per Cent of Faculty Turnover in Selected Departments, 1962 to 1967	108	31.7
Per Cent of Change in the Membership of the Governing Board, 1962 to 1967	109	52.9
Term of Office of Department Chairmen, according to the President	98	unlimited
Tendency of Department Chairmen to Serve in Office until Retirement	89	no
Proportion of Faculty Holding Tenure, 1968, according to the President	97	40.5

Perceived Participation of Members in Educational Decisions

Total Faculty of the College Votes on the Addition of New Courses	103	not usual
Governing Board Votes on the Addition of New Courses	103	no
Perceived Number of Hurdles in Adding a Course to the Curriculum	103	1.8
Perceived Number of Hurdles in Adding a Major Program to the Curriculum	103	2.7

Appendix D

PREDICTOR VARIABLES USED IN TESTED HYPOTHESIS REGARDING ACADEMIC CHANGE

Environmental Variables	Number of Institutions	Mean
Perceived Amount of Influence in Determining Educational Policy of Various Internal Groups. Seven-point scale, with 1 indicating no influence and 7 indicating a great deal of influence.		
Administrators	103	6.3
Department Chairmen	103	6.2
Other Senior Faculty	103	5.5
Junior Faculty	103	4.6
Faculty Coalitions and Blocs	103	3.8
The Faculty in General	103	5.2
Particular Faculty Committees	103	5.6
Departments	103	5.6
Students	103	3.4
Perceived Amount of Student Influence on Curricular Decisions. Nine-point scale, with 1 indicating no influence and 9 indicating a great deal of influence	103	4.0
Perceived Importance of Curriculum Committee in Curriculum Development. Nine-point scale, with 1 indicating no important role and 9 indicating an all-important role	103	6.1
Department Chairmen Selected by Appointment or Election	98	appointed
Proportion of Curriculum Committee Consisting of Department Chairmen	91	43.4
Perceived Amount of Faculty Voice in Promotion Decisions. Nine-point scale, with 1 indicating no voice and 9 indicating much voice	89	4.6
Perceived Limitations on Junior Faculty from Participating in Policy Decisions. Five-point scale, with 1 representing great limitations and 5 representing no limitations	88	3.9

228

Variables Employed in Analysis

Environmental Variables	Number of Institutions	Mean
Perceived Extent of Faculty Contacts with the Governing Board. Five-point scale, with 1 meaning regular contacts and 5 meaning none	89	3.7

Attitudes Toward Participation and Education

Respondents' Attitude toward Student Participation in Curricular Policy Decisions. Nine-point scale, with 1 favorable and 9 opposed	103	3.4
Respondents' Attitude toward Trustee Participation in Curricular Policy Decisions. Nine-point scale, with 1 favorable and 9 opposed	103	6.5
Respondents' Attitude toward Academic Innovation. Six-point scale, with 1 unfavorably disposed and 6 favorably disposed	103	5.0
Respondents' Perception of the Faculty's Orientation toward their Discipline or toward the Institution. Six-point scale, with 1 indicating an orientation toward the discipline and 6, institution	103	3.0
Respondents' Perception of Faculty Attitude toward Prescription or Election of Courses. Six-point scale, with 1 favoring prescribed curriculum and 6 favoring elective programs	103	3.3
Respondents' Perception of Faculty Satisfaction with the Present Program. Six-point scale, with 1 satisfied and 6 dissatisfied	103	2.8
Perceived Orientation of the Most Influential Members of the Institution. Five-point scale, with 1 indicating an orientation toward the status quo and 5, toward change in the academic program	103	3.4

Expectations Regarding Faculty Responsibilities. Five-point scale, with 1 indicat-

229

Appendix D

PREDICTOR VARIABLES USED IN TESTED HYPOTHESIS REGARDING ACADEMIC CHANGE

Environmental Variables	Number of Institutions	Mean
ing the expectation and 5 indicating no expectation.		
Faculty Members are Expected to Notify a Superior of their Absence	89	1.6
Faculty Members are Expected to Take Attendance of Students	89	3.1
Faculty Members are Expected to Give Examinations in Classes	89	2.1
Degree of Faculty Role Specification, based on above expectations. Ten-point scale, with 1 representing highest possible specification and 10 representing the lowest possible specification	89	2.9
Perceived Orientation of the Curriculum Committee. Six-point scale, with 1 indicating an orientation toward the status quo and 6, toward change in the educational program	84	3.5

While much of the published material was concurrent with the period 1962–67 which we were analyzing, we had to rely on a good deal of post hoc information from the telephone interviewees, where we were limited to their retrospective impressions and opinions as of 1968. Thus, for example, if the respondents at a college reported that until 1966 department chairmen in their institution had served indefinite terms of office as chairmen, but now had begun serving three-year terms, we used the information relevant to the earlier period. But inevitably this method of reconstructing the past contains errors, and so our data are not as reliable and accurate as we wish they were.

The greatest unreliability may lie not in these post hoc data, or even in the catalog material that we used for much of our data, but simply in the different perceptions that individuals have of conditions and standard operating procedures at their own institutions. In our interviews, we attempted to ask the same factual questions of at least two members of each institution to check this information; yet the disagreements among many of them over seemingly empirical information were far more common than we had believed possible.

We had been prepared to find wide differences of opinion among our respondents about issues and events, but since our results are only as reliable as the data on which they stand, we were unnerved by the discrepancies that we found about facts, particularly on three items. The first was the term of office of a department chairman, which would appear to be a purely factual item. Yet when we asked both presidents and department chairmen this question, "Do department chairmen serve for a set number of years or indefinitely as chairmen?" we found that at ten of the institutions, the administrator and chairman disagreed. Eight of the chairmen, interestingly enough, claimed that they served indefinitely, while the presidents said that chairmen served terms of from two to six years. Even more strange, at the two other institutions the chairmen said that they each served three-year terms, while the presidents claimed that chairmen served indefinitely. These discrepancies may stem from different interpretations of a tradition of reappointing chairmen on the expiration of their terms; but on this question, we avoided the discrepancy by accepting the administrators' interpretation.

At thirteen of the institutions, the chairmen we interviewed disagreed with the professors about whether or not a professor was supposed to notify the chairman if for some reason he could not meet his class as scheduled. In some of the cases, the differences probably stemmed from different policies among the departments at these institutions, since in each case the professors and chairmen were selected from separate disciplines. But in every case, the thirteen chairmen expected to be notified, while the professors claimed it was unnecessary or only expected in some circumstances. Here we felt we should follow the opinions of the professors, since we were particularly interested in their own perceptions of their duties. This

231

discrepancy, incidentally, appears to illustrate one tendency of organizational life: that subordinates look upon norms which subjugate them to be less important than superiors do.

The greatest amount of disagreement occurs among perceptions of the number of decision points or hurdles involved in making a curricular change. We asked this question:

> If your department decided to offer several new courses and require students majoring in the department to take them, what steps would be involved at your institution in deciding whether or not to implement this idea? That is, what individuals or groups or committees would have to give their approval?

At over 40 per cent of the institutions, some people reported the number of steps to be at least two or more in number than did others. For example, a university president reported that only one step would be involved at his institution: "The college council would take action—nothing more." The chairman of the theology department said it would involve at least four steps: the departmental curriculum committee, the curriculum committees of the university's two liberal arts colleges, the deans of the colleges, and then the college councils. And a professor of physics saw none. He averred that if the faculty of a department submitted the proposal to the dean of the college, it would be automatically approved. Although these three responses showed a particularly wide discrepancy, the extent of others almost as varied led us to treat this information gingerly in our thinking and place little faith on it in our analyses.

Index

A

AAUP: on academic professionalization, 15n; on election of department chairmen, 180; on role of administrators, 182–183

Abstraction, trend to, 62–63

Academic change (*see* Academic reform)

"Academic" focus of departments, 60–63

Academic reform: academicians' role in, 75–104; and adaptability, 4; agents of, 40–49, 73–104, 146–151; causes, 32–49, 109, 130, 189; causes as perceived by academics, 77–81; characteristics contributing to, 32–49, 154–187; conclusions about, 140–189; correlates of, 105–135; correlation among measures of, 207–208; creation of new structures, 2–3, 22–23; described, 51–72; dynamics of, 17–32; history of, 2, 4, 23–32; hypothesis about sources of, 107; influence of external environment, 32–40, 142–152; influence of faculty shortage, 147; influence of institutional autonomy, 146–150; influence of market pressures, 154–

Index

156; influence of students, 131–132; measures of, 52, 204–208; need to understand, 9; obstacles to, 99–104; patterns of, 22–32; problem of, 2–16; processes of, 17–49; sources of, 105–190; synthesis of knowledge, 31–32; techniques of, 22, 24–31, 53; techniques of measuring sources of, 108–109; transformation of existing institutions, 22, 23–24; trends, 71–72

Academic self-interest, 150–151

Accretion and attrition in the curriculum, 24–31, 53, 188–189; examples, 58–59

Adaptability and academic reform, 4

Administrators as initiators of change, 75–77, 79, 87–104; influence of, 182

Advocacy, need for, 20–22, 40–44, 141

Agassiz, Louis, 41

Angell, James Rowland, 137, 139, 183

Antioch College, 23–24, 40, 43, 155, 185

Ashby, Eric, 151n

Attitudes: change of, 46–47; influence of, 132–133, 165

Attrition of knowledge in the curriculum, 24–31, 53, 188–189

Autocracy, 22, 166–167

Autonomy of institutions, 149–150

"Available Jones" colleges, 108

Avuncular institutions, 177–187

Avuncularity defined, 178–179

Aydelotte, Frank, 43

B

Babbidge, Homer D., 7, 151n, 192

Baker, George P., 22

Barber, Bernard, 44–45

Barnard, Henry, 30, 42

Barr, Stringfellow, 24

Barzun, Jacques, 5

Bell, Daniel, 68

Ben-David, Joseph, 145, 193

Bennington College, 23, 40

Bennis, Warren, 9

Beverly, R. M., 12

Black Mountain College, 155

Blau, Peter M., 149n, 192, 193, 197

Bloom, Benjamin, 12

Brandeis University, 26

Brewster, Kingman, 15n

Brick, Michael, 124n

Brickell, Henry M., 195

Brown University, 23, 33

Bryce, Lord James, 186

Buchanan, Scott, 24

Burgess, J. W., 42

Butler, Nicholas Murray, 30

Butterfield, Victor, 48, 183

Butts, Freeman, 35n

Byrnes, Robert F., 34–35

C

California, University of (Berkeley), 2, 32, 156, 168

Cambridge, University of, 146, 150, 186

Canadian universities, 148

Capen, Samuel P., 4

Caplow, Theodore, 151n

Carter, C. F., 198

Catholic colleges, 55, 143, 193

Centralization of power, 166–169

Change (see Organizational change; Academic reform)

Change Magazine, 159, 199

Charters, W. W., 159, 184

Chicago, University of, 22

Chronicle of Higher Education, 199

Clark, Burton R., 3n, 11n, 24n, 192

Clark, Terry, 41, 193

Cohen, I. Bernard, 149–150n

College programs, 63–67; requirements for majoring, 70

Index

Colleges and universities, differences among types: in academic reform, 125–126; in course reform, 56, 58; in faculty influence, 94–96; group studied, 52, 201–204 (see also Higher education)

Collegiality, definition, 174–175

Collegium orientation, 175–177

Columbia University: curricular changes, 27–28, 30, 42–43; general education, 68

COMMAGER, HENRY STEELE, 50

Community colleges (see also Junior colleges), 23

Conclusions from study, 39–40, 140–189

Conservatism of academic institutions, 13, 102

Consultants, 183–185

COOMBS, PHILIP H., 195

Cornell University, 35

CORNFORD, F. M., 14

CORSON, JOHN, 183, 192

"Cottage industry" colleges, 14

Course change: accretion, 24–25, 58–59; by areas of knowledge, 55–57, 60; correlates of, 111–118; dominant trend in, 63; by level and type of institution, 58; as measure of academic reform, 52, 54–63, 204–206; perceived initiators of, 79–84; rate of, 54–58

COWLEY, W. H., 35n, 103n, 192–193

Crisis, reform through, 2–4

CRONBACH, LEE J., 5n

Curricular change (see Academic reform)

Curriculum: changed by accretion, attrition, and synthesis, 27–32, 58–59; percolation of knowledge in, 28–30, 59–60; recent trends in, 64–70

D

DAHRENDORF, RALF, 151n

Danforth Foundation, 159

DAVIS, RICHARD H., 193–194

DAY, EDMUND, 39

Degree requirements, change in, 52, 54, 67–69, 206–208; correlates of, 120–123; initiative for, 87–90

DeLISLE, FRANCES H., 5n, 72n

DEMERATH, NICHOLAS J., 174n

Denominational support for higher education, 35

Department chairmen: importance in academic reform, 112–114; influence of, 132; initiative for change, 75–76, 84, 87, 94, 96; selection of, 180; tenure of, 170, 171–172

Departments: contrast between static and dynamic, 112–116; increasing "academic" focus of, 60–63

Disciplines: comparison regarding course reform, 55–56; comparison regarding changes in majors, 64, 87; history of origins, 36–39

Discretionary funds, 179–181

Doctoral-level institutions (see Universities; Higher education)

DRESSEL, PAUL L., 5n, 72n

Dynamic departments vs. static, 112–116

Dynamic institutions vs. static, 123–130

E

EBERLE, AUGUST, 173n

Economics, 36–37

Efficiency, 15–16

Electives, 29–30

ELIOT, CHARLES W., 30, 42, 47

ENGLE, PAUL, 47

Environmental influence: impor-

Index

tance of, 39–40, 131, 142–
146, 149–150, 154–156, 182;
local vs. national, 155
Equalitarian organizations, 21–22
ERSKINE, JOHN, 21
ETZIONI, AMITAI, 14, 197
EURICH, ALVIN, 7–8
EVANS, RICHARD I., 77, 194
Expansion of programs (*see* Accretion)
External influence (*see* Environmental influence)
Extracurriculum, changes in, 51

F

Faculty: as initiators of reform, 79,
82, 84–85, 87, 94, 96, 99–
101, 102–104; perceived initiative for change, 75–77;
power of, 10; shortage of, 147
Fads in higher education, 5, 156–
157
Fields of knowledge (*see* Disciplines)
FISHMAN, JOSHUA, 26
Foundation support for higher education, 37–38
Fragmentation, vertical, 13–14
France, university reform in, 4
FRANK, GLENN, 43
Free universities, 30
FRIIS, ROBERT, 210n

G

GARDNER, JOHN W., 1, 8–9, 196
General education: at Harvard, 176;
in secondary schools, 6, 59;
trends in higher education,
67–69
Georgia, University of, 155
GERARD, RALPH W., 193
German universities, 151n, 186
GIBBON, EDWARD, 146
GILMAN, DANIEL COIT, 20, 22, 23,
47
GOODMAN, PAUL, 21, 27

GOULDNER, ALVIN W., 18
GRAMBSCH, PAUL V., 72n
GREEDWOOD, ISAAC, 42
GREELEY, ANDREW M., 163, 193
GROPIUS, WALTER, 47
GROSS, EDWARD, 72n
GUEST, ROBERT, 198
GUETZKOW, HAROLD, 26, 38
GUSFIELD, JOSEPH, 41

H

HALL, G. STANLEY, 43
HAMILTON, WILLIAM, 136
Hampshire College, 23
HANUS, PAUL, 30
HARCLEROAD, FRED F., 147n
HARKNESS, EDWARD S., 137–138,
143
HARPER, WILLIAM RAINEY, 20
Harvard University: electives, 29,
30; general education, 176;
origins of house plan, 137–
139; role of Board of Overseers, 185–186n
HAWKES, HERBERT, 20
HAYDEN, TOM, 21
Hierarchical organizations, 21–22
Higher education: conservatism of,
13; denominational support
for, 35; distinctive problems
of reform in, 13–16; effectiveness of, 3; efficiency in, 15–
16; fads in, 5, 156–157; foundation support for, 37–38;
general education in, 67–69;
goals of, 71–72; innovation
in, 5, 9, 124n, 137–139, 156;
new clientele for, 23; new
models of, 22–23, 156–157;
new units in, 90–92; quality
not studied, 153; reputation
in, 14; self-interest in, 150–
151; self-selection for, 14–15;
sellers' market in, 146–147;
structuring, 16, 141–142; ver-

Index

tical fragmentation in, 13–14; vested interests in, 12, 150
History, first professor of, 36
HODGSON, RICHARD C., 178n
House plan at Harvard, 137–139
HUGHES, EVERETT, 108, 173
HUTCHINS, ROBERT M., 11–12, 21, 164

I

Illinois Industrial University, 22
Impediments to change (see Obstacles to change)
Inertia in institutions, 6–9, 10–12, 144–146
INGHAM, R. J., 192
Initiative for change, 40–49, 75–79, 141
Innovation in higher education: criticism of, 5; example, 137–138; introduction of, 29; measure of, 124n; sources of support for, 32–40, 156, 189; study of, 124n
Instability of institutions, 107, 135, 163–164
Institutional autonomy, 149–150
Institutional inertia, 6–9, 10–12, 144–146
Institutionalization of organizations, 11–12
Institutional openness, 163, 178
Institutional status, changes in, 92–94
Institutions (see Colleges and universities; Organizations)
Interviews used in study, 74–75, 209–219
Iowa, University of, 47
Isomorphism in higher education, 61

J

JAMES, WILLIAM, 42
JEFFERSON, THOMAS, 4, 20, 22, 23
JENCKS, CHRISTOPHER, 176
Johns Hopkins University, 22, 23, 26, 35, 43, 47

Joliet Junior College, 23
Junior colleges included in sample, 53; course reform in, 56; programs at, 63, 66
JUSSERAND, J. J., 20

K

KERR, CLARK, 151n
KETTERING, CHARLES, 43
Knowledge, percolation of, 28–30, 59–60
KRATHWOHL, DAVID R., 12
KRISTOL, IRVING, 6, 151n

L

LAND, EDWIN, 26, 39
LANGDELL, CHRISTOPHER COLUMBUS, 47
LASKI, HAROLD, 143
Latitudinarian institutions, 164, 168
Lawrence Scientific School, 36
LAZARSFELD, PAUL, 47, 159n
Leadership of change, 79–94
LEWIN, KURT, 13
LEWIS, WILMARTH S., 187
LEWISON, DANIEL J., 178n
Liberal arts college majors, 64–65
Linguistics, 38
LOWELL, A. LAWRENCE, 17, 137–138, 185–186n

M

McCOSH, JAMES, 19
McGRATH, EARL J., 194
MACHLUP, FRITZ, 31
MACKENZIE, GORDON, 46
McLAUGHLIN, FATHER LEO, 22
Majoring, changes in requirements for: correlates of, 120–123; as measure of reform, 52, 54, 69–70; at various types of institutions, 69–70
Major programs, change in: as measure of reform, 52, 54, 63–67, 206; correlates of,

Index

118–120; initiative for, 84–87; trends, 66; in various fields, 64–67, 68; at various types of institution, 63, 64–65, 66

Marginal members of institutions, 40–41, 159–161, 181, 182–187

Market pressures, 32–34, 154–156, 189

MARTIN, WARREN BRYAN, 61, 156

Massachusetts Institute of Technology, 22, 26

MAYHEW, LEWIS B., 159n

MEIKLEJOHN, ALEXANDER, 20–21, 43

MENDENHALL, THOMAS C., 15n

MERTON, ROBERT K., 164–165

METZGER, WALTER, 20

MEYERSON, MARTIN, 61

Michigan State University, 23, 184–185

MILES, MATTHEW B., 195–196

MOHR, LAWRENCE B., 198

Monopoly, effects of, 146

MORGAN, ARTHUR, 23–24, 43

MORISON, ELTING E., 198

MORISON, SAMUEL ELIOT, 139

MORT, PAUL, 196

MOTT, NEVILL, 3

MUSCATINE, CHARLES, 2

Muscatine Committee, 2, 4, 32

N

Newcomers, importance of, 44–49, 161–163

New models of academic institutions, 22–23, 156–157

New School for Social Research, 175

New units of institutions, 90–92

NIXON, JIM, 27

NOTT, ELIPHALET, 172

O

Obstacles to change, 10–16, 99–104

O'CONNELL, WILLIAM R., JR., 167–168

Ohio State University, 155

Oligarchy, 167, 169

Openness of institutions, 163, 178

Organizational change: advocacy and, 20–22; conclusions about, 9–13; examples, 18–19; history, 18–22; literature on, 192–199; as response to pressure, 18–19

Organizational inertia, 10–11 (see also Inertia in institutions)

Organizational survival, 12–13

Organizations: characteristics of, 10–13; equalitarian and hierarchical, 21–22; institutionalization of, 11–12

Outside influence (see Environmental influence)

Outsiders, importance of, 44–46, 92–94, 114–115, 145

Oxford University, 146, 150, 186, 190

P

PARSONS, TALCOTT, 13n, 96n, 174n

Parsons College, 23–24

Passive structure of organizations, 10

Patriarchy, 133, 169–174

Patrons, importance of, 41–44

PELLEGRIN, ROLAND, 196

PERKINS, JAMES A., 44

PERLIN, SEYMOUR, 26

PIERSON, GEORGE W., 29–30, 138n, 139

PLANCK, MAX, 45

PLATT, GERALD M., 96n, 174n

Polarized provincialism, 103–104

Political economy, 36

Powerlessness, 115, 166

Presidents (see also Administrators): patriarchal, 172; power of, 182–183; term of office, 172–173

Pressure for change, 18, 133–134

Professionals in academic institutions, 15, 178

Professors (see Faculty)

Proliferation of courses, 58–59

Index

Public interest and self-interest, 150–151

PURKES, J. HARRIS, 25

PUSEY, NATHAN, 48

Q

Quality of educational institutions, 110, 153

R

Reed College, 155

REEVES, FLOYD, 184–185

Regulations, change in: correlates of, 120–123; as measure of reform, 52, 54, 70–72, 206–208

Rensselaer Polytechnic Institute, 23

Reputation of academic institutions, 14, 127

Resources, importance of, 32–40, 156, 189

Reward, importance of potential, 19, 140–141, 189

RIESMAN, DAVID, 41, 61, 159, 193

ROBERTS, MILLARD, 24

Rochester Institute of Technology, 184

ROGERS, EVERETT M., 198–199

ROGERS, IDA LONG, 6

RUDOLPH, FREDERICK, 7, 147

RUDY, WILLIS, 34

RUML, BEARDSLEY, 194

S

St. John's College, 23–24

Sample of institutions used in study, 201–204

SANFORD, NEVITT, 21

San Francisco State College, 26–27

Sarah Lawrence College, 23

Scheffield Scientific School, 36

SCHLESINGER, ARTHUR M., JR., 44n

SCHON, DONALD A., 20n, 197

SCHRAG, PETER, 199

Science: influence of, 35, 145

Secularism, 35–36

Secular support of education, 35–37

SELDEN, WILLIAM K., 172n

Self-interest and public interest, 150–151

Self-selection in organizations, 10–11, 14–15

Seller's market in higher education, 146–147, 189

Seniority, 169–174

SEWELL, ELIZABETH, 22

SHEWHART, WALTER, 19

SHRIBERG, ARTHUR, 210n

SILLIMAN, BENJAMIN, JR., 29

SIMON, HERBERT, 33

SIMS, WILLIAM A., 197

SMITH, ADAM, 151n

Smith College, 23

SNYDER, RICHARD C., 26

Social change, and academic reform, 35–39

State colleges, 61, 84, 86–87, 92–94

Static departments, 112–116

Static institutions, 123–130

STEINER, GARY A., 197

Stephens College, 184

STERN, BERNHARD J., 7, 192–193

STODDARD, GEORGE, 47

Structuring of institutions, 16, 141–142

Students: current influence of, 114–115, 131–132, 148–149; historical influence of, 147–148; perceived role in change, 79–82, 87, 94, 96

Study of Institutional Vitality: interviews used, 209–217; procedures, 106–107, 201–221; summary of, 188–190; variables employed, 222–230

SUDMAN, SEYMOUR, 210

SULKIN, SIDNEY, 8

Swarthmore College, 43

Synthesis of knowledge, 31–32, 53, 65

Index

T

Technical proficiency as educational goal, 71–72
Telephone interviews, 74–75, 209–219
Tenure, 127
Term of office: for department chairmen, 170, 171–172; for presidents, 172–173
TICKNOR, GEORGE, 20, 29, 41, 42
Trustees, influence of, 185–187; as initiators of change, 79, 92–94, 96; patriarchal, 173
TURNER, JONATHAN BALDWIN, 20, 22, 41
Turnover of personnel (*see also* Newcomers), 44–49, 125
TUSSMAN, JOSEPH, 156, 168
TYLER, RALPH, 11, 184

U

Union College, 172
Union for Research and Experimentation in Higher Education, 159
Universities: graduate school constraints on undergraduate reform, 125–126; requirements for majors, 70; undergraduate course reform in, 58; undergraduate majors in, 63, 64–65, 66

Upper-division colleges, 22
UPTON, MILLAR, 24

V

VEBLEN, THORSTEIN, 103
Vertical fragmentation of educational institutions, 13–14
VEYSEY, LAURENCE R., 34
Virginia, University of, 22, 23, 155
VOLKART, EDMUND, 8, 192
VOZICK, MIKE, 21, 27

W

WALD, ABRAHAM, 47
WATSON, GOODWIN, 6
WAYLAND, FRANCIS, 2, 21, 23, 33, 41, 105
Wesleyan University, 29, 48, 183
WHITEHEAD, ALFRED NORTH, 2
WILLETT, WILLIAM M., 29
WILLIAMS, B. R., 198
WINTER, WERNER, 47
Wisconsin, University of, 43
WRISTON, HENRY, 160, 176

Y

Yale University: drama workshop, 22; electives, 29–30; origins of college system, 137–139

Z

ZELEZNICK, ABRAHAM, 178n
ZINSSER, HANS, 45